The Architect and the Animal

The Architect and the Animal

edited by Kostas Tsiambaos

THE MIT PRESS
CAMBRIDGE, MASSACHUSETTS
LONDON, ENGLAND

The MIT Press
Massachusetts Institute of Technology
77 Massachusetts Avenue, Cambridge, MA 02139
mitpress.mit.edu

The MIT Press would like to thank the anonymous peer reviewers who provided comments on drafts of this book. The generous work of academic experts is essential for establishing the authority and quality of our publications. We acknowledge with gratitude the contributions of these otherwise uncredited readers.

Supported by:

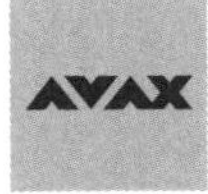

This book was set in Arnhem Pro by The MIT Press. Printed and bound in China.

Library of Congress Cataloging-in-Publication Data is available.

ISBN: 978-0-262-04969-6

10 9 8 7 6 5 4 3 2 1

EU product safety and compliance information contact is: mitp-eu-gpsr@mit.edu

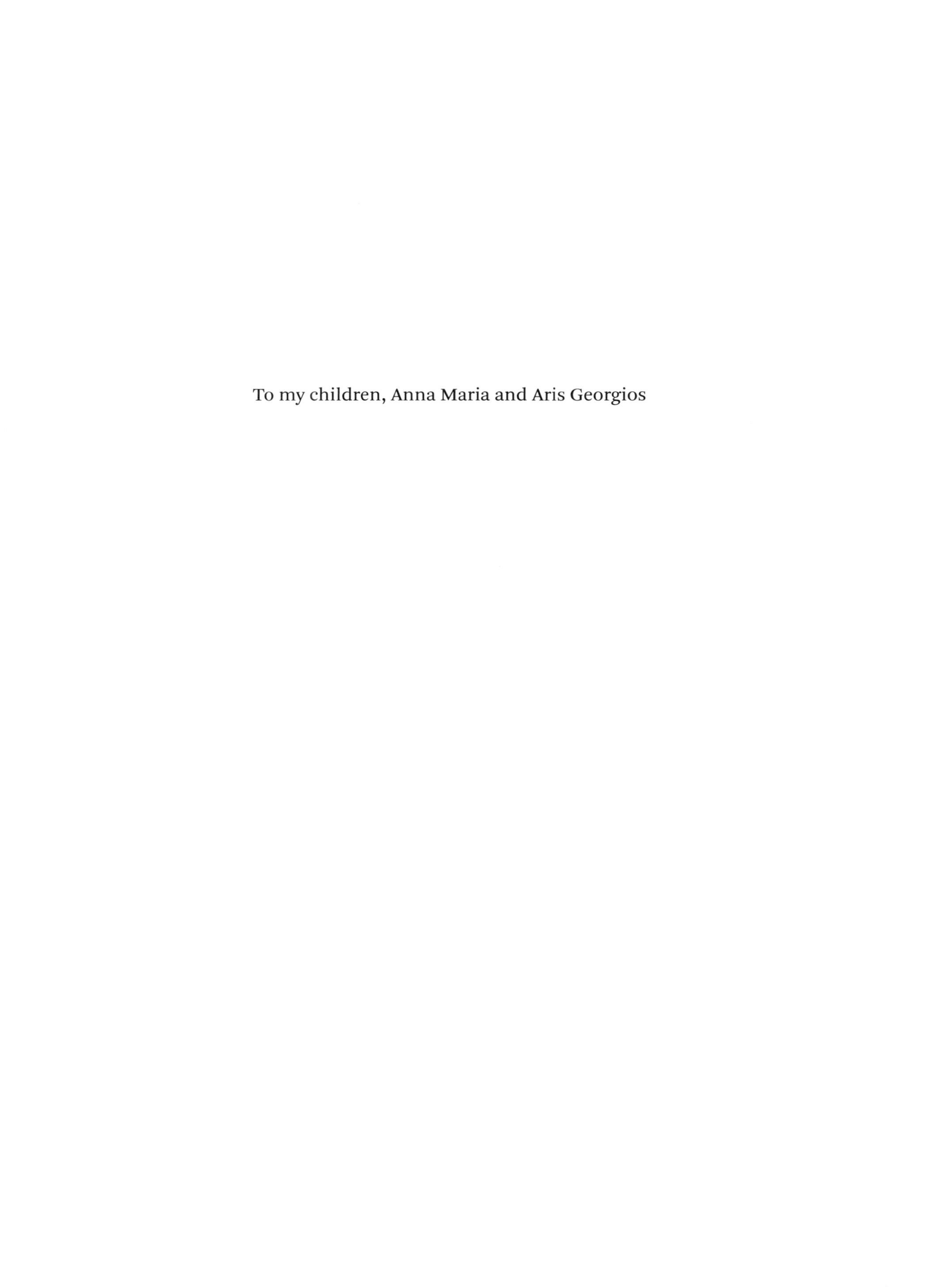

To my children, Anna Maria and Aris Georgios

Contents

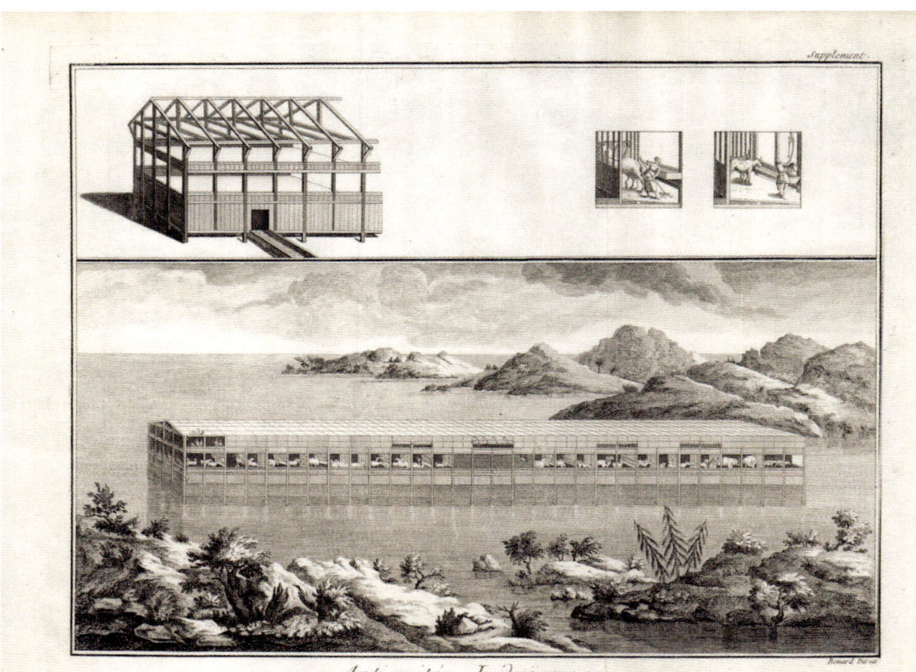

Antiquités Judaiques.

Preface

> It is not in mines or natural caves nor in graves that we must search for the origin of architecture . . . it is to the ark, the first object of the second world and the last of the first.
>
> JOSEPH GANDY, "The Art, Philosophy, and Science of Architecture," unpublished manuscript (1826)

A wooden construction 300 cubits long, 50 cubits wide, and 30 cubits high, with three decks divided into rooms in rows, and one single door at its long side. Inside it, Noah, with his family, a male and female pair of each species of animal (what about hermaphrodite worms and snails?), and enough food and water for everyone to survive long enough. According to both the Bible and the Quran, the only living creatures existing on earth, for a short period of time, were a master builder with his family and a few thousand animals; and the only construction that survived the deluge was a huge wooden container, the ark that Noah made, following God's instructions. An architect, his family, and their animals were the only seeds of the future.

In the representation of Noah's ark printed in the pages of the Supplement to Diderot and d'Alembert's *Encyclopédie*, a huge box floats on the waters, with its exposed timber frame and its gable roof. As sophisticated as an architectural construction may be, the simple geometry of this floating building is a result of the simplicity of the given instructions. Noah's ark is not just an archetype for architecture, being the architectural origin (the *arché*) of the new post-flood world; it is also a model of rational thought resulting from an act of speech: (God's) words translated into architecture are a primary example of how to do things with words.

At the same time, the Cartesian geometry of the building designates the presence of human rationality in the natural world. In vivid contrast both with the rocks, trees, and clouds that surround it and with the organic forms of the

Figure 0.1
Noah's Ark. Unattributed engraving supervised by Robert Benard, c. 1770. Supplement to Diderot and d'Alembert's *Encyclopédie*.

animals standing in the standardized rooms inside it, the orthogonal grid of Noah's ark attests to a new paradigm of knowledge that follows a modern system of thought. The presence of the animals in the ark, during the flood, is also a metaphor for their transition from a natural state to another state, a repositioning in a world of science through their selection, organization, classification, and dislocation inside the cells of a three-dimensional wooden grid. The grid, in this case, is crucial as a structuring structure against the fluidity, inexactness, and *resistance* of the wildlife; and the wilder the things inside the building, the bigger the need for a new order of things.

The Architect and the Animal performs as another kind of ark in the sense that it collects various references to, and representations of, animals in the architecture of the long twentieth century. But, in contrast to the rationalistic ark represented in the *Encyclopédie*, animals that appear in this book reclaim their agency as media of criticism and resistance against the modern systems of knowledge and the techniques that had marginalized them. By bringing forward icons, myths, dreams, and symbols that are both common/shared and personal/private, animal references and representations bear the visceral excessiveness of architecture as a cultural theory and practice that exceeds mere technocratic competency. These animals, which had always been present on the most important works of architecture since prehistory but gradually disappeared from the buildings of the twentieth century, resurface as actors of an ignored, forgotten, or latent content that raises questions on history and place, culture and identity, autonomy and creativity. If the ark in the Age of Enlightenment was a modern *dispositif* in the form of an architectural taxonomy imposed on Animalia, then animals in this book demand to move freely again, outside the "box," in order to expand, enrich, and enliven an architecture that often failed to honor its potential for inclusiveness, empathy, and critical awareness.

Moreover, *The Architect and the Animal* talks about a kind of mirroring, as animals replace, disguise, or extend the particular subjectivity of the architect's work. By including animal references and representations in their buildings, texts, sketches, drawings, photographs, and so on, architects question, more or less consciously, the creative vector of their praxis: what happens to architecture when an animal appears in the scene? Or even, what happens to architecture after the architect tries to imagine the experience of an animal by *becoming* an animal themselves? In many chapters of this book, animals appear as such an "other" for the human in general, or the "other" of the author-architect in particular. This kind of projective critical interrogation, which initiates from the personal, gradually ends up becoming a general questioning of architecture. Thus, the micro scale and the macro scale converge; the object, "out there," contains and protects the person's "in here."

Eventually, the animals in this book, either as specific living beings or as imaginary creatures, invite us to reconsider what affect means for architecture.

If architecture is a prerequisite for the human life to be evolved, then relationships with other living beings are just as necessary, if not more. In a sense, animals' protection in couples inside Noah's ark-itecture is not only an indication of care for the survival of all living beings but also a choice that safeguards the importance of relating itself. With the company of human and other animals, even the end of the world, as we know it, can be tolerated and lived through. Sooner or later, another architecture will follow.

KOSTAS TSIAMBAOS

Tout le monde de mes amis est gentil
mais je suis ~~un~~ le danger public.
L'autre soir dans le train Venise Milan,
Roger, prétendant que je suis un génie
et moi je certifiais être un âne,
j'ai alors ~~fait~~ posé la posture par ~~un~~ ce
graphique :

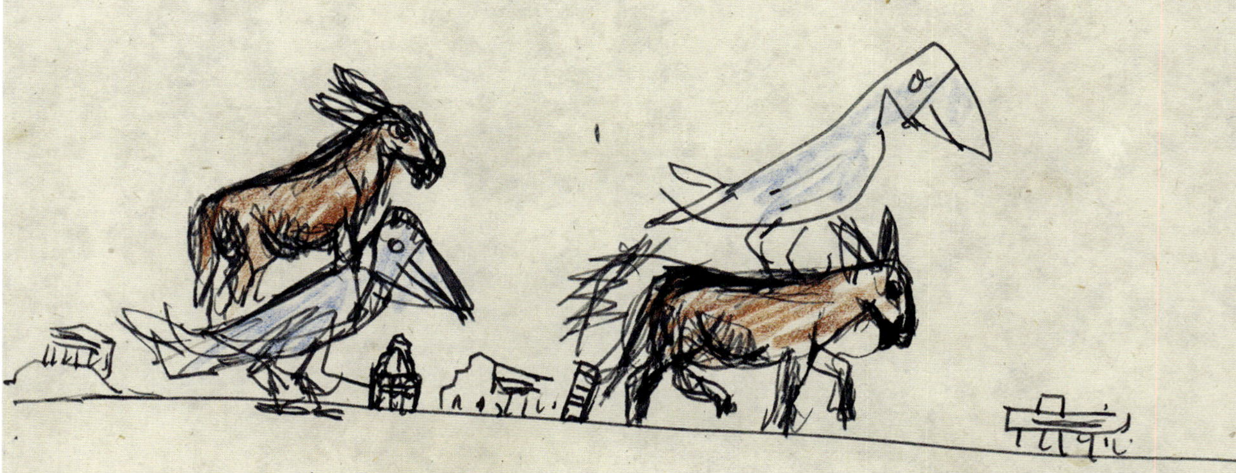

~~Le~~ génie porte-t-il l'âne
ou l'âne porte-t-il le génie ?

Ass

M. Christine Boyer

A donkey, or *Equus asinus*, is a domesticated form of *Equus africanus*. While the origins of the words "donkey" or "ass" are lost, they have developed multiple meanings. In English, "donkey" refers to a beast of burden that is stupid, foolish, obstinate, patient, and stubborn. The French *âne*, a derivative of *asinus*, is translated into English as "ass" and has even more semantic associations: a foolish person "makes an ass of himself"; a sly person "covers his ass," while a stupid person is a "jackass"; and a person who works hard "works their ass off."[1] This asinine tale reveals some of the contradictory meanings that Le Corbusier deployed in reference to a donkey or ass (the terms are used interchangeably in English translations).

Throughout his life, Le Corbusier referred to himself as a donkey (*âne*). In his last interview, "Mise au point" (1965), he declared: "I carry within me one consolation. I bring consolation like an honest donkey who has done his work and accomplished his task! I know that the horizon is free and that the sun is going to rise again. . . . Far from the hustle and bustle, in my den (since I am a meditative person, I have even compared myself to a donkey, out of conviction), for fifty years now I have been studying 'Everyman,' his wife and children. One preoccupation has concerned me compulsively: to introduce into the home a sense of the sacred; to make the home the temple of the family."[2]

And the refrain he repeatedly used: "I am an ass, but with a sharp eye. We are dealing here with the eye of an ass who has the capacity of feeling. I am an ass with an instinct for proportion. I am, and remain, an impenitent visual person. It is beautiful when it is beautiful . . . but it is according to Modulor! I don't give a damn about Modulor, what do you want me to do with Modulor? And yet, no! the Modulor is inevitably right, and it is you who feel nothing. The Modulor elongates the ass's ear. (Here I mean the ass other than myself mentioned earlier.)"[3]

When Charles-Édouard Jeanneret wrote on architecture in the pages of *L'Esprit Nouveau* (1920s), he took the pen name of Le Corbusier, transforming

Figure 1.1
Le Corbusier, *Paraphrase of the Entry into Jerusalem*. © F.L.C./ADAGP, Paris/OSDEETE Athens, 2023.

Lecorbésier, the name of his grandmother's father, into a new meaning: the raven-archer. He often called himself "Le Corbu," the raven, and signed his paintings and letters with the sign of this bird. In 1952, Le Corbusier wrote a letter to Sigfried Giedion from Chandigarh in which he called himself an ass, not a genius as some have called him. He included a sketch to illustrate the point, later titled *Paraphrase of the Entry into Jerusalem*. On the right side of the drawing, he placed a raven on the back of an ass promenading by the Parthenon, then the Leaning Tower of Pisa, and in the future the Villa Savoy, all favorite symbols of the architect. On the left side, he placed a standing raven with an ass on his back. Underneath the sketch he wrote, "Does the genius carry an ass or is the ass carrying the genius?," for this is the walk of the honored transposed into the walk of the crucified.[4] It remains an open question whether Le Corbusier's self-image was that of a painter or a writer, both misunderstood and crucified by the critics, while his pseudo-self, the architect, was avidly admired and called a genius.

Obviously, Le Corbusier is referring to Jesus's triumphant entry into Jerusalem on the back of a humble ass, one of the most enduring images of Western culture. It was the prelude to his crucifixion. Henceforth the ass became a symbol of piety, martyrdom, and a sufferer for humanity, even though this lowliest of beasts is more often a symbol of foolishness, stubbornness, sometimes stupidness. Donkeys are also pack animals—a core technology for moving goods, especially in the mountainous terrain of the Mediterranean basin. They are hardy and resilient animals working tirelessly with little maintenance. Although they are slow-paced, they are steady and sure-footed. They are also strong and sturdy, able to carry heavy burdens relative to their size. And donkeys are also commonplace, or at least were in earlier times, and thus generally considered beneath notice. Or if noticed, they are met with hilarity and scorn. The language used to describe them usually involves demeaning comparisons. The term "asinine," for example, describes someone who is foolish, a bit dumb, even devoid of intelligence, although that label may not be true of donkeys themselves. Donkeys have been associated with the poor, marginalized, or oppressed in society. And they are humble enough to be associated with women.

Le Corbusier's asinine tales begin with his early unpublished manuscript "La construction des villes" (1910), where he praises the meandering paths laid down by donkeys. Inspired by Camillo Sitte's admiration of organic, curved street patterns with varied widths and views along the way, Le Corbusier developed his well-known theory about donkey paths, proclaiming that town administrators must avoid implementing modern gridiron street plans and instead learn the lessons of how the donkey travels, following the contours of the land and stopping for picturesque views.

Looking out a window on a rainy day, Corbusier saw the rain falling on the pavement of a sloping street and the sinuous lines it made as it descended the street. The lesson of the donkey was held in this scene.[5] In effect, if the beast with long ears had been part of a city planning office, it would have proposed the following. When it is a matter of rising streets, you geometers, think of others, poor beasts condemned to carry heavy burdens. We do not like your continuous slopes that you draw so straight in keeping to the budget of your office. Rendered sullen by these taxes, we are paid by being whipped. We like better a slope less inflexible, then smoother, a little flat; after that a normal slope, and we will make a series of big efforts. But don't forget us four-legged beings; on your continuous slopes, we constantly have to make the same effort. A little variety in the work of our muscles would be less fatiguing. You say: rest is a matter of changing occupations. If you make roads as we propose, then they will be amusing, through their variations, and our drivers will forget their whips and our skin will benefit.[6]

Le Corbusier's sympathy for donkeys was enhanced in 1911 when he and his friend Klipstein took a trip to Istanbul, Mount Athos, and Athens. Wide-eyed, he absorbs these scenes as they open before him: cafes where men smoke the narghile, the strangely powerful shaved heads of Turkish men, and little over-burdened donkeys going up and down the streets. He loves these small beasts plodding away with all their might, for they seem to represent the humorous juxtapositions of the East. Their lazy masters load them down with bundles of cut grass, stacked so crookedly that they will eventually fall to the ground. Or they are loaded with baskets of tomatoes, onions, and garlic. So loaded, the donkey, the baskets, the Turk fill the entire width of the street.

He writes about the little donkeys and young women of Istanbul. The donkeys from the first moment won him over, for he was always attracted to simple things. But the women he hated for three weeks—all the time in which his heart was heavy with his failed expectations of an "exotic" East. The donkeys were innumerable and took part in all occupations: messengers, carriers of debris, vegetable and fruit providers. They were slow-paced, roped together along steep paths, or they trotted with poise and thoughtfulness while their bells chimed like a carillon.

When it came to writing about the donkey path in *Urbanisme* (1924), Corbusier does an about-face with respect to the brute donkey. Now this stupid, lazy animal meanders along, zigzags to ease his climb, always trying to gain shade. He takes the line of least resistance and sidesteps every obstacle in his path. He stubbornly resists modernity. Conversely, man is rational; he thinks ahead and seeks the straight line because man has a goal and knows where he is going. Unfortunately, the pack donkey is responsible for every plan in every European city. These cities have no arteries, only capillaries; thus growth brings sickness, and survival necessitates an operation. In the age of motorcars, a modern city must live by the straight line. It is paralyzed by the curving line. Man reasons, he practices order, and his toil is dictated by the straight line and the right angle. Nature is all confusion and the accidental, full of surface appearances. Man's way is the straight line, he is in control of himself and has reached a condition of order. The pack donkey is feminine to Le Corbusier; seeking the winding road, it reveals animality and lack of concentration.

One of Le Corbusier's favorite books, even in his childhood yet reread during the last weeks of his life, was Cervantes's *Don Quixote of La Mancha* (1605). Le Corbusier was a man engaged in battle, full of idealism and with a crusader's zeal. He took the image of Don Quixote for himself—abused, beaten up, yet spiritually pure, working without reward for many years, receiving many blows, as he went about battling for the city of tomorrow. The beloved donkey is in the story as well, in the image of Sancho Panza riding his donkey Dapple, a down-to-earth, faithful companion to Don Quixote while he goes about tilting windmills astride his horse, Rocinante.

No doubt *Don Quixote* is the most famous novel to feature a donkey as both animal companion and allegory for human nature. The Don's old horse Rocinante and Dapple, Sancho Panza's beloved donkey, are both true companions and mentors to their respective masters, as well as reflections of their characters: the arrogance and caprice of the horse and the humble steadiness of the donkey. Don Quixote's efforts are frustrated. He is ignominiously defeated by things, or rather by his miscalculation about things, their resistance and stubborn opposition to his will.

In Le Corbusier's last interview "Mise au point," mentioned above, he interrupts his thoughts to give thanks to both Cervantes and Rabelais. Don Quixote and Sancho Panza had shown him how to hammer away with persistence, including optimistic outbursts, confidence, faith, and love. They survived, they made compromises, they landed on their feet, and they were full of humorous episodes. Cervantes utilized the horse and the donkey/ass as metaphors for the men who rode them—one arrogant, the other humble, one tilting at windmills, the other patiently and loyally enduring as the comic foil to Quixote's idealism, no matter the latter's many setbacks, frustrations, and struggles. Le Corbusier would never see any of his visions for urbanism implemented. He proclaimed again and again: "I am an ass" (Je suis un âne).

Bull

Rodrigo Pérez de Arce

"The animal scrutinizes him across a narrow abyss of non-comprehension. . . . This is why the man can surprise the animal. Yet the animal—even if domesticated—can also surprise the man, the man who is looking across a similar, but not identical, abyss of non-comprehension."[1] Such is John Berger's assumption about the unbreachable gap that excises us from animals—all of them—domesticated and wild ones, large and small, sweet and menacing, pets, beasts, and pests.

Every tradition that had previously mediated between man and nature was broken in the nineteenth century, according to Berger: "Before this rupture," he reasoned, "animals constituted the first circle of what surrounded man." Not so long ago, horse carts brimming with fruits and vegetables rattled across residential neighborhoods, breeding a certain sense of familiarity with domesticated animals, their pace, odor, countenance, and also tokens in the form of manure. In Berger's vision, only peasants nurtured the ancestral rapport between humans and animals, while modernity was increasingly banishing both peasants and animals toward the margins of society. Similarly, Peter and Alison Smithson observed that "in societies full of serving animals . . . man had to share his grown food, his space of countryside or city, with his four-footed help mates."[2] Up to the mid-1950s, scenes of this kind characterized in some way or another the ordinary landscape in places like my hometown, Santiago.

Thinking in terms of modern political economy, banishment and exclusion form part of the modern urban drive. Indeed, the city can be explained by what it leaves out as much as by what it embraces. Such is the way José Ortega y Gasset defines its ground zero, the urban square:

> But . . . how can man withdraw himself from the fields? . . . Quite simple; he will mark off a portion of this field by means of walls, which set up an enclosed, finite space over against amorphous, limitless space. . . . The square . . . this lesser, rebellious field, which secedes from the limitless one, and keeps to itself, is a space sui generis, of the most novel kind, in which man frees himself from the community of the plant and the animal . . . and creates an enclosure apart which is purely human, a civil space.[3]

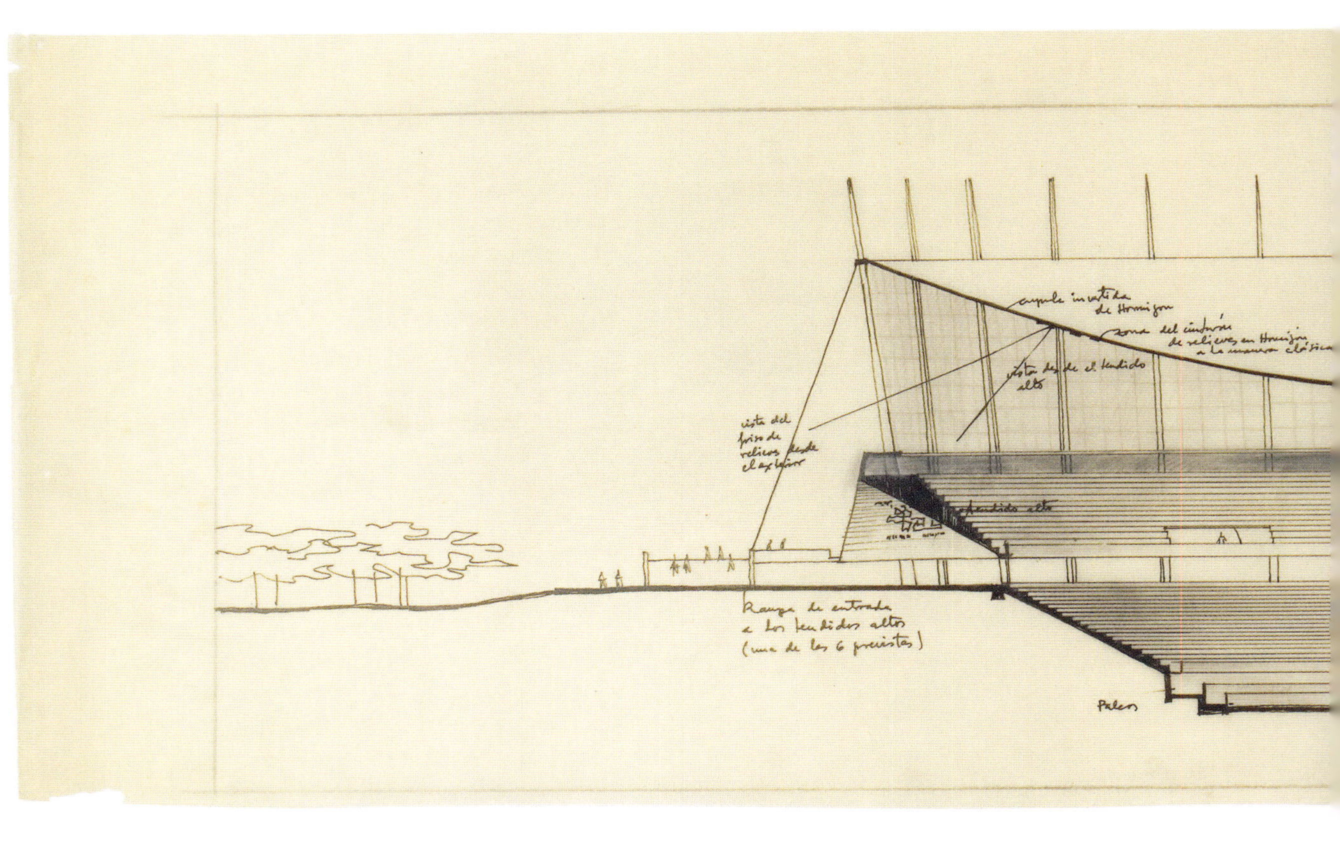
cupula invertida
de Hormigon
zona del cinturón
de relieves en Hormigon
a la manera clásica
vista desde el tendido
alto
vista del
friso de
relieves desde
el exterior
tendido alto
Rampa de entrada
a los tendidos altos
(una de las 6 previstas)
Palcos

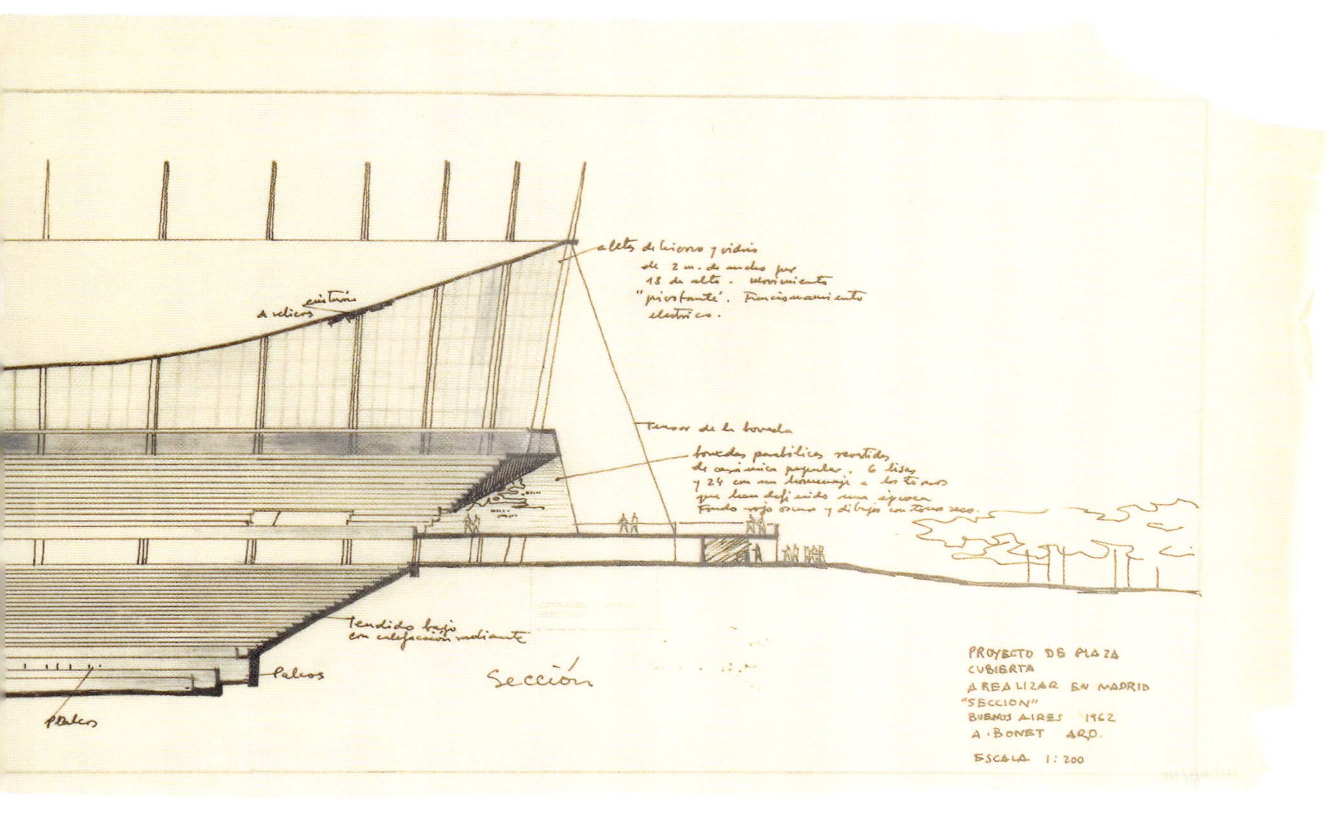

Figure 2.1
Antonio Bonet Castellana, Bullring, 1962. © Bonet Castellana Archive. Arxiu Històric del Col·legi d'Arquitectes de Catalunya.

One should notice how Ortega's wall excludes both "the community of the plant and the animal" so that the square primarily makes a statement about difference vis-à-vis all expressions of rough nature, with the sole exclusion of the celestial forces. Henceforth, as expected, this human-made distinctiveness should set the scene for the highest modes of human interaction. No doubt Ortega drew inspiration from the luminous Mediterranean "dry" squares and their mysterious allure. Such was also the format embraced by the Iberian conquerors in Latin America, till the mid-nineteenth century when—as if instigated by revenge—their creole successors filled the emblematic urban voids with dense bouquets of exotic flora.

The zoo, the race course, and a host of legal and semilegal enclaves mostly devoted to gambling staged the living presence of animals within this highly artificial urban domain. As noted by Berger, the impulse gained momentum by the nineteenth century, precisely when the presence of many domesticated animals was receding while the wild was becoming ever so unreachable. These animal enclaves mainly surged either due to the agonistic drive or else with the aim of instruction and recreation. Play became therefore one significant sponsor of the animal presence in modern urban scenarios. Harking back to European antiquity, this particular ludic drive fashioned its agonistic arenas in formats that recast the ancient Roman circus and amphitheater.

Such is also the case with bullfights. Purposefully bred in vast fields and far away from all human contact, the *toros de lidia*, as they are called, were usually kept as wild and alien as feasible, until the fateful day when they were dragged away from their habitat into the bewildering setting of the empty arena, a geometric tabula rasa that was unlike anything these noble beasts had experienced before. Nothing in there whatsoever resembled their familiar grounds, for the sacrificial arena was monomaterial, flat, abstract, essentially featureless, and inert. The *albero*, a yellowish sand strewn over its surface, was raked after each episode so that the bull always stepped into a virginal soil, one totally devoid of imprints, a field that—unbeknown to it—would sooner rather than later be splattered with its own blood.

Historians trace the evolution of *tauromaquia*—the art of bullfighting—through stages.[4] First, there was a semirural period when the contest took place in open fields. The practice admitted then a certain amount of chaos, as the rules were not yet drawn. The next step brought the duel right into the main square, which was turned into a huge theater by means of removable stands and other devices. Here the citizenry witnessed the wild, as incarnated by the bull, entering their most refined urban domain, as if a crocodile had entered an exquisite lounge. The occasion was mediated through a sophisticated ritual with an impressive display of pageantry. As in play, no prescribed outcome was admissible except that ultimately a corpse was dragged out of the arena. Both the bull and the matador faced death. Unlike modern sport with its caustic and puritan overtones, the bullfight was characterized primarily as a feast (instead of just a game), the fiesta *de toros* where passion, cruelty, gaiety, and drama converged.

The third stage in the process is highly significant, for in it the *plaza* de toros emerged as a freestanding coliseum, a monument exclusive to bullfights locked well within the city. Its designation as a *plaza* de toros—a bull (fight) *square*—is paradoxical, as it stresses the arena's ultimate civic status while referring to animals/citizens of different biopolitical statuses: free versus captured, trained versus wild, authoritative versus controlled. Once it was established, during the eighteenth century, the coliseum's circular format remained largely unchallenged; and as with stadia, its walls substituted the command of the urban horizon for the all-around presence of the multitude. As if bypassing academia's fixation on the classics in order to meet primeval impulses, this was just one expression of a linkage between modernity and the most ancestral rituals involving beasts; in fashioning stadia, architects reverted to archetypally violent Roman precedents.

Bulls had attracted the interest of diverse avant-garde figures, notoriously Pablo Picasso and Le Corbusier, who were both equally drawn to the timeless figure of the minotaur. Aside from memorable etchings and drawings of bulls, Picasso's enthusiasm for bullfights drew him to organize such (bloodless) events within an impromptu arena staged in his own grounds in Vallauris between 1948 and 1961. Along with Luis Miguel Dominguin, a well-known *matador* and quite a public figure, Picasso even considered constructing a permanent bullring in his own chateau in Vauvenargues. Sometimes he even dressed up as a matador.

In 1962 Catalan-born architect Antonio Bonet Castellana was approached by Picasso for the creation of a monumental bullring in Spain. Dominguin was also involved in this collaborative quest, where the artist would play the role of promoter, as a sort of client partner in a continuous interchange with the architect. There was no prescribed site, although Madrid was apparently the best option. The ploy was to first make the project and then negotiate official sponsorship. Picasso was then at the height of his fame, and as such, he was the one who could do most to persuade the public and the authorities. However, as the architectonic format was firmly established, all possible innovations were confined by the building type.

Bonet offered Picasso a set of parabolic vaults, twenty-four in all, for the display of his ceramics that alluded to the bullfighting tournament. The artist also took advantage of the inverted cupola as an occasion for a circular frieze to be inscribed with bas reliefs all along its 225-meter rim, which could be seen from within and outside the precinct.[5] In roofing the bullring with an inverted concrete cupola, Bonet was doing away with the age-old tradition of open-cast arenas, with the distinction of bleachers—*sol y sombra* (light and shade)—according to the solar orientation. Casting a lid upon the arena, he was also removing it from that particular linkage to the celestial forces and rough nature, thus consolidating, in Ortega's terms, "an enclosure apart which is purely human, a civil space."

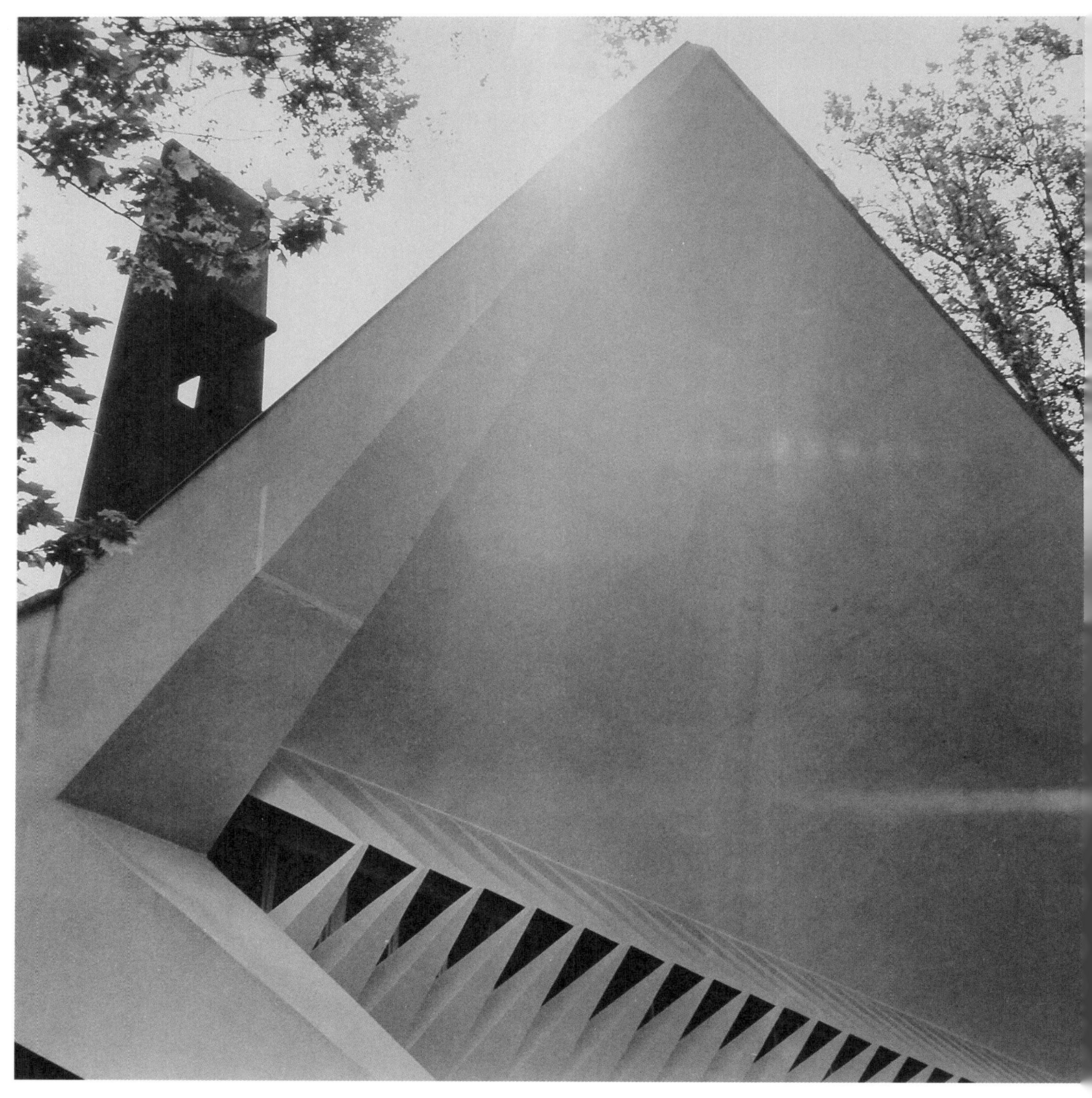

Figure 3.1
Enzo Venturelli, Turin Zoo aquarium, detail of the entrance, circa 1960.
© Archivio di Stato di Torino.

Cetus

Gregorio Astengo

On the morning of September 9, 1961, Walt Disney entered the doors of the local zoo in the northern Italian city of Turin. Accompanied by journalists and a camera crew, the sixty-year-old cartoonist was seen walking among the enclosures of the animal park, observing the giraffes, feeding the elephants, and admiring the monkeys, all within the naturalistic setting along the southern bank of the river Po. Disney's short visit was the last in an intense program of public appearances in the city, which had culminated a few days earlier with the opening of his own 360-degree cinema, the Circarama. The entertainment set had been built by the automobile manufacturer Fiat for Italia '61, the nationwide public celebration of the centenary of Italy's unity. However, given Disney's popularity within the animal kingdom, his visit to the zoo attracted at least as much public attention as the more high-profile events of the previous days. Interviewed by journalist Carlo Mazzarella, Disney was asked to draw fanciful parallels between the small Turinese zoological garden and his own Californian amusement park of Disneyland, both inaugurated exactly six years earlier. Indeed, seen through the lenses of the television broadcast produced for the eventful visit, the naturalistic animal garden appeared as a covert theme park in itself: decorated as a bucolic village of stone grottoes and timber cottages, the zoo was, in reality, made mostly of metal enclosures and concrete boxes and pools, clad with brick and mortar in order to translate into "elegant lines" the owners' slightly inconsistent motto, "Few cages, lots of freedom." Seen in this guise, the zoo revealed its contradictory artifice as both an enclosure for exotic beasts and a popular source for public entertainment.

Indeed, at the time of Disney's visit, the Turin Zoo was at the peak of its success and had already gone through two subsequent building expansions, in 1957 and 1960. The second one, in particular, was the boldest but also the most uncomfortable addition to the otherwise familiar and modest architecture of a zoological garden: a building containing an aquarium and reptile house. The building was designed by Turinese architect Enzo Venturelli (1910–1996), who was commissioned by the zoo's owner, the animal retailer Società Molinar, to create a signature showpiece for their park. Located at the entrance of the zoo, the building looked like nothing seen before in the park, nor probably anywhere else in Turin. A large rectangular body, 46 meters in length and 22 meters in width, was organized on two levels. Inside, five double-height cages for the reptiles could be observed from a flying bridge, with ten aquariums located along the main space on the ground floor. Visitors entered the building under a large, cantilevered canopy that crowned the glass facade by projecting seven meters forward, decorated with a metal brise-soleil just above the doors.[1]

Because of its loud appearance, the building stood uncomfortably in the plain, mimetic setting of the zoo—the metaphoric elephant in the room. Perhaps for this reason, the brand-new building was purposely left out of Disney's televised visit, despite clearly being the newest and most memorable object in the zoo. The other reason the building did not really fit in the populist narrative of the event was its spatial introversion. Unlike all other enclosures in the park, the aquarium could not openly display its animals to the public. Instead, it was only through the large biomorphic mouth of the building that one could access the universe of amphibian glass cages and water tanks inside its bowels.

It was exactly due to its metaphorical nature that the building, and especially its facade, soon became the most remarkable and discussed piece of the zoo. In the public eye, the aquarium's fanciful exterior suggested an explicit connection with its contents, promoting the image of a giant beast, perhaps a crocodile or a whale, ready to devour its visitors. And so, while the journal of structural engineering *Informes de la Construcción* suggested the entertaining image of a toothed reptile, Bruno Zevi's editorial team at *L'Architettura. Cronache e Storia* saw an evident reference to Melville's whale and polemically nicknamed the building "Moby Dick."[2] Given its allusion to an aquatic predator, perhaps *cetus* is the most suitable way to identify this analogy. The word appropriately comes from the mythological *kētŏs*, the first word adopted to categorize "unnamed" creatures of the sea, at times serpents, whales, dragons, crocodiles, or monstrous compounds of their parts.[3] And while it is not clear what inspired Venturelli to create such a design, the few sketches left in his archive suggest that the building's facade was conceived largely independently of the rest.[4] Just like an ancient monstrous *cetus*, the aquarium and reptile house was a collection of biological elements, assembled to compose an inhabitable totemic archetype: the mouth-shaped facade, the lung-like tanks, the intestinal nave, the ectothermic air conditioning.

While Zevi saw an impulsive and contradictory caprice, the building's biomorphism was the aquarium's greatest success. The point of its ambiguous allusions was to present visitors with an unmissably attractive constellation of popular images: the curious exploration of the intestines of a stranded sperm whale, as in classic early modern accounts; the examination of the bones of a leviathan, as in a nineteenth-century scientific exhibit; or the fantasy of being ingested by a marine beast, like Jonah, Captain Ahab, or especially Pinocchio. Indeed, Disney's own rendition of Collodi's 1883 novel, which appeared in Italian cinemas in 1947, must have been the most immediate reference for a Turinese audience. While the original story saw Pinocchio devoured by a *pescecane*, a giant shark, Disney turned the monster into a sperm whale called Monstro, making the narrative all the more immediate.

Through a combination of specificity and universality, the building was able to project onto its visitors an attraction close to wonder. Unlike any other enclosure in the park, Venturelli's building could not be mistaken for anything *but* both an aquarium and a reptile house, an inhabitable *cetus* filled with the exotic beasts that had inspired it. By turning into a literal experience the idea of inhabiting the bowels of a monster in order to explore its natural habitats, the Turin Zoo truly became a theme park, an animalistic Disneyland. Any ambiguity between the environment and its occupants, evident in the rest of the naturalistic simulation of the park, was dropped. Instead, Venturelli's building explicitly declared its intentions and presented to its visitors a Collodian or Melvillian story, one which until then they could only have read in a book or seen on a screen.

It may appear contradictory, then, that the most Disney-like of all Turinese buildings did not make it into the short interview documenting the American animator's visit to the zoo. However, in many ways this ambiguous attitude perfectly embodied the reticence of local architects and critics toward any sort of audacious gesture, a stance famously noticed just two years earlier by Reyner Banham as a timid, infantile, and bourgeois revivalist "retreat."[5] Venturelli's building, a marine monster in the middle of a corny natural setting, could be seen as an attempt to stir the proverbial pot of local Turinese architecture. While perhaps not discursively successful, the aquarium and reptile house provided a bold gesture that successfully attracted and disturbed its public. The *cetus*, the sea creature whose empty remains now sit in the largely abandoned Turinese park, still plays with the local imaginary as a reference to a recent yet already mythological past, one in which legendary beasts could come to devour the jaded inhabitants of a dormant industrial city.[6]

Dog

Gabriele Mastrigli

The presence of animals in the narrative and iconography of Superstudio is one element of its multiform metaphoric language. From this point of view, animals for Superstudio are *tout court* representations of Nature—that is, the representation of what architecture is destined to embrace and, literally, comprehend. Although initially cows, horses, dogs, or monkeys appear simply as sparring partners in Superstudio's architectural collages, by being living things placed in opposition to the abstract monumental background (or foreground) of squared architectural volumes, they progressively become active characters of tales tuned as parables. In those narratives, animals are not just living things but *agents* of living nature, a wide, symbolic, and cultural sphere read as the counterpart of rationality. In such a category—which ends up including humans too—architecture is not represented in abstract monumental forms anymore but is investigated as an anthropological fact through which modernity is questioned about its real functioning as a system, its purpose, and its forms of life.

At the beginning of 1969, Superstudio realized the prototypes for its *Istogrammi d'architettura* (Architectural histograms), inspired by the idea of a "single design," the last pretext on which architecture can be based in order to try to find a place for itself in modernity. The contradictions of modern architecture are here radicalized in a "system" capable of absorbing the entire range of claims that architecture and design have to take into account. *Istogrammi d'architettura* are wooden objects finished with sheets of white laminate produced by print, on which a 3 × 3 cm grid was silk-screened. Generated by the variations of the squared surface in a type of *écriture automatique*, the *Istogrammi* produce a catalogue of "noncontinuous three-dimensional diagrams" that rationally organized the entire corpus of design actions via a material where everything, ultimately, resembles everything else. This "reductive" process demonstrates that in order to reproduce itself, the system needs to exploit creativity that is desperately seeking new forms. Hence, every search for definitive objects—the utopia of modernity—is physiologically destined to fail. Life is not a matter of "functions" anymore but a free expression of a vital status that can interact with objects in any unpredictable way. The more a design is generic, the better existence can liberate its potential, as we can see in the images of the Natalini family dining and sleeping on one of these white-gridded objects.

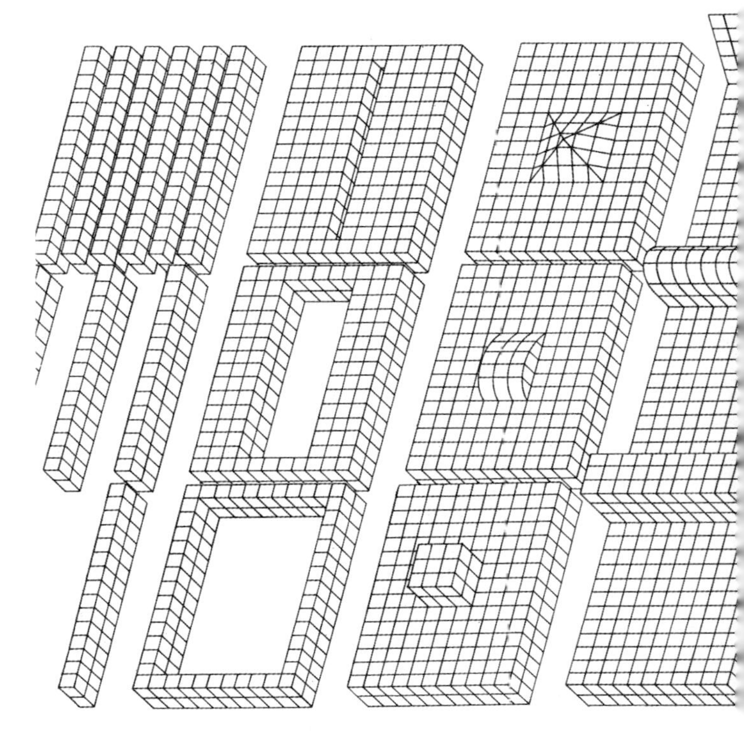

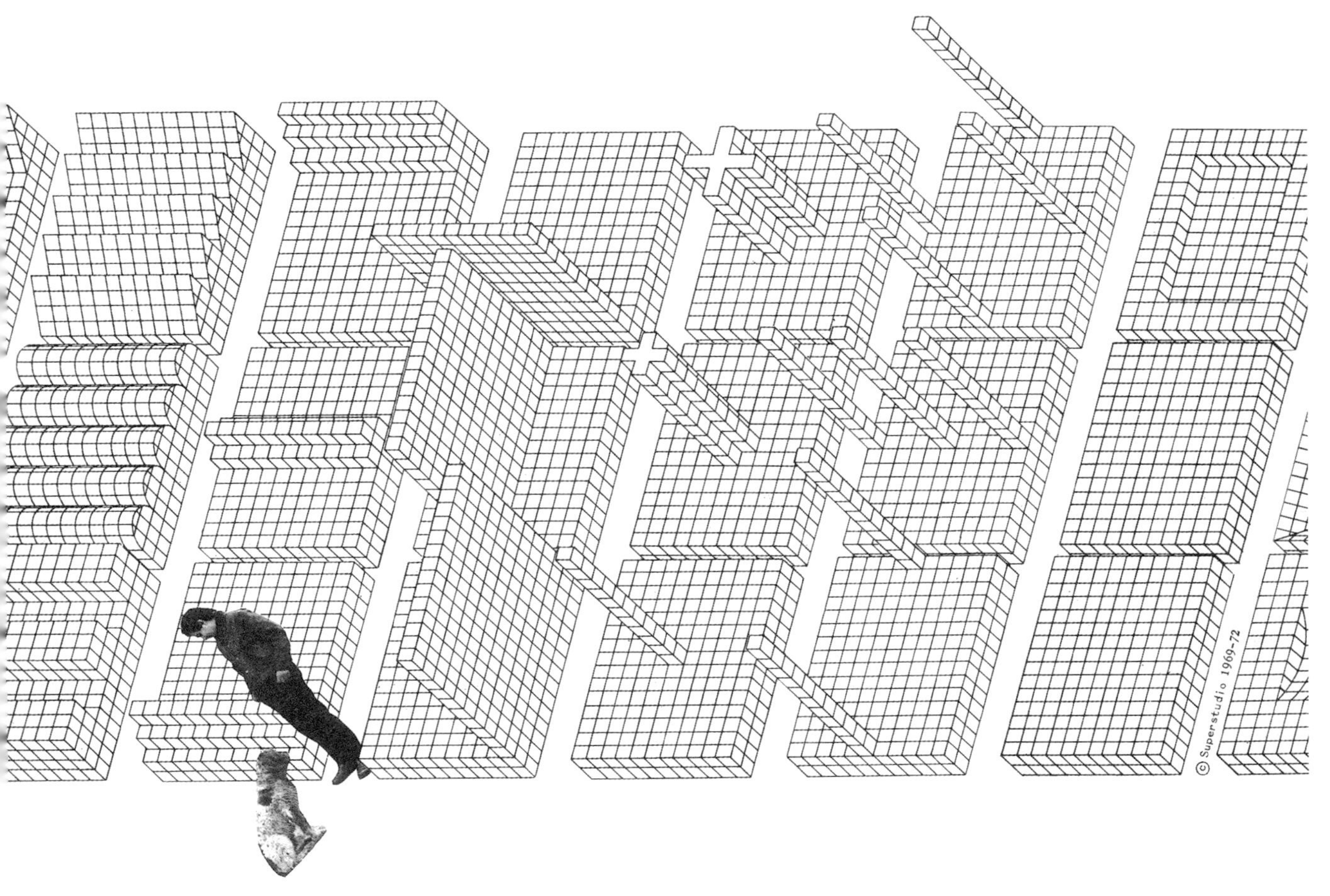

Figure 4.1
Superstudio, *Istogrammi*, 1970. Black-and-white poster.
Courtesy of Gian Piero Frassinelli/Superstudio.

In one of the catalogues of histograms, this world with "no quality" is precisely measured by the ironic, blatantly dysfunctional presence of another Superstudio member, Gian Piero Frassinelli, with a dog. The animal was a stray dog living in Piazza Bellosguardo, where the group had its office, and the picture was taken by Cristiano Toraldo di Francia during one of their lunch breaks, when they went out for some sandwiches at the grocery nearby and the dog came to claim its part. From that moment on, *Piero e il cane* (Piero and the dog) became almost an icon of "life in the age of single design," also appearing in the catalogue of Misura furniture, a series of objects designed with the same material and logic as the histograms but related to more conventional functions (chairs, benches, tables, etc.). Yet the presence of the animal doesn't aim to contextualize or domesticate the abstractness of the object. Quite the opposite: here the dog is not the faithful friend of man, but the representation of life liberated from all symbolic obligations of culture and returned to a relationship with things mediated just by their formal—that is, geometric—aspect.

In 1972, the New York MoMA show *Italy: The New Domestic Landscape* became both the stage and the battlefield allowing visitors to compare the designs of the masters (from Castiglioni and Magistretti to Zanuso) with the ideas of the young representatives of counterdesign. Superstudio took the event as an opportunity to further develop the project that summed up the research it had been conducting until then, paving the way for an even more radical turnaround. By interpolating the rationale of *The Continuous Monument* with that of the histograms, *Supersuperficie* (Supersurface) consists of a sort of two-dimensional histogram on a planetary scale, an imaginary grid that covers the entire surface of the earth intended as "a visual-verbal metaphor for an ordered and rational distribution of resources."[1] For Superstudio, the peak of the processes of modernization corresponded to a "life without objects" on a planet transformed into a single device that organizes human existence and makes it possible. Architecture ceases to be the mediation between humans and the environment or to represent such mediation. Humans' very existence—that is, life itself, in an ultimate overlap between nature and technology—is the public image of truly modern architecture. Not by chance, *Supersuperficie* was immediately included by Superstudio in a broader series of narratives called *Atti Fondamentali* (Fundamental acts). *Vita*, *Educazione*, *Cerimonia*, *Amore*, and *Morte* (Life, Education, Ceremony, Love, and Death) are the five chapters in an ambitious attempt to deal with life and design via a radical anthropological refoundation of architecture.

Among the five chapters of the *Atti Fondamentali*, *Cerimonia* is the one that more than the others deals with the very essence of life, which, according to Superstudio, is first of all a *ritual*. Here the discourse about architecture leads to a convergence between symbolic ethos, rooted in Adolfo Natalini's literary background, and immaterial culture, as investigated by Gian Piero Frassinelli, the anthropologist of the group. The result is a series of tales, published in another issue of *Casabella* in February 1973, in which life is explored as a continuous sequence of unconventional rites. "Beyond the use of architecture as a service (shelter, microclimate), another type of use is continually happening,"

Superstudio writes. "This is the symbolic use of architecture. Architecture as the formalization of the symbols of knowledge, dominion, procreation and immortality."[2] That is why, it concludes, we can say that "every building on earth is destined for some unknown ceremony . . . and beyond all illusion, we could try to build a reality for ourselves in which all ceremonies and rites are exclusively ours and could perhaps be very quickly forgotten."[3]

In this therapy of taking "architecture to pieces bit by bit and [putting] it on the table, until it is finally available for use," animals represent a significant *agent*. Such is the case of the chapter called "Los Esclavos" (The slaves), in which the citizens of a rigidly organized society inhabiting a square village leave their town only on June 21 each year. On that day, they go out into the surrounding plain and catch wild horses, brutally killing them in a violent, exorcistic massacre perpetrated in the name of the god that they fear, whose name is *Libertad* (Freedom). In other cases, the tone of the tale is that of a true parable, as in "The Great Pilgrimage" (*Cerimonia "Il Grande Pellegrinaggio"*), to which Superstudio dedicated one of the famous lithographs of the *Atti Fondamentali*—and, for sure, the most cryptic. The tale tells the story of the island of Kon-Su-Mi (a play on the term "consumption") discovered by a "missionary from General Motors," where natives worship as a living god a hermit living in a cave on an inaccessible rock. It's worth hearing the story in the words of Superstudio:

> The missionary succeeded in reaching the hermit and talked with him for twenty years, trying in vain to persuade him to purchase an 80,000 HP turbine. Finally, in desperation, he killed himself. His letter of goodbye, published throughout the world, caused a sensation, and thus began the spread of the cult of the "Naked God" in all nations of consumer faith. Every good consumer today holds it his moral duty to visit the Naked God at least once in his lifetime. Each day, the magnates of industry and commerce can be seen arriving at the feet of the red statue of Consumerism. Having abandoned their Cadillacs, Rolls, and private jets, and dressed in the most modest clothing available, they climb the 5,273 grey stone steps that now replace the original native liana ladder. At the end of the stairway, the pilgrims raise their arms and are subjected to an inspection by the chief of the 3,000 guards watching over the Naked God.
>
> Today, the original search has become a mere formality, because no one would dare commit the grave sacrilege of introducing any object into the god's grotto. Access to the small cavern is a very moving moment, almost no one manages to hold back his tears, hysterical scenes often take place, and many women faint. In the grotto, lit only by the light coming through the door, one can glimpse behind the grille separating him from visitors, the mystical figure of the hermit, "the One without Objects," as he is called. There exists but one rare photograph of the Naked God, wrapped in a soft white blanket, which we are proud to be able to offer to our readers; it was taken by a Japanese reporter

who managed, at the risk of his life, to enter the holy cell, eluding the watchful guards, with a micro-camera hidden in a wart on his nose.[4]

Following the story, Superstudio published in the pages of *Casabella* the "rare photograph" of the Naked God: the curious face of a chimp effectively wrapped in a soft white blanket. What better than a monkey to evoke human life without objects?

They wanted to use the same picture for the main lithograph, but the quality of the image did not allow the necessary magnification, so they fell back on the picture of a scary red-headed ape, realizing that, in the end, it worked much better. After all, life without objects is not a matter of aesthetics.

Earthworm

Teresa Stoppani

Architects do not draw earthworms, as they are disturbingly inconvenient when it comes to form. Modular and iterative, their repetition of rings (Latin *anellum-anelli*, hence the name of the phylum Annelida) could have been the envy of both modernist and organicist experimental architectural projects. But no, there is no reference to worms of any sort in the Plan Obus for Algiers, where Le Corbusier is intent on celebrating speed with the motorway running atop the long ribbon of social housing, a linear segmental sequence of concrete frames to be occupied by apartments.[1] There is no mention of worms in relation to Luigi Carlo Daneri's Forte Quezzi INA Casa social housing complex in Genoa, nicknamed "Biscione"—the snake, not the earthworm[2]—by the press and the public for its long linear undulations along the slope of the Quezzi valley.

The earthworm is inconvenient for architecture. It is not that the earthworm does not have a "head" and a "tail," but it is difficult to tell its mouth and anus apart at first glance. Architecture likes its fronts and backs, its beginnings and ends. Earthworms are variable in length and they are rarely isolated, they wriggle and dig, their entanglements further supporting the misplaced impression that they may have no beginning and no end. The earthworm questions measures and boundaries. Made of intestine for most of its length, it is oblivious to the vertical and the horizontal, surface and ground, which it disturbs as it stirs, digests, and mixes soils.

Its modularity notwithstanding, the earthworm is not form-friendly. For architecture, it raises an ontological problem. As such, it is a threat. For Georges Bataille, the earthworm (along with the spider and spit) is the epitome of the formless (*informe*) that "has no rights in any sense and gets itself squashed everywhere."[3] The formless must be crushed "because it has no right in any sense, because it does not make any sense, and because that in itself is unbearable to reason," glosses Yve-Alain Bois.[4] It is "the unassimilable waste that Bataille would shortly designate as the object of heterology."[5]

Georges Didi-Huberman has explained the relation of the formless to the earthworm with the idea of "formless resemblance" (*ressemblance informe*),[6] a relation in which are embedded figure, morphology, and metaphor. Bois instead proposes that the *informe* cannot be "mapped onto the idea of deformation [as it] resembles nothing [and] the 'something like' [used by Bataille is]

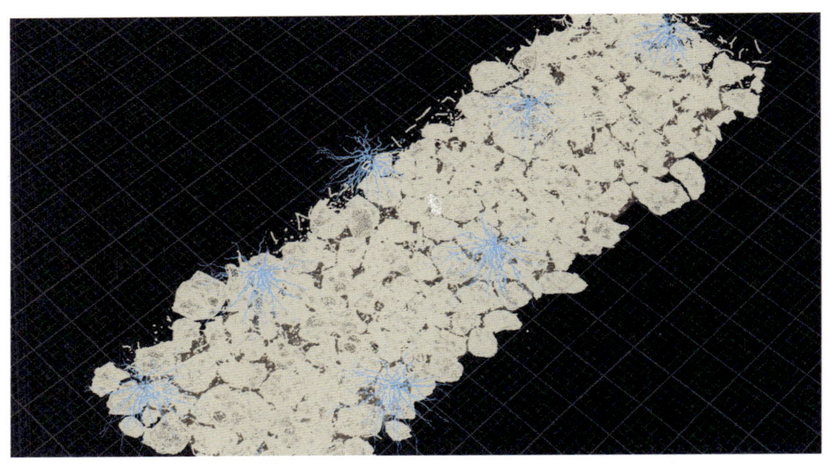

Figure 5.1
Forensic Architecture and David Wengrow, *The Nebelivka Hypothesis*, 2023. Soil structure. Wireframe view of the structure of the soil composed by worms' channels, debris, minerals, and plant roots. Sunflower roots are highlighted in blue. © Forensic Architecture.

not referring to a resemblance but to an operation." The *informe*, then, is not a figure but an operation that crushes "metaphor, figure, theme, morphology, meaning—everything that resembles something, everything that is gathered into the unity of a concept."[7]

The disturbing formlessness of the earthworm is not in its shape but in its operation. Science realized this a long time ago. Drawing from observations by Charles Darwin and by Otto August Mangold, Jakob von Uexküll explains how the earthworm identifies the different parts of a leaf or a pine needle to more easily pull it into its tunnel. The identification of the more convenient form does not occur by shape; the worm distinguishes the stem from the apex of a leaf by their different taste. Uexküll concludes that there is "nothing to the notion of shape perception in earthworms," "the worm is in no condition, by its constitution, to develop shape schemata," and it is the change in taste that becomes the "form symbol for the earthworm."[8]

No shapes for the earthworm, who smells and tastes and operates by moving matter around and through its body. It is this that the architect can grasp and represent, through a process of mapping: representing not the icon but the trace, and of the traces making a map, possibly a dynamic one. The traces left behind/around by the earthworm are not only the marks of its movements and the spaces of its making, but the product of the transformation of the soil it performs: the transferring, the processing and digestion of matter.

In *The Nebelivka Hypothesis*, a collaboration of Forensic Architecture with archaeologist David Wengrow,[9] the earthworm becomes not only a clue and an investigative tool, but indeed the co-constructor of the rich substratum that supported the sustenance of ancient communities and is now the fertile black soil of central Ukraine. Forensic Architecture's research project, concentrated at first around the village of Nebelivka, spread across a wide area of the Ukrainian steppe to explore the traces of 6,000-year-old settlements and study their physical aggregation, in order to advance hypotheses on the form of their society and their relation to the land. The investigation combines archaeology, paleobotany, and soil science with the tools of Forensic Architecture (aerial photography, satellite imagery, image processing, electromagnetic scanning, remote sensing, multispectral dataset analysis, and parametric modeling) to reveal the presence under agricultural land of the remains of cities "organized as concentric rings of domestic buildings, around a mysterious open space"[10] that remains empty. The remains of these large ring-shaped settlements appear to be centerless, and show "no traces of temples, palaces, administration, rich burials, nor any other signs of centralized control or social stratification."[11] The Nebelivka hypothesis therefore proposes the model of an ancient nonhierarchical, noncentralized, collaborative urban settlement. But the true finding of the project is revealed when the analysis, from space and ground, enters the soil of the region to discover its "architecture": the chernozem[12] is an anthropogenic soil (anthrosol) produced by humans with the collaboration of the earthworm. The practice of the rotational "sacrificial" burning of houses (those more internal within the concentric rings) in the settlement, and their reduction to compressed platforms of incinerated wattle and daub, provided the ideal environment for the action of the earthworms, mixing sediments in a process of soil enrichment.

The Nebelivka hypothesis not only challenges the hierarchical and extractive nature of the city's relation to "its" territory but proposes a productive collaboration of human and nonhuman (buildings, fire, earthworm, soil) in the making and maintaining of the environment: "soil becomes an artifact and the artifact becomes an extension of the soil."[13] Making soil is a complex and collaborative process, and a very slow one. It can be diagrammed and mapped, but not drawn.

There are many wormlike critters[14] in John Hejduk's architectural parables, but they are not earthworms: serpents rather, tentacles, Medusa's mane, even unruly garden hedges, all performing the architectural detours[15] that Hejduk so wonderfully stages. Yet there are worms in his illustration of Aesop's fable "The Hare and the Tortoise,"[16] accompanying Tortoise to the finish line of the race. They are fable earthworms: they have a crowned head, eyes, and a smile even if they do not have a mouth. Or maybe they are victoriously mocking us, as one of them seals the moral of the fable. *Slow and steady wins the race.*

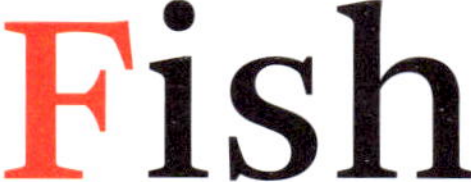

Fish

André Tavares

There is not much literature on the work of Eduardo Iglésias (1926–2014).[1] Having graduated in Porto in 1958, he designed an acclaimed beer factory in Vialonga, on the outskirts of Lisbon, with brutalist concrete patterns contrasting with a large aluminum curtain wall, whose transparency exposed the facility's machinery. In the 1960s he was keen on rational structures, the Miesian tones of his geometries softened by the juxtaposition of textured materials. That was the case with a modest structure designed for the Matosinhos refrigeration company, an ice supplier and cold storage facility built in one of Europe's largest dedicated areas for the production of canned sardines.[2] The section highlights the structure of the horizontal wooden ceiling, offset by a vertical exposed brick wall that signposts the pavilion. Prominent in the brick wall was a distinctive smiling creature, with a round eye, visible scales, a mouth, a fin like a fancy haircut, and a peculiar tentative tail. It was a fish. Was the generic appearance of the sea creature equivalent to the corporate anonymity of mid-century international architecture?

Iglésias could have drawn a complete abecedary, starting with albacore and ending up with *Zeus faber*, popularly known as John Dory. Each letter would correspond to a different species, with the physiology of each species providing the cue for different architectural outcomes. In that scenario, *G* would stand for *Gadus morhua*, or *C*, since it is known as cod; *S* for *Sardina pilchardus*, and *T* for tuna, or *Thunnus thynnus*.

Cod is a demersal fish that preys on other fish: it has a strong muscular mass and is low in fat. The fact that it inhabits the zone where warm and cold currents meet allows it to seek out the particular water temperature and food that accord with the various stages of its life cycle. Before being preyed upon by fisheries, which led to cod's commercial extinction in the Grand Banks, architecture for processing cod consisted of large areas of open-air drying racks, combining the "stage" where the fish were landed and processed, the "flake" where the fish were dried, the "office" used for work, and the "cook room" for the fishermen to eat in and possibly sleep.

Letter *S*, for sardines, would feature a different architecture. The sardine is a pelagic fish that lives in the upper levels of the water column and occupies a lower rank than cod in the trophic chain. Rich in fatty acids, it benefits from strong upwellings, where the upper layers of the water column are

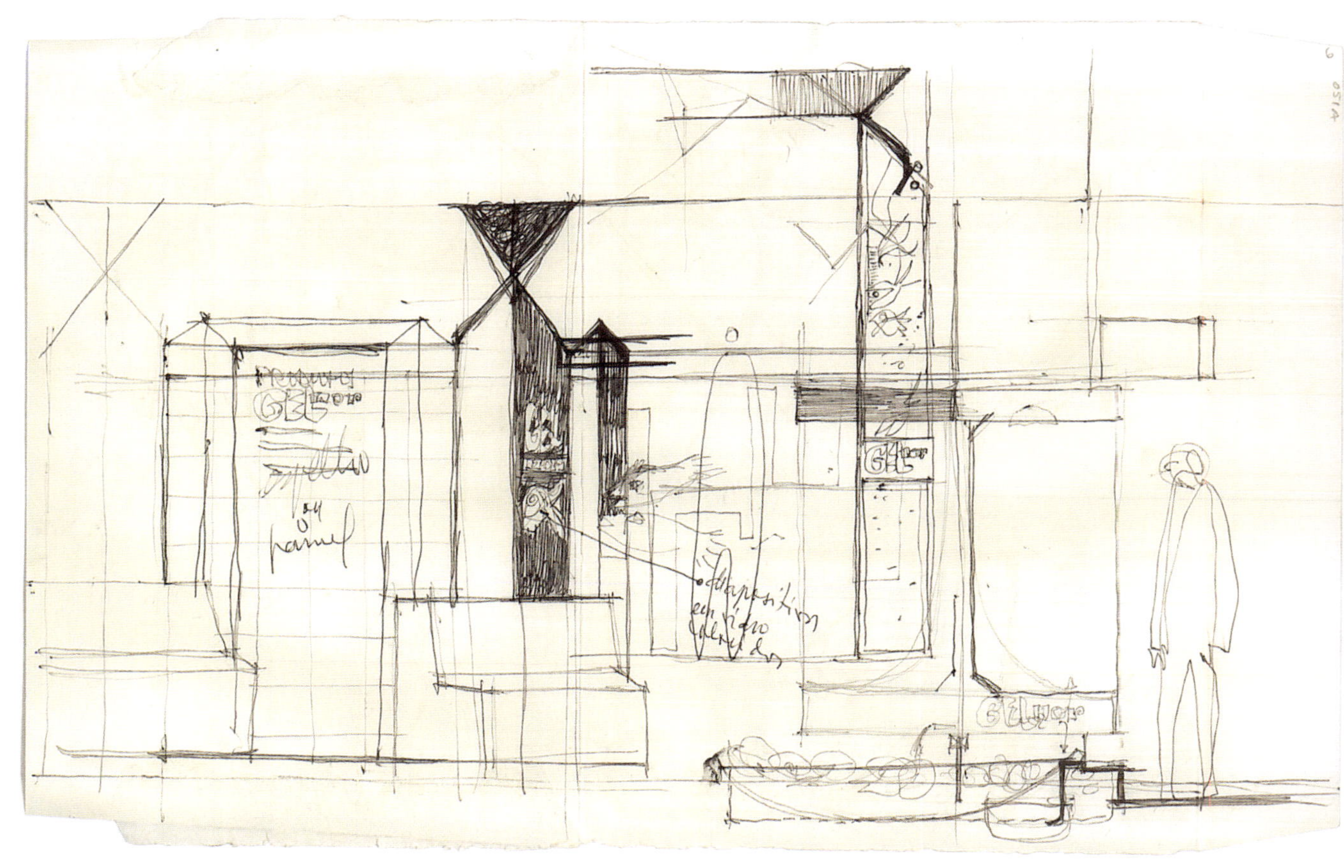

Figure 6.1
Eduardo Iglésias, Frigoríficos de Matosinhos, Grémio e Gelnor (section drawing), 1973. Ref. code: FAUP/CDUA /EI /ARQ/051_pd011-014. Courtesy Faculty of Architecture of the University of Porto.

simultaneously cold and rich with nutrients. It migrates in large schools, which protects it from predators, moving in deeper layers of the water column during the night and moving up to feed near the surface during the day. The fact that it occupies a lower rank in the trophic chain makes it sensitive to environmental cycles, with volatile populations responding to better or worse recruitment years. Eventually, it was such volatility that led to the collapse of famous industrial districts like Cannery Row in Monterey, California, when the fishing pressure on the local sardine populations was higher than the sustainable yield. Its industrial architecture was made of large ordinary concrete buildings, its most distinctive feature being the floating hoppers that drove the sardines, after they had been unloaded, through an underwater pipe and up into the factories over a pier in the harbor.

The letter *T* would feature structures on top of the dunes, *arraiais*, built as camping facilities in the southern Iberian Peninsula to support the seasonal operation of *almadravas* catching tuna on their migratory passage toward the Mediterranean. Atlantic bluefin tuna is a large apex predator capable of swimming at great speed, and it is part of a large family of tuna with a variety of related species and subspecies. They can average between 2 and 2.5 meters in length and are found throughout the Atlantic since they can adapt to cold and warm water temperatures, diving down to depths of 500 to 1,000 meters. They congregate to spawn, which they do mostly in the Mediterranean and in the Gulf of Mexico, and they are highly migratory, crossing the Atlantic at speeds of up to 88 kilometers per hour. The *almadravas* are complex systems built on the water to divert the swimming tuna into an enclosure. Once trapped, the beasts are an easy prey for fishermen, who catch them in violent bloody battles.

Cod, tuna, and sardine are thus very different fish, easy to characterize in a drawing made by a skilled draftsman. Iglésias's drawing did not represent any of them but rather depicted a generic fish. The cartoon-like figure resurfaced in a sketch he made for the facade of a frozen fish shop in downtown Porto.[3] Designed in 1973, its angular shapes were supposed to be built in glass and wood, emphasizing the colors of a modern life where consuming fish no longer involved long hours of gutting and washing (not to mention the powerful odor of salted cod left soaking for days in a row) and could be bought cheaply in hygienic frozen fillets. Instead of the *C*, *S*, and *T* fish and architectural varieties, the representation of *F* as a standard animal echoes the *F* that stands for "frozen" and "fillet." The naïve drawing by Iglésias is a reminder of an entire history of architecture that we can record by following ice as an agent of change.

Ice was used in fishing vessels from the late eighteenth century on. It allowed English fishermen to look for new fishing grounds further from the shore when the sole and flounder inshore populations were becoming scarce after decades of continuous exploitation. When the Manchester railway line was inaugurated in 1830, connecting the harbors of Grimsby and Hull to Sheffield and Liverpool, ice and refrigerated wagons expanded the commercial range of fisheries and the distance that could exist between fishing grounds and marketplaces, and the shore harbor became a pivotal point connecting two independent infrastructural systems (on sea and on land). The growing urban population demanded more food, and the capacity to link resources to consumption increased the pressure upon fish populations. Trawling became economically viable, with ice making it possible to keep the so-called fresh fish for a few days before selling them. Increasing the supply of fish for urban consumption was the genesis of fish and chips, an urban product whose purpose was to sell the remnants of the previous day's unsold fish. It became popular to deep-fry chunks of fish remnants, selling them just before they lost their commercial value, with the fried oil masking the somewhat unappealing smell.

Freezers were introduced as an experiment intended to expand the meat industry. Meat can maturate, and even if the first freezers did not exactly improve its taste, the technology seemed appropriate as a means to connect the distant markets of England and the United States to Australia or Argentina. In technological terms, frozen fish was a logical extension of frozen meat. Its performance as a logistical operation was advanced by the Great War, when in 1915 the French government had recourse to refrigerated carriages to supply the army at the front. The system prompted the construction of large concrete refrigerators in the nodes of the French railway system. In the 1920s, these monolithic Hennebique-style functional structures were the harbingers of a new era. In Lorient, a prominent new freezer was paired with an American counterpart built in the French Newfoundland domain of Saint Pierre and Miquelon. The idea was to fish cod off Newfoundland, freeze it immediately (instead of the long and laborious curing process required for dried and salted cod), and ship it in boats equipped with freezers to the French refrigerated railway system. Despite the erection of the buildings, the government program was a fiasco.

When, in the 1930s, the Norwegians imagined building a network of freezing facilities throughout the northern coastal settlements of Finnmark, the plan was to increase the value of their fisheries, notably cod and herring. At the time, while Norwegians were extracting from the ocean twice the volume of British fisheries, Norwegian sales of salted and dried products were worth half those of the British. Selling frozen fish, even if less profitable than fresh fish, was more lucrative than salted fish and was seen as a way to rescue northern villages from poverty. The plan came to completion after World War II, when the government had to rebuild the villages from the destruction caused by the German army's retreat. The Germans, like the French, had recourse to frozen fish to feed their armies, and northern Norway was an important source for the purpose.

Postwar industrial development, especially in the United States, provided the ideal context in which frozen fillets, and later fish fingers, could enjoy commercial success. Precooked meals and domestic freezers, promoted by electric companies as a means to ensure permanent domestic consumption of energy, catered to the high demand for proteins which, with the support of an efficient cold chain, could be sourced from far away. It was this distance, from the fishing areas to the consumer's table, that did away with the differences between fish species and created the global idea of fish. The geometric shape of the fish finger, deprived of bones and other encumbrances, was fried in butter with a bread crust to become a worldwide standard. No longer cod or halibut, but simply fish.

Iglésias's cartoon embodies this complex history as an architectural synthesis, the urban frozen fish shop. Its logic is the Atlantic as a commercial space, and the networks created by transformed fishing technologies and improved logistical networks connect the shape of the drawing to the ecological impact of architecture. Whereas the drying racks for cod were an emblem of the substantial impact of fisheries on the Grand Banks cod populations, it was the fish finger and the frozen capacity of European and American fleets that depleted the gargantuan biomass of Atlantic cod. This was the difference between the *C* for cod, the *G* for *Gadus morhua*, and the *F* for fish. The selection of the letter of the alphabet to classify Iglésias's sketch had a significant architectural and ecological impact.

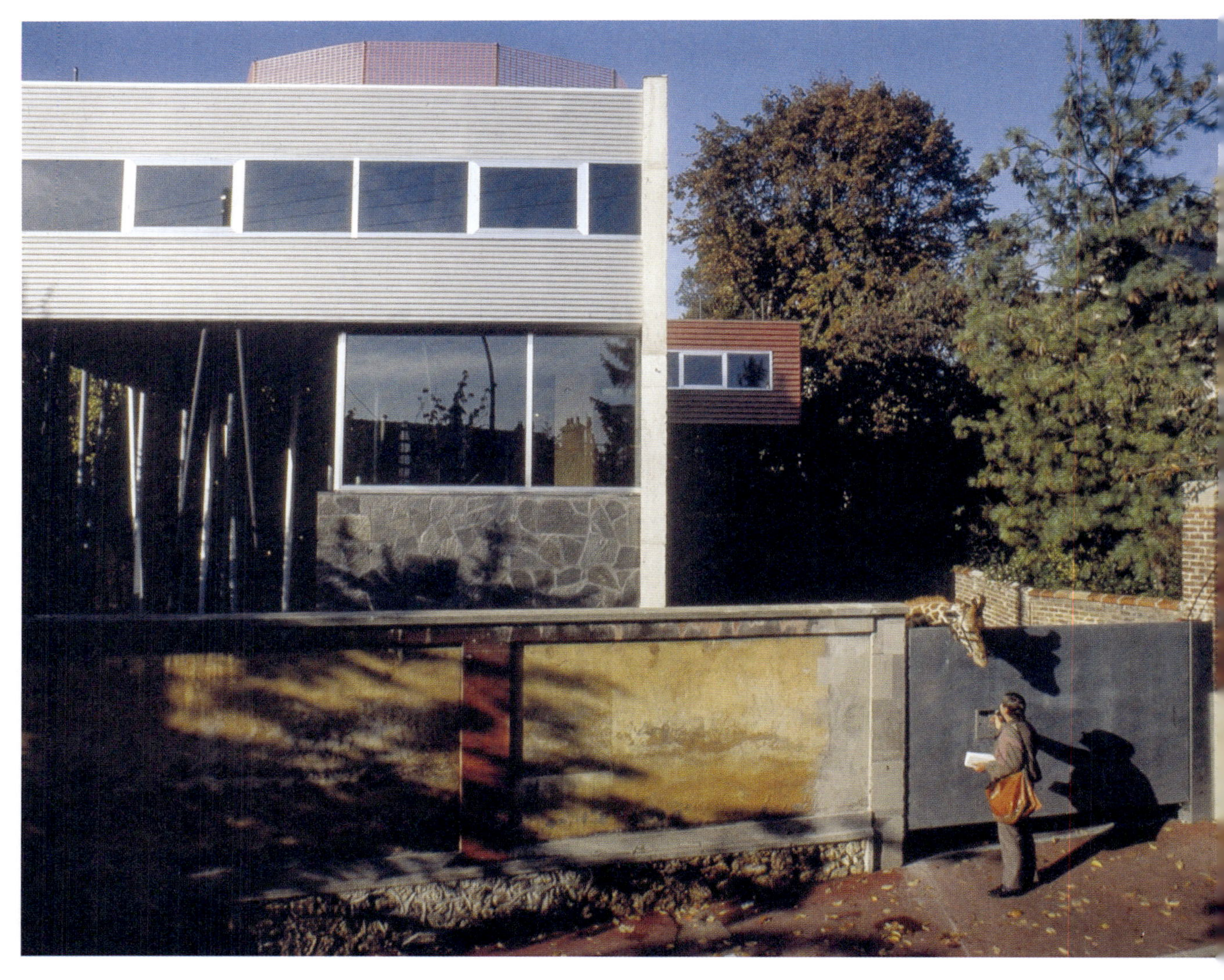

Figure 7.1
OMA/Rem Koolhaas, Villa dall'Ava, Saint-Cloud, 1984–1991.
Photograph by Hans Werlemann, Courtesy of OMA.

Giraffe

Françoise Fromonot

Rem Koolhaas's automonograph *S,M,L,XL* is full of puzzling images.[1] Strange inserts, unlikely collisions, and mysterious iconographic encounters punctuate a volume organized as if to solicit the reader's interpretive capacities constantly. The photographic tour of the Villa dall'Ava—one of the smallest buildings presented in the book—is one of its most extraordinary visual sequences.[2] Pictures are from a one-week photo shoot in the villa by two preferred collaborators of OMA, the photographer Hans Werlemann and the videographer Chiel van der Stelt. Conceived as an antidote to the clichés of architectural photography, the pictures were generated "to test the perennial qualities of the villa by imagining it in twenty situations fifty years from now," explained Werlemann.[3] A number of potential pets were planned to be part of this scenario, including a large snake, but the film directors had to make do with a young giraffe, Romeo, borrowed from a nearby zoo. In one of the photographs reproduced in *S,M,L,XL*, Romeo is led in the driveway by a mysterious attendant, seen through the glazed facade along the house's ramp. OMA's archive contains several less-known pictures of the same series, all showing the graciously awkward animal wandering around the house as if to address certain aspects of its architecture.

The giraffe scene in *S,M,L,XL* has often been considered as a pleasant if inexplicable anecdote. But to bring a real giraffe into a house of the Paris suburbs it is no easy task. What could be the architect's underlying intention there? To stage and fix an analogy between this strangely built animal and the inversion of gravity displayed in the villa, where the mass of the swimming pool is carried by indecisive *pilotis*?[4] And therefore to insist on the creative strategy adopted by OMA in order to fulfill the programmatic desire of the client—a glass house and a swimming pool, on a plot too narrow to accommodate both—resulting in their counterintuitive superimposition? Or, in a more Freudian manner, is the physical presence of the giraffe meant to trigger a free association between several elements of the project which otherwise would have remained latent, designating in the process some theoretical intentions embedded in the project itself? Obviously, there are the slender Mikado sticks that raise the block of the street-side living quarter as if by magic, but also the pattern of the *opus incertum*—brown with light mortar—that clads the base of the villa. The stone, cold and mineral, evokes by antiphrasis the warm and sensual skin of the giraffe, paradoxically underscoring the artificiality of the building. And then there is the resonance of both of these metaphors with the distant silhouette of the Eiffel Tower to which the long axis of the pool is directed. The recurrent analogy found in popular representations between Paris's symbol of modernity and a giraffe accredits this hypothesis, confirming the metropolitan ambition of this small project.

An animal of strange proportions, with the head of a ruminant and the coat of a wild cat, the giraffe has been an enduring source of fascination for scholars, artists, and the population at large ever since its arrival in Europe. Science had to invent a portmanteau word to name this unique biological collage. In his magnificent *Icones Animalium* (1560), the Swiss naturalist Conrad Gessner called it *PantheraCamelo*, panther-camel, and featured it twice among portraits of more common beasts. The usual species name of the giraffe, *camelopardalis*—camel-marked-like-a-leopard (*pardus*)—describes a chimerical creature, an aberration, an overturning of nature's order. Hieronymus Bosch painted a giraffe in symmetry with a unicorn in the *Eden* panel of his *Garden of Earthly Delights* (1503–1504). The prodigious creatures that inhabited the iconography of the Middle Ages continued to prowl around the margins of the Renaissance, kept alive by the Flemish artists that the surrealists would find so appealing. Years later, Carel Willink—a Dutch surrealist still active when Rem Koolhaas and Madelon Vriesendorp were students[5]—produced a series of canvases showing large African animals wandering around famous classical French gardens, including one of a couple of giraffes stationed at the foot of the Orangerie staircase at Versailles (*Two Giraffes*, 1956). These were part of Willink's style of magic realism where the imaginary landscapes and scenes are assembled out of existing elements documented by photography.

Koolhaas's giraffe would therefore point toward a Flemish iconographic tradition spanning over four centuries, in which animals, familiar or fantastic, occupy a place of choice. The alphabetical glossary running in the margins of *S,M,L,XL* has an entry on "Animals," a quote from Demetri Porphyrios quoting Foucault quoting Borges quoting the famous taxonomy of animals found in a "Chinese encyclopedia."[6] Is it a way to establish a link here between animals and the endless circulation of references, the rhizomatic propagation of their possible meanings that culture is made of? In this respect, the giraffe, with its iconographic fortune over time, might have a more personal, biographical resonance for Koolhaas. His father, Anton (1912–1992), was an acknowledged expert on wildlife, a writer and producer of documentaries on the subject. He is famous in the Netherlands for his animal novellas, which have largely remained untranslated and are therefore little known outside the Dutch-speaking world.[7] Their favorite theme is the animal view of the world, and among their little heroes are a spider, a dog, a bear, a sparrow, or a bat (aka a "flying rat," another example of nature's talent for fabulous hybridization).

But more than anything else, the giraffe is a totem in the bestiary of Salvador Dalí. In his paintings, drawings or installations, the Catalan surrealist obsessively inserted one or several specimens, their mane in flames. The burning giraffe appeared first in *L'Âge d'or* (1930), whose set Dalí designed for Luis

Buñuel. The year that he painted the image for the first time (*Girafe en feu*, 1937), he had planned to shoot a film with the Marx Brothers, to be called *Giraffes on Horseback Salad*;[8] some preparatory drawings for the sets show a formal dinner on a terrace lit by giraffes transformed into candelabras, and a swimming pool in a grand piano. Could the giraffe, then, be another of Koolhaas's nods to the Eiffel Tower, ritually turned into an animal of fire by the Bastille Day fireworks, which the owners of the villa never miss, watching from their pool terrace? Riffing on the imagination of Bosch, Dalí then modified the anatomy of other animals to conform to that of the giraffe. In his famous *Temptation of St. Anthony* (1946), for instance, he gives a horse and elephants spidery legs and has them carry heavy burdens on their backs: an obelisk, a baroque basilica, a gigantic sculpture. With its phallic neck, the burning giraffe represented "the masculine cosmic apocalyptic monster," Dalí proclaimed in "The Terrifying and Edible Beauty of Art Nouveau Architecture," in which he held forth about his loathing of rationalist modernism—in other words, of Le Corbusier—and his love for Gaudí and art nouveau.[9]

Is Koolhaas borrowing once again from surrealism, and more specifically from Dalí, in order to mock and overtake Le Corbusier? In *Delirious New York*, he analyzed Le Corbusier's negative reaction to the Manhattan skyline, contrasting it—in order to make it his own—with Dalí's wholehearted adhesion to the surrealism of New York.[10] Since the Villa dall'Ava displays a systematic mishandling of the "five points of modern architecture,"[11] as if to deliberately turn the canon of Le Corbusier's purist villas into a theater of delirium, the presence of the giraffe could point to Dalí being the secret agent behind this *détournement*. All the more so since the villa enacts, and the giraffe recalls word for word, the anatomical fiction that Le Corbusier deployed to denigrate the skyscrapers of Manhattan: "Imagine a man undergoing a mysterious disturbance of his organic life; the torso remains normal, but his legs become 10 or 20 times too long."[12] The importation to the Villa dall'Ava of an African herbivore in a pretty coat may also be a response to a 1930 painting by the English surrealist Christopher Wood, depicting a zebra—another *objet à réaction poétique* of flesh and blood—posing on the terrace of the Villa Savoye.[13] In fact, everything conspires to designate Le Corbusier as the main target of Koolhaas's architectural parody. A naturally mannerist animal, the giraffe epitomizes the Dutch architect's provocative deformation of the language of high modernism, in search of an experimental domestic architecture for the present day. A surrealistic reinterpretation of the modernist suburban villa, the Villa dall'Ava appears, in this respect, as a small manifesto.

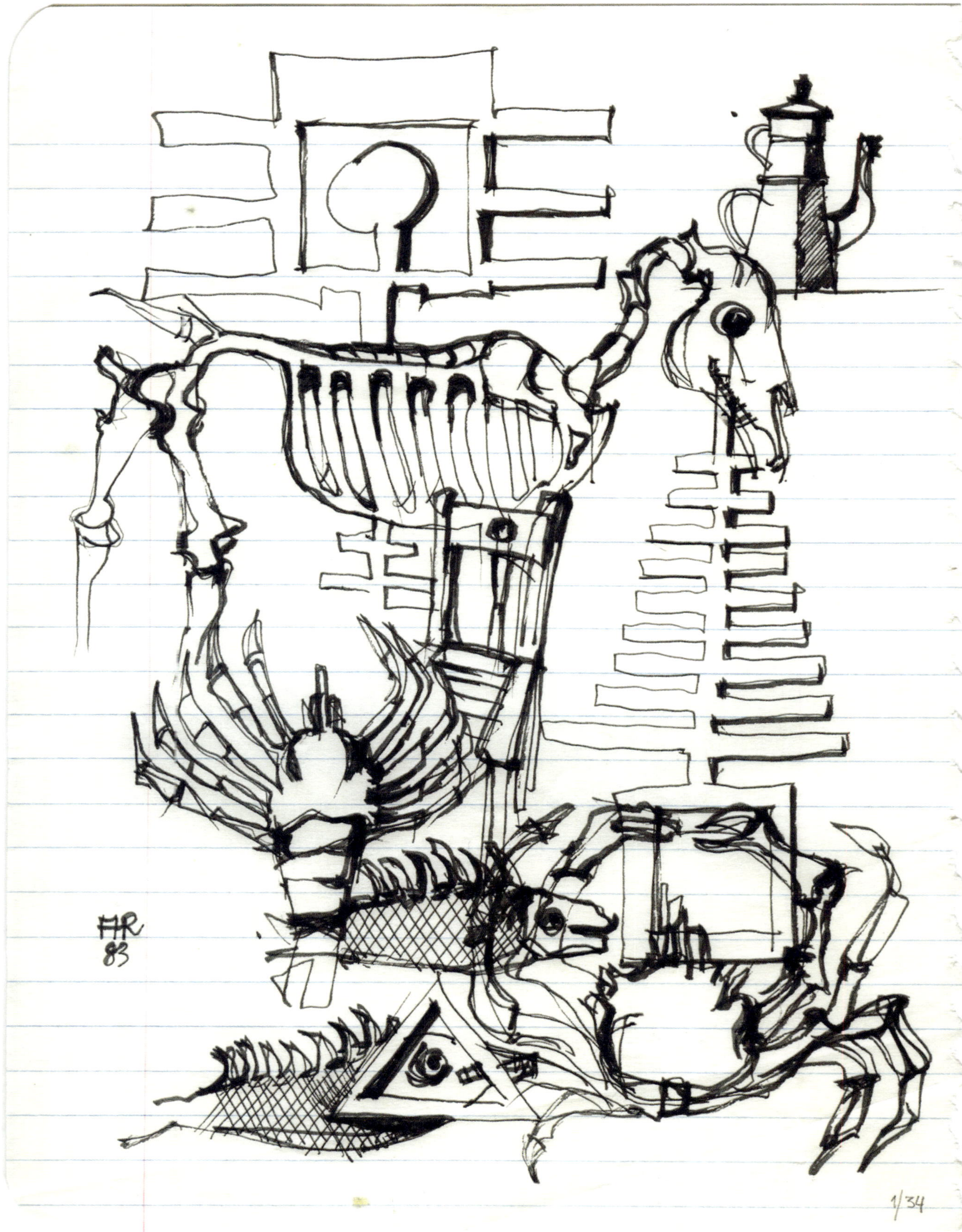

1/34

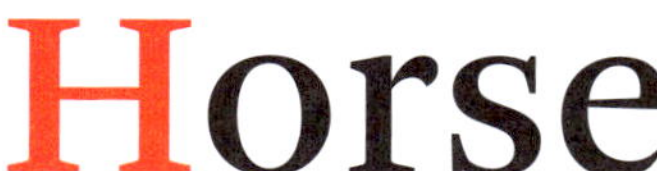

Horse

Iwan Strauven

Drawings of horses only appear relatively late in Aldo Rossi's graphic work: in 1982, sixteen years after the publication of his book *The Architecture of the City* and eight years after the completion of his contribution to Monte Amiata in Milan's Gallaratese district. At that time, the quadruped makes its appearance along with other animals—such as fish, lobsters, and crabs—but within this exquisite cenacle it claims most of Rossi's attention. He makes countless sketches and drawings of horses, horse skeletons, and horse heads, as an apparition in and part of the urban landscape, as a floating element in a pure composition or in close-up, with only the horse's head in view. This specific, emphatic, and repeated attention to the horse will continue until 1983, after which the noble animal will return only sporadically: in a drawing of the theater of Genoa (1990) or in a late presentation sketch for a Project for Stables (1991). The focal point of the series of horse sketches marks a very specific moment in Rossi's oeuvre: it forms a caesura that marks the transition between the brilliant young Rossi of the early years and the more mature master after 1984.

Rossi's sudden fascination with horses coincides with and was perhaps triggered by the organization of an exhibition of his own work in Mantua titled *Aldo Rossi a Mantova* that took place in 1984 at the Casa del Mantegna. Although it was a monographic exhibition about his own work, Rossi invited his favorite photographer, Luigi Ghirri, to contribute. This resulted in a dialogue between architect and photographer that was also reflected in the publication *Architetture padane* accompanying the exhibition. Instead of photographing Rossi's architecture, Ghirri was inspired by the specific context in which the exhibition took place: that's why he made images of horses: on the one hand, the horses that were portrayed by Andrea Mantegna and, on the other, the horses that, applied to the frescoes on the walls of the Palazzo del Te in Mantua, seem to be the real inhabitants of Giulio Romano's Mantuan masterpiece. In a very

Figure 8.1
Aldo Rossi, Untitled, 1983. Pen on paper, 24 × 7 × 19 cm. Private collection.

personal, brief text in the publication, Rossi provides additional explanation for their shared fascination with horses:

> In contrast to the horses of Palazzo del Te, the horses of Mantegna, sought after in Luigi Ghirri's photographs, represent fantasy here: they too are white, and they seem white not by race but rather pale with this pallor of which Virgil tells us, and this pallor contrasts with the powerful anatomical, earthy structure with which they are represented. In Palazzo del Te the "interior" becomes an "exterior"; and the horses that always return to Mantua are the inhabitants of a Project for Stables, which I never completed or only began, and which we present in this small volume.[1]

For his own sketches and drawings of horses presented in the catalogue, Rossi went back to the publication *The Anatomy of the Horse* by the well-known English horse painter George Stubbs. According to Rossi, Stubbs's work interested him more because of the structure of the skeleton than the form; he explained that he had "a primarily clinical interest in bones and their pathology, pathology that every Lombard relates to the dampness of our land, which is probably true, but which is also perhaps the result of ancient and internal deformations. Thus the study of these horses became confused with the study of chairs and furniture as supporting structures."[2]

In his drawings and sketches, we see how this analogical transposition between the skeleton of the horse and the supporting structure of the furniture is gradually subjected to a scaling up, not only to clarify his design of furniture but also to shed light on earlier work, such as the cemetery of San Cataldo in Modena or the already cited condominium of Monte Amiata in Milan's Gallaratese district, both of which are among Rossi's most iconic works of the early period. In his sketches from 1982 and 1983, the juxtaposition and, in some cases, even superimposition of horse and building establish an analogical transposition between animal and building and between skeleton and structure. But while, in the case of the simultaneously designed furniture, this operation is actually active in the creation of the project, this does not really seem to be the case with the older projects. Here it is, rather, an analogy encountered a posteriori that can be used to make the projects more understandable; the analogy is active not at an operational level in the project, but rather at an exegetic level in its interpretation.

This is not to say, however, that skeletal structure per se as an analogy played no significance in these earlier projects. On the contrary. In his *A Scientific Autobiography*, Rossi refers to the serious car accident he suffered in the spring of 1971 on his way to Istanbul, between Belgrade and Zagreb, which caused him to spend time in a small hospital in Slawonski Brod, where he was working on his project for the Modena cemetery:

> I lay in a small ground-floor room near a window through which I looked at the sky and a little garden. Lying almost immobile, I thought

> of the past, but sometimes I did not think: I merely gazed at the trees and the sky. This presence of things and of my separation from things—bound up also with the painful awareness of my own bones—brought me back to my childhood. During the following summer, in my study for the project, perhaps only this image and the pain in my bones remained with me: I saw the skeletal structure of the body as a series of fractures to be reassembled.[3]

Twelve years later, the study of the skeleton of the horse allows Rossi to represent this personal experience that would have so much influence on his own practice, thanks to the work of Stubbs, in a very visual and powerful way. More than with the other beasts that appear in his graphic work in those same years for the same reasons—the bone structure of fish, the carcasses of lobsters and crabs—the analogical transposition of the skeleton of the horse to the structure of a piece of furniture or a building is obvious: Rossi does not refer to the metaphor of the Trojan horse himself, but of course, as mobile architecture par excellence, capable of installing a new condition, it is never far away. Whatever the case, after the exhibition in Mantua and after the introduction of the horse as an operative analogy, Rossi's work gradually begins to lose some of its original intensity and seems to have begun to suffer from increasing self-consciousness and complacency—a turn in his oeuvre against which even the horse could not safeguard him.

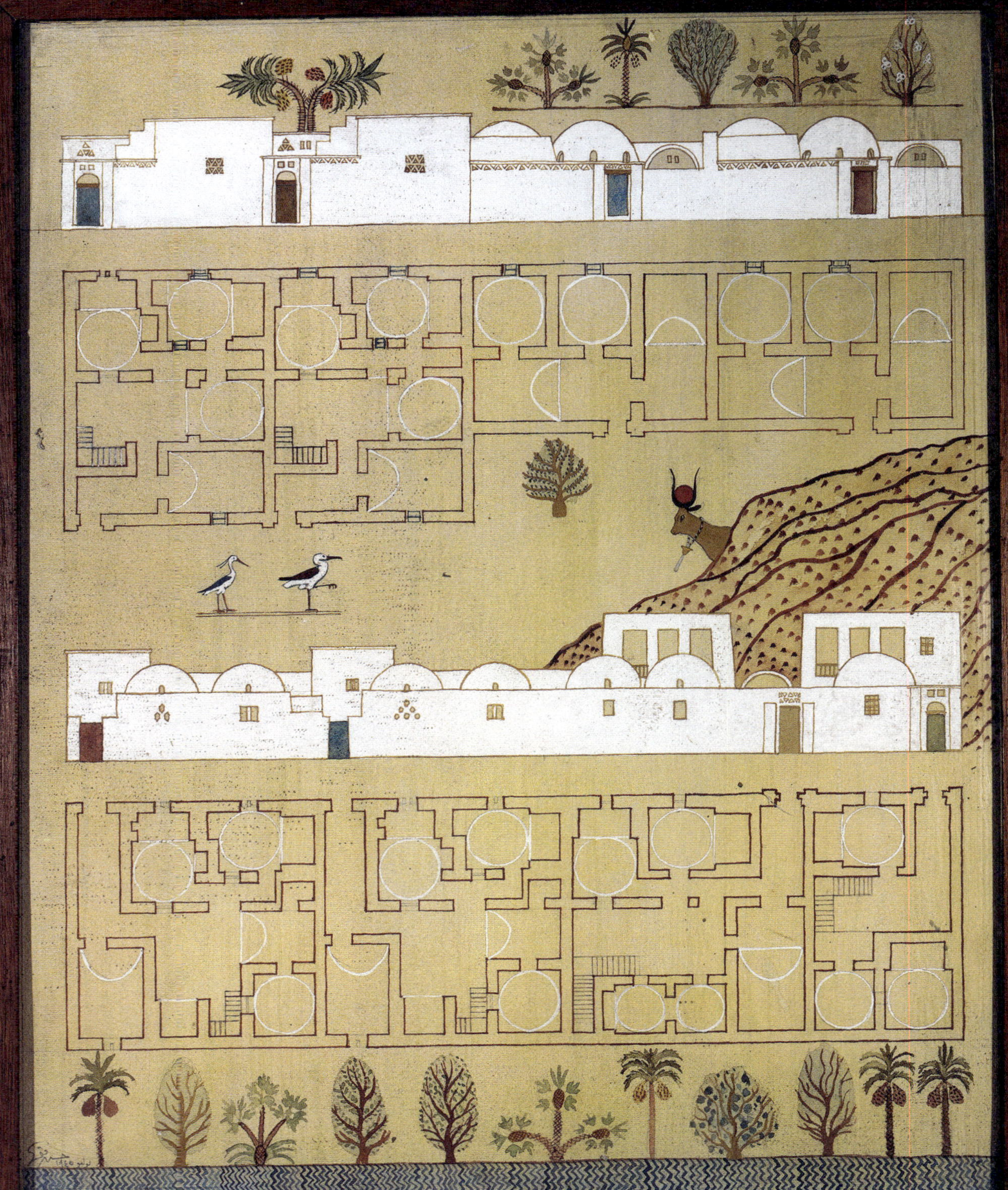

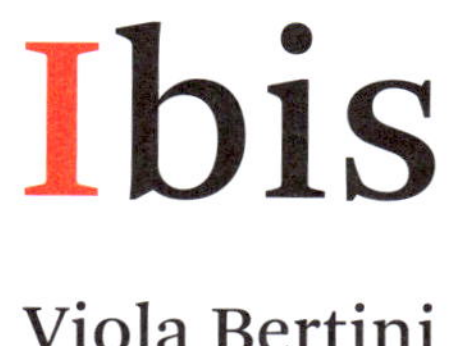

Ibis

Viola Bertini

I is an Ibis,
Who wanders in bogs,
And lives upon lizards,
And fishes and frogs.[1]

In 1946, the Egyptian architect Hassan Fathy painted the gouache titled *New Gourna Houses*. The design was both abstract and iconic, and the two-dimensionality of the representation constituted a direct reference to the ancient paintings of the Pharaonic age. Two groups of houses, drawn in plan and elevation, are the main objects of the composition. Colored white, they stand out from the background and refer to an idea of architecture with a strong character and strictly linked to the Egyptian context. The sacred mountain of Gourna is the only direct reference to the specific site; however, many symbols populate the watercolor, among which are the two ibises that occupy a central position within the image.[2] Placed between the two groups of houses, one with one foot raised and the other with both feet resting on the ground, the birds are facing the sacred mountain of Gourna, from which goddess Hathor emerges, represented here in the form of a *heavenly cow*.

The gouache, like the other pictorial works produced by Fathy during his long career,[3] represents a kind of manifesto of his architectural poetics, where logical realism and lyrical realism overlap and coincide. The two-dimensional geometric representation intersects with the dimension of the fable, as suggested by the inclusion of symbolic elements borrowed from popular culture and ancient mythology. Moreover, most of the topics characterizing Fathy's approach to history, context, and architecture can be retraced in this painting. The design of the houses, indeed, is nourished by many paradigms, bringing together several architectural elements: vividly colored doors, buttresses placed to mark building entrances, multiform *claustra*, domes, vaults, lodges,

Figure 9.1
Hassan Fathy, *New Gourna Houses*, 1946. Gouache. Plan and elevation with image of Hathor. © Aga Khan Trust for Culture/Gary Otte (photographer).

etc., all being typical architectural elements that belong to that broad Arab tradition to which Fathy looked in his attempt to define a modern architecture that would refer to culture and place. By transposing those elements from different places and times, by rewriting them and assembling them into a new design, Fathy gave birth to an Egyptian architecture which was new but, at the same time, strongly rooted in a collective memory. This design process, which makes use of this valuable reservoir of past forms, expresses a specific approach to architecture's correspondence to history and tradition: architecture not as a crystallization of the past, but as a critical rewriting of it.

In the gouache, the same approach is revealed by Fathy's choice to paint in the manner of the ancients and to inhabit the drawing with antique symbols that assume a double meaning: on the one hand, they affirm the architect's will to relate to the Egyptian past; on the other hand, they are a communication tool aimed at establishing a plan of shared dialogue between the architect and those who will inhabit his architecture. Indeed, the gouache *New Gourna Houses* was conceived by Fathy within the context of the project for New Gourna village, located close to Luxor, in ancient Thebes. In 1945, Fathy was commissioned by the Egyptian government to plan the new settlement, a task that proved to be extremely demanding, since it entailed designing an entire town from scratch intended to house the inhabitants of the ancient village of Gourna.

The people of Gourna, historically settled within the archaeological area of the Valley of the Kings and Queens, had made the illegal trade of ancient artifacts their main economic vocation. When an entire corner of carved rock was detached from the mountain and smuggled away by the Gournites, the Department of Antiquities was forced to take drastic measures. As a result, it was decided, after issuing a ministerial decree, to expropriate and demolish the houses of the old village built directly on top of the Pharaonic tombs, and to rebuild them outside the archaeological enclosure, in an area just a few kilometers away. However, the inhabitants of ancient Gourna were hostile to their relocation, which in practice meant abandoning their ancestral homes and their established ways of life.[4] In order to persuade them to move to the new village, Fathy involved the inhabitants in the design process, initiating a consultative mechanism as a sort of visionary experiment in participatory planning. His first aim was, in fact, to build spaces that could reflect the sensibilities of the people, in an effort to meet both the specific needs of the individuals and those of the entire community. Within this context, the gouache was intended by the architect as an instrument through which he would communicate to the Gournites his ideas for the new settlement; in this, the use of symbols had the purpose of stimulating the community's sense of belonging to the place.

Egyptian farmers, wrote Fathy, used to unconsciously decorate their houses with ancient hieroglyphs:

> while building the village of Gourna, . . . I asked Moallem Aladin Mustapha to decorate the doorway of one of the houses himself, in the way

> he liked. He reproduced some hieroglyphic symbols representing the sky, Noot, and the earth. By asking him how he arrived at this form he answered simply that it was a common figure against the evil eye. He did not realize, however, that it was a hieroglyphic inscription he was using. . . . When peasants are given the chance to build their own villages, they can express themselves in the same colorful and empathic visual language of their forefathers, which is suited to their character and to their environment.[5]

This incident explains, at least in part, the presence of the two ibises in the *New Gourna Houses* gouache and its multiple meanings. In the first place, they are emblematic of a vast context—the country of Egypt as such—in which the village is located and to which other presences also allude, such as the *doum* palm, a typical plant of the region, and the River Nile which lies along the bottom edge of the painting.

The ibises, like the goddess Hathor or the vegetation, constitute an explicit reference to the paintings of the Pharaonic period and declare a symbolic and spiritual belonging to Egyptian history. In fact, a mythological aura has solidified over time around the symbol of the ibis, deriving from the veneration it received in ancient Egypt, as testified by the many pictorial and sculptural representations of ibises to be seen in Egyptian art, and by the numerous mummified specimens found at burial sites.[6] In the context of the gouache, the presence of the two birds takes on further symbolic meanings, directly translated from antiquity. Two types of ibises were in fact the object of worship by the Egyptian civilization. The hermit ibis—*Geronticus eremita*—was represented by the term *Akh* in hieroglyphics, which indicated one of the nine elements of which the human body was believed to be composed.[7] The *Akh* expressed the quality of the individual who, after death, was destined to become part of the circumpolar stars, or stars that "know nought of perishing" and remain a constant of the night sky.[8] The term, which is difficult to transpose into contemporary language, can be interpreted as "soul" or "spirit" and translated as the word "resplendent," the latter quality attributable to the thick, polychrome brown plumage of the hermit ibis, whose hieroglyph was associated with this very concept. The cult of the sacred ibis—*Threskiornis aethiopicus*—was instead linked to that of the god Thoth, of whom the bird was considered an incarnation. Thoth was the god of wisdom, knowledge, and writing, and the inventor of language, the one who ruled over anything involving an intellectual operation. A lunar deity and a deputy of the god Ra, he also ruled mathematics and magic and was alternately represented in the form of a baboon, as a man with the head of an ibis, or entirely in the form of an ibis. According to mythology, the sacred ibis was in fact created by Ra, starting from Thoth, and given the role of messenger between the earth and the celestial sphere. Therefore, if the hermit ibis defended death, the sacred ibis protected life.[9] Apart from the symbolic figurations, the ibis was also adored as a purifying animal.[10] "The ibis is honored in Egypt," wrote Plutarch, "because it destroys snakes whose bite is deadly."[11]

By representing the ibises in the design of the village of New Gourna, Hassan Fathy was acknowledging the original matrix of his own culture and placing himself in a historical and cultural continuity. This approach expresses a vision of circular time for which past and present, ancient Egypt and modern Egypt, coexist without the slightest contradiction. By introducing the ibises into the painting, Fathy was suggesting that the maintenance of the eternal order of the universe was guaranteed by the eternal becoming, the perpetual renewal, the daily journey of the sun god Ra, the periodic flooding of the River Nile, and therefore the cyclical trend which, according to ancient Egyptian cosmogony, overlaps the linear flow of time: "The first perception of infinity, an infinite circle, as the ancient Egyptians used to represent it by a snake biting its own tail."[12] As incarnations of the god Thoth and as purifying animals associated with the initial stages of creation, the two ibises in the gouache may also be a good omen for the success of the project, placed there to protect the houses and their inhabitants and to guide the intellectual work of the architect who, also under the watchful eye of Thoth, is called to design the new village with rationality and wisdom.

By the mid-nineteenth century, the African sacred ibis had gone extinct in the country that once glorified and venerated it; only with great luck, looking toward the sky, can someone today catch sight of some of these birds migrating from sub-Saharan Africa across the land of the Pharaohs. The ibises represented in the New Gourna gouache have survived a much longer flight: the one from antiquity to modernity.

Japanese Dragon (*Ryū*)

Thomas Daniell

While the European dragon and the Asian dragon share obvious visual characteristics, there are also some essential differences. The former tends to be a cave-dwelling, fire-breathing, malevolent man-eater (or princess-eater) that terrorizes the local community, with just enough animal cunning to hoard treasure and obstruct the path of questing knights. Physically, it is a chimera, a hybrid animal: bat-winged, snake-scaled, goat-horned, tiger-taloned, but fundamentally reptilian. Though occasionally tamed for use as a flying steed, the Western dragon is irredeemably evil, wild, even demonic; its most extreme manifestation is the world-destroying, seven-headed Dragon in the biblical book of Revelation. In contrast, the dragons of East Asia—all of which, including the Japanese *ryū*, derive from Chinese mythology—tend to be benign symbols of nobility, intelligence, health, wealth, peace, and imperial authority. The only fictional animal in the Chinese zodiac, the dragon is also considered the most desirable (more babies are born in dragon years, due to deliberate planning by the parents) and believed to possess attributes of the other eleven zodiac animals, thereby comprising all possible human archetypes. It too is a hybrid, though with huge taxonomic variation, usually possessing a head that evokes both horse and crocodile, deer horns, the legs of a lion or bird, a serpentine body decorated with tufts of feathers or fur, and prismatic, scaly surfaces like a fish or eel. While the European dragon is symbolically associated with fire, the element of the Asian dragon is water. It dwells within lakes or storm clouds, almost always wingless, gracefully and silently undulating through the air.

The Origin building, built in 1981 as a showroom for a venerable manufacturer of silk kimono sashes, is not Shin Takamatsu's debut work, but it is arguably the true start of his career. Located in Nishijin, Kyoto's traditional garment district, Origin sits on a typically narrow and deep lot known as an *unagi no nedoko* (eel's bed), a consequence of medieval laws that calculated property tax based on the width of the street frontage rather than the area of the land. It presents a facade—indeed, a face—that seems to contradict every expectation of Japanese traditional architecture: a totemic, symmetrical mask of polished brown granite, the apparent weight and density negated by a recessed black podium that allows it to levitate slightly above the ground. Entry is through a vertical orifice or raphe, the upper part of which narrows and

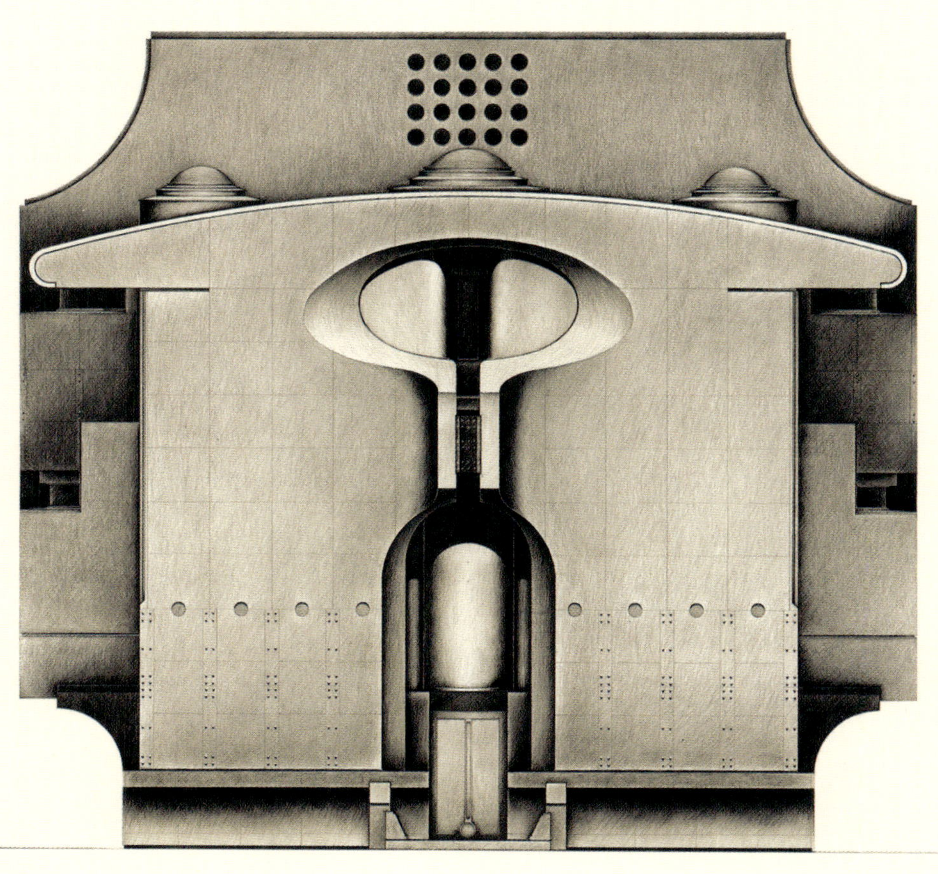

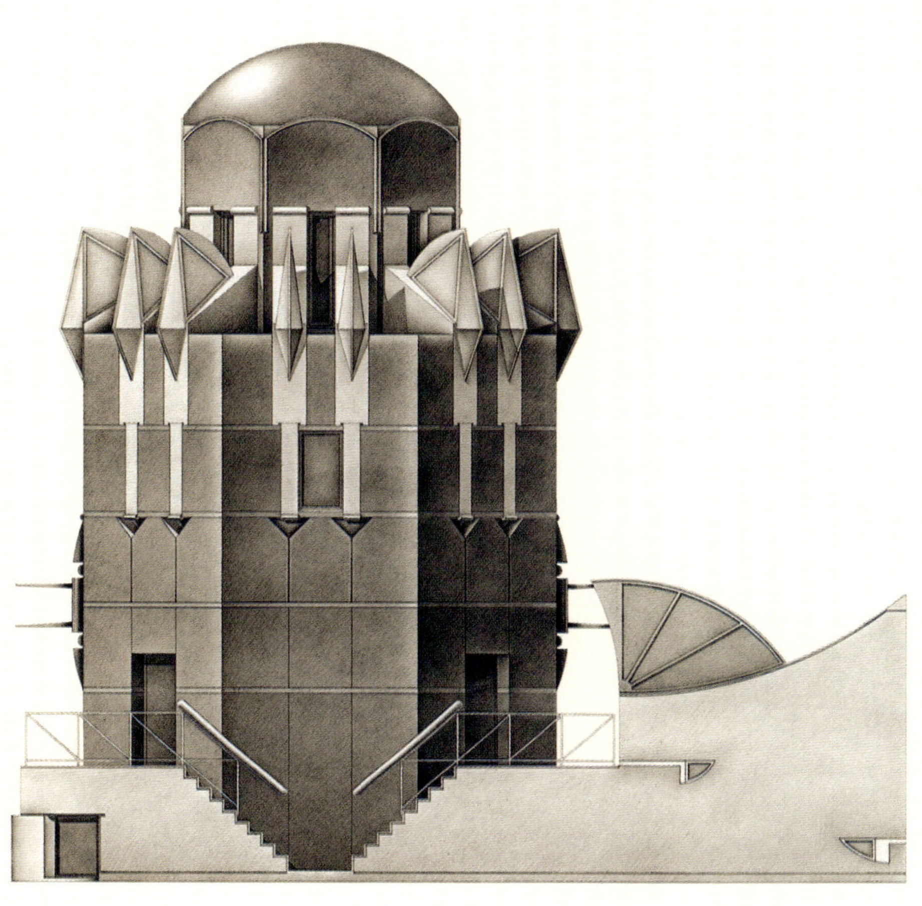

Figure 10.1
Shin Takamatsu, Origin I and Origin III, street facades (Kyoto), 1981/1986.

protrudes to form a snout or pout, then widens again to outline a glazed oval oculus (or clitoris?). Gill-like bulges on either side support a gently vaulted roof profile, with no projecting eave. The smooth, almost baroque stereotomy of the stone is punctuated by an array of oversize metal bolts and ferrules that recall the architecture of the Viennese Secession, in particular Otto Wagner's Austrian Postal Savings Bank (1906). But if Wagner's ornamental rivets were intended as a statement about material honesty, indicating that the stone is not structural but a relatively thin cladding for hidden reinforced concrete walls, in Takamatsu's case it appears that this archaic monolith has been subject to contemporary body modifications (nose, tongue, nipple, and labia piercings, perhaps) or futuristic technological enhancements, a saurian beast with cybernetic implants that augment its intelligence and abilities. To be sure, Takamatsu did not begin the design with the image of a dragon in mind, but the result has a brooding Sphinx-like presence in the street. Facing east, its single eye reflects the morning light, then by night glows with a serene stare—or for some observers, no doubt, a gaze blank and pitiless as the sun.[1]

A couple of years later, Takamatsu added an annex (Origin II) that extended the building deeper into the eel's bed, then in 1986 he completed Origin III, creating a linear sequence that extends across the entire city block, with a second facade on the parallel street to the west. He published an essay explaining the genesis and evolution of the Origin series titled "Double-Headed Dragon," written in Japanese but using the English word "dragon" rather than the Japanese *ryū*.[2] Indeed, a metamorphosis had taken place over those five years. In medical terms, it could be described as a change from cyclopia, an incomplete cleavage of the brain hemispheres that leaves the face with a single eye, to dicephaly, an excessive cleavage that leads to duplicate heads conjoined on a single torso. The calm, static Asian dragon of Origin I is now sutured to the aggressive, dynamic European dragon of Origin III, yonic introversion has become phallic extroversion, and the latent robotic qualities have overtaken the animal, producing a biomechanical phantasmagoria, a Mechagodzilla. This was surely the transitional moment in the shift away from zoomorphic modeling toward the technological expressionism that was to obsess Takamatsu for the following decade or so.

The architecture of Origin III comprises both the dragon and its lair, uncoiling asymmetrically across its site, burrowing underground and leaving curvilinear terraces in its wake, sending a tail-like extension toward a small circular stage in a rear corner, then rearing up at the street edge in an octagonal tower with a venomous red cupola. Thin, sharp skylights encircle the tower, and much larger skylights slice through the broad flight of exterior steps leading to a sunken terrace, like shark tooth jewelry or mechanical batwings. The building surfaces are a mixture of gray concrete and polished black granite, embellished with elaborate metal and glass details that evoke blades and needles—perhaps the weapons of a cybernetic monster, or perhaps merely a metaphorical representation of the implements being used inside the building to cut and embroider silk.[3] In some cases, they are poised threateningly across porthole windows, alluding to the most disturbing moment in Luis Buñuel's 1929 surrealist film *Un chien andalou*.

Aside from the Chinese Hong (rainbow dragon), an ominous creature that is very occasionally depicted with a second head instead of a tail, and the Greek Hydra, which usually has multiple heads sprouting from the same set of shoulders, a two-headed dragon has no real European or Asian precedent, though it does recall the amphisbaena: a serpent with a head at each end, spawned by the blood dripping from the Medusa's severed head as it was carried by Perseus flying over the Libyan desert on winged sandals.[4] Though the amphisbaena originated as a snake, it is often depicted as a miniature dragon, with bird-like feet, feathered wings, and vestigial horns. But perhaps the opposite-facing heads of Origin should be more generously regarded as an independent yet linked pair, like Ao Guang and Ao Run, the benevolent Chinese Dragon Kings of the Eastern Sea and Western Sea.

King Cobra

Vera Simone Bader

Balkrishna Doshi's involvement with the king cobra is no coincidence but is based on a tradition that goes back thousands of years. The king cobra is an important symbol in ancient Vedic and Hindu mythology. With 1,000 heads or a raised neck shield, it offers protection to the gods and appears again and again in this form as a symbolic representation throughout Indian cultural history. The bas-relief of the coastal temple at Mamallapuram, for example, built during the Pallava dynasty around 720 CE, shows it in a central position. Like many other animals, it plays an extraordinary role in the transmission of mythological content and is therefore closely associated with art, sculpture, and architecture. Through such myths and stories, Doshi ties his work to the spiritual-cultural traditions of India, using them, as he put it in several interviews, to "better understand and clarify his ideas and thoughts."[1] In his opinion, "a sure way to do away with the rigidity of a project is to come up with a myth about it."[2]

Clearly, this is an approach he also chose for the design of the Amdavad Ni Gufa, the underground art space in Ahmedabad that he created for sculptor Maqbul Fida Husain in the early 1990s. Doshi and Husain wanted to design an object that defied any conventional notions of constructing. Instead, the goal was to create an organic place, almost like a living being. For Doshi, the building was a statement: although the art space was located off to the side, it was still built on the campus of CEPT University. He was a major influence on the founding of this university and its orientation, namely, to bring education in art and architecture together in one place, thereby making connections possible. The collaboration with Husain was thus a logical consequence of the ideas Doshi had propagated early on. Moreover, Doshi deliberately did not want to continue the architectural language he had developed for the main building of CEPT University in 1968. At that time, he conceived of a brick and concrete structure characterized by clear vertical and horizontal lines and by open and closed structures. This globally recognized canon of modernist forms was to play no role in the design of the Gufa. The contrast between the two buildings could not be greater.

The decision to use the king cobra as an associative model was made very consciously. After all, it is a genetically ancient creature perfectly adapted to its environment. Its patterned, shimmering skin dress, which defies all dryness

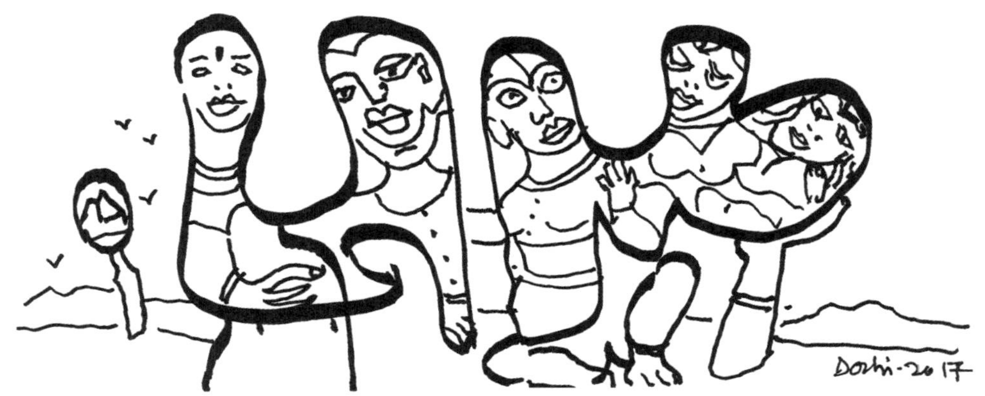

Figure 11.1
Balkrishna Doshi, sketch, 2017. Courtesy of Khushnu Panthaki Hoof.

and heat, appears to be the ideal model for an organism in the often-sweltering heat of Ahmedabad. And this is precisely what Doshi and Husain wanted to translate into an architectural language. In this context, it's fitting that the king cobra lives in caves. Doshi had often thought about these spaces before. The use of vaults that protectively drape over the space like a cocoon was an idea he pursued in his earliest projects. For the Gufa, however, he went a step further. He had visited sadhus in Mumbai, sages who live in cool, dark caves. He was deeply moved by the cosmic radiance of these places and, based on that, began working on his design for the Gufa.[3]

In fact, Doshi developed a floor plan of intersecting circles covered by smaller and larger domes. The outer walls are vaulted. Inside, reminiscent of a reptile's stomach, there are only pillars, which are not straight but slanted like ribs, standing askew in the space; the rooms flow fluidly into one another on uneven levels. Local workers transferred the computer-simulated curvatures into wire-frame structures, which they fabricated on site and filled with mortar by hand. The thin-shelled construction was lined with shards from a nearby ceramics factory that shimmer now in the sun like white mosaics. The protruding round openings that provide subdued light in the art room even look like the eyes of a crocodile or frog. In addition, access to the art room is through a muzzle-like opening. The entire complex is thus deliberately designed to be reptilian. Husain further shaped the amorphous space with color surfaces, giving it a dynamic energy of its own. Depending on where one stands, the interior of the building takes on a completely new, fluid character. Doshi also asked Husain to paint a cobra on the domes. This cobra spreads its linearity, connecting the two large rotundas with each other.

It is not that the king cobra formed the template for the design; rather, the design and a story emerged in parallel, influencing each other. In a text entitled "The Revelation," which Doshi wrote at the same time in 1994, he remembered a dream he had had the night before his first visit to the building site. In it, Kurma, an incarnation of Vishnu, appeared to him and spoke with him about architecture, about the meaning of space and form, which can be timeless, illusionary, and fluid. The Hindu god had a wafer-thin skin covered with a bright shiny layer: "The modulation of this skin was complex due to the intermingling of many rounded shapes of varied heights, dimensions, and inclination."[4] At the end of the text, Doshi makes the connection to Shesha, the thousand-headed cobra that serves as a resting place for Vishnu between his creations, by having Husain paint it on the domes at the opening ritual for the art space. In the story, Doshi thus mythologizes his ideas of design and creation, transferring his concept into linguistic and architectural images.

"It is not just architecture! It is an experience, it is a narration, it is a thought. The main idea is that I really look at everything as if it is a living organism."[5] Doshi had developed this design method over the years, and it increasingly influenced his work as a very personal response to the reality of life of the local people, whose lives are shaped by customs, ceremonies, and spiritual beliefs. Consequently, his many sketchbooks contain not only depictions of cityscapes, buildings, and design ideas; there are also numerous drawings of lions, lizards, and cows, and animals of a clearly mythological nature, such as the elephant god Ganesha. These animals influence Doshi's deeply personal dream world and play an equally important role in the architectural shaping of forms. Against this background, the Gufa can certainly be seen as a decisive high point in his creative period.

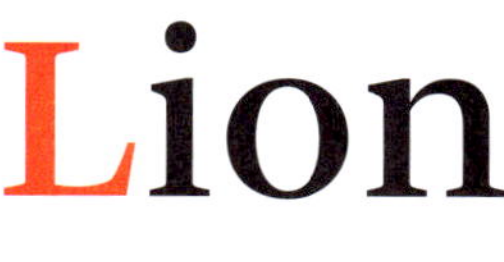

Lion

Martin Søberg

> When first the Fox saw the Lion, he was terribly frightened and ran away and hid himself in the woods. Next time, however, he came near the King of Beasts, he stopped at a safe distance and watched him pass by. The third time they came near each other, the Fox went straight up to the Lion and passed the time of day with him. Finding the Lion a bore, the Fox turned his tail and parted from him without much ceremony.[1]

The first project that the American architect John Hejduk (1929–2000) designed when he started studying at Cooper Union's school of architecture in New York in 1947 was an illustrated book of Aesop's fables, eventually published in 1991. It included several fables featuring lions: "The Sick Lion," "The Four Bulls and the Lion," and the one printed above: "The Fox and the Lion." The moral of the fable states: "Familiarity breeds contempt." Indeed, Hejduk's architectural oeuvre presents itself as a continued exploration of the unfamiliar. Perhaps this explains his fascination with animals including lions: on the one hand so like human beings, on the other hand so enigmatic, so opaque.

Indeed, animals and their representations occur in various stages of Hejduk's oeuvre, especially in its very early stages during the late 1940s and early 1950s and in its mature stages from the 1980s onward. They appear in different ways: Firstly, *programmatically*, as part of the program of projects, for instance in the design of a zoological park, that is, as relating to houses for animals. Secondly, *formally*, on a formal-symbolic level in creaturely, zoomorphic fabrications. Thirdly, *ontologically*, as part of Hejduk's imaginary world-making, expressed through drawings, accompanying or contrasting human beings, for instance, in the projects *The Lancaster/Hanover Masque* (1980–1982), *Victims* (1983–1984), and *Bovisa* (1986). Hence, only decades after 1947 did the lion, King of Beats, return to Hejduk's work among other animals such as snakes, horses, peacocks, and armadillos in his drawings and poems, inhabiting the poetic worlds that were his architecture.

Inherently dialectic, Hejduk's creative method implies exploring the contrast between presumed dichotomies such as flatness and depth, black and white, man and woman, human and animal, playing with those terms. What seems to fascinate him, in particular, is the transition from one state or identity

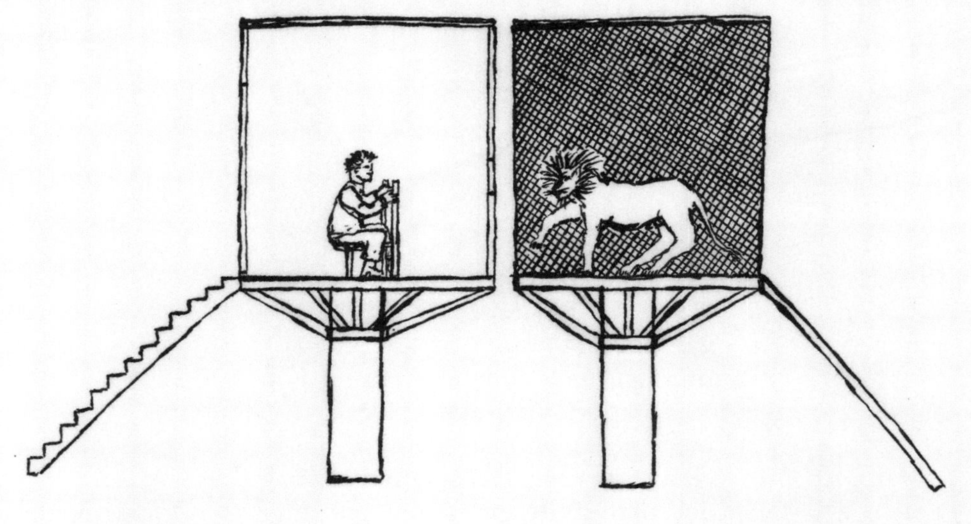

Figure 12.1
John Hejduk, "House of the Zoologist" from *Bovisa*, 1986.
John Hejduk fonds, CCA Montreal. © CCA.

to another or at least the liminal condition between those states. Hence, his dichotomies are not necessarily stable. We might say that in the case of Hejduk, life and form are never separated; indeed, his work is based on the exact assumption that such a separation is impossible. As he famously stated: "I cannot do a building without building a new repertoire of characters of stories of language and it's all parallel. It's not just building per se. It's building worlds. It's building worlds."[2] This is most clearly expressed in Hejduk's projects for specific and often urban sites such as Venice, Berlin, Lancaster, Bovisa, Vladivostok, and Riga, projects which relate directly to the stories and traumas of those places.

Bovisa is Hejduk's proposal for a redevelopment of Milan's Bovisa district. The project was his response to an invitation to participate in the XVII Triennale di Milano as part of the theme "Nine Projects for Nine Cities." The project, based on a document termed "MZ7" which included site information and photographs, comprises a number of drawings that present various built structures of the area, some of them named "machines," others described as "houses." The structures assemble elements of particular architectural typologies: pitched-roof houses, the slender towers which were once part of many medieval Italian towns, and cylindrical buildings resembling both baptisteries and silos. Yet to these structures Hejduk has added spikes, scaffolds, wheels, or long and slender, snake-like corridors wrapping around them. Some of the structures are even placed on top of cars, while others are pulled by horses.

Hejduk's exploration of the relations between humans and animals, as well as of objects/subjects or subject/subjects, is demonstrated in the *House of the Zoologist*. It is a hybrid drawing, both section and elevation, presenting to us two buildings of similar dimensions: a room with an almost square section, lifted from the ground by a pillar and supported by slender beams. Whether the rooms are cubic or cylindrical is impossible to tell. The room to the left houses a man sitting backward on a chair, which allows him to look through what appears to be an opening in the wall toward the adjacent building. He gazes toward his neighbor, a male lion, who returns his gaze. The lion is represented on a background of crosshatches, indicating a wired cage. The eyes of man and lion meet on the same horizontal line; the doubling of the buildings is echoed in the man's frizzy, mane-like coiffure. These living bodies, these species, are different yet similar, separated yet connected by their gaze, questioning who is actually studying whom. In *Victims*, Hejduk also included a zoologist as one of his sixty-seven characters, linked to a structure which, enigmatically, was to house *Copies of Recaptured Creatures*. What does this mean? Had the creatures somehow escaped but been recaptured? Hence, processes of repetition and mirroring permeate both projects.

Other lions occur in Hejduk's work throughout the 1980s. Lions are sitting like dogs in his poem "On a Bridge" from *The Silent Witnesses and Other Poems* (1980). A black-and-white photograph of a sculpture of a lion is pasted into his *Berlin Sketchbook* (1982). In his book *Mask of Medusa* (1985), Hejduk quotes Gustave Flaubert's *Salammbô*, which contains a description of a file of lions crucified by the Carthaginian peasants with the purpose of terrifying other lions to deter them from attacking.[3] *Berlin Night* (1989), one of Hejduk's most disturbing projects, exploring relationships of terror, judgment, and surveillance, comprises a *Lion Tamer's House and Work Space*. Hejduk states: "The lion is afraid of the trainer."[4] As often in his projects, he establishes a catalogue of characters relating to the plots of the scene and its various spatial elements. This includes nine silent jurors, all of them animals: lion, tiger, panther, snake, porcupine, bull, monkey, peacock, and chameleon. It is not clear what trials they are about to participate in, yet they are supposedly residing in some peculiar sort of viewing boxes. As was the case of the *House of the Zoologist*, Hejduk's architectural structures are, indeed, rather often viewing machines, constructed as part of a staging of relationships, for instance between humans and animals.

In an essay on Hejduk's architecture as a matter of encounters, K. Michael Hays argues: "Like the animals in a fable that speak with human voices, Hejduk's objects seem, impossibly, to be aware of us. And yet we see not the gratifying reflection of ourselves we had hoped for but another thing looking back at us, watching us, placing us."[5] Yet perhaps these built structures are not so immobile after all, but merely resting or sleeping. Hejduk's drawings seem to articulate a liminal situation in which architecture functions not only as a framework, as the facilitator of specific functional programs, but as an accomplice in the expulsion of the condensed human-animal relations. Hejduk's lions are mute yet vivacious companion species, as are his built structures.

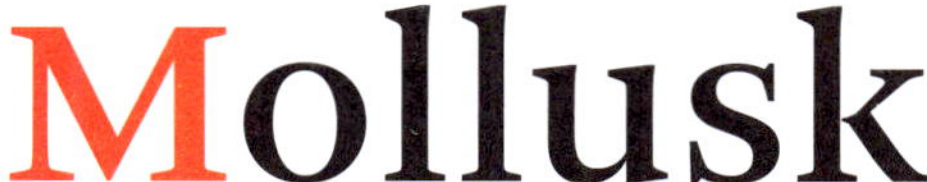

Mollusk

Aron Vinegar

The invocation of mollusks—a highly diverse range of animals, members of the phylum Mollusca, the second-largest phylum of invertebrate animals and the largest marine phylum, which includes oysters, mussels, clams, scallops, snails, octopuses, and squid—is ubiquitous in the writing and practice of architectural modernism and in aesthetico-modernism more broadly speaking. Many of us are familiar with the role mollusks play in edifying narratives and metaphors of dwelling, which invoke them as a privileged way to think through and mediate metaphysical dualities, such as interior and exterior, life and death, mineral and organic. At this point, what more can be said about and with the mollusk?

As an opening gambit, let's consider a more excessive and ultimately disturbing staging of the creature than is often invoked in architecture through a conchological focus on the beautiful form, structure, and geometry of its shell.[1] This building fragment replete with mollusk shells was easy to overlook at first, casually placed on a long worktable along with a few other examples of building materials and student projects, in the Preservation Technology Lab at the Graduate School of Architecture, Planning and Preservation at Columbia University. But once it caught my attention, I was transfixed. The small-typeface label placed next to it is cryptically titled "Ruin Fragment" in bold font, followed by the briefest of descriptions simply noting that its material is concrete, and that the fragment is derived from the ruin of an early nineteenth-century building located on the southeastern coast of the United States. To add a bit more specificity to the label, it is an example of what is called tabby concrete, in which the lime is produced by burning oyster shells in a kiln at high heat, then slaking the shells by adding water, local sand, and often ash. As one can readily see, a plethora of broken pieces of mollusk shell (predominantly oyster)—ranging in size from small fragments to entire left and right valves wrenched apart at the hinge—are then added to the lime to speed hardening, and to increase durability and volume. This is a basic technical explanation of the production of tabby concrete, which hardly addresses the unruly energy and originary traumaticity that is captured by this fragment.

The first thing one notices about the fragment is that the mollusk shells make an appearance in excessively plural states of brokenness, inconsistency,

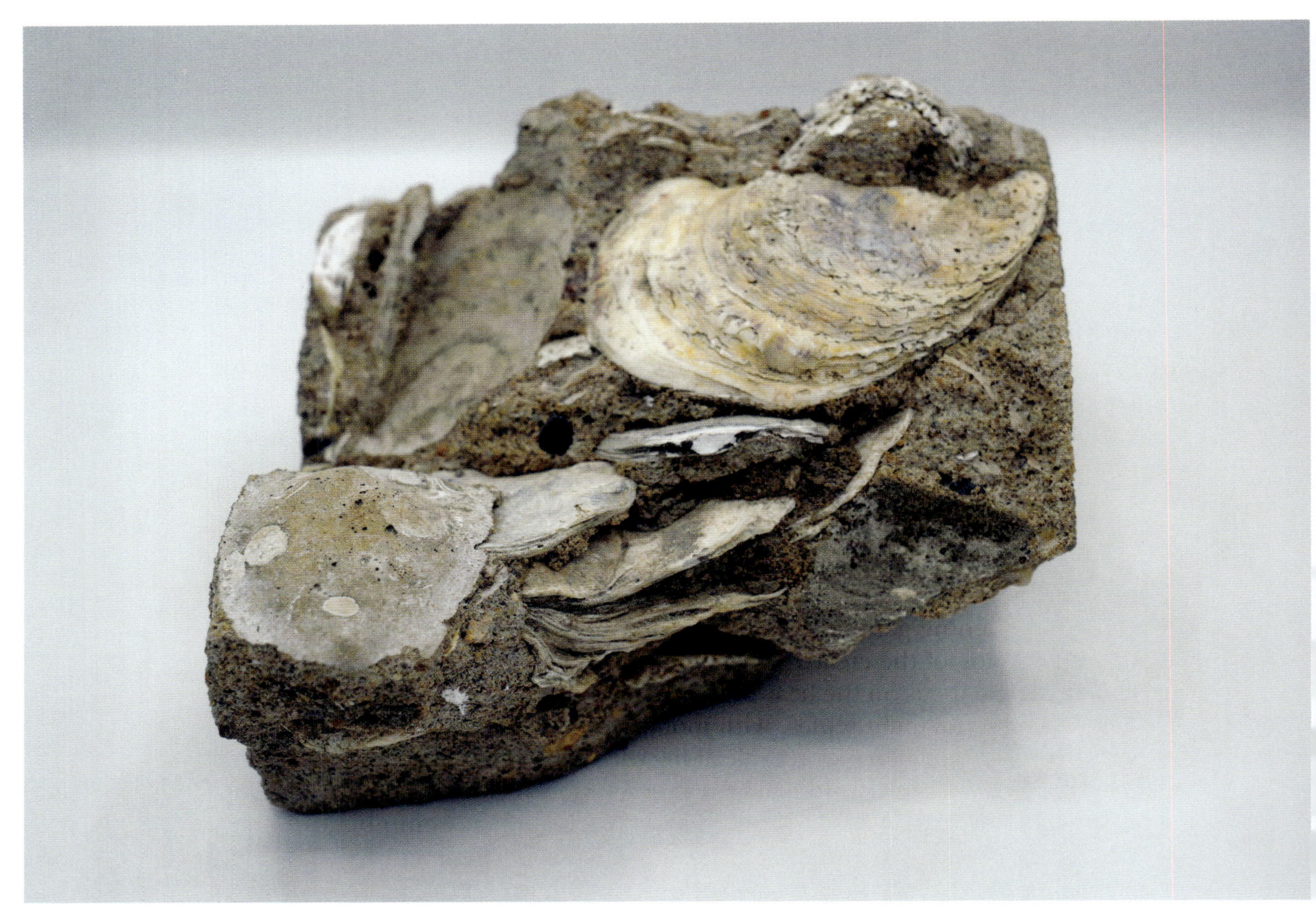

Figure 13.1
Fragment of tabby concrete from the ruin of an early nineteenth-century building located on the southeastern coast of the United States. Preservation Technology Lab, Graduate School of Architecture, Planning and Preservation, Columbia University. Photograph by Mika Tal, 2024.

and aggregation, rather than being depicted, via drawing or photograph, as an isolated bivalve or gastropod shell that emphasizes its form, structure, and geometry. In the ruin fragment, the mollusk is a messy "heap," not an autonomous shell that can be grasped, conceptualized, and authorized (think of Le Corbusier's many visual and written analogies between the grasping hand and the shell, or more critical accounts of this gendered analogy, such as Dora Maar`s untitled photograph of a woman`s mannequin hand emerging from a shell on a stormy beach).[2] The oyster shells are flaky, broken, and stick out at odd angles from the fragment, such that from a certain perspective they seem indicative of a "heaping" and a "strewing," a *struere* (a Latin verb meaning to build or assemble but, in its less cohesive significations and etymological derivation, also meaning to heap, pile up, amass, or strew) that unbinds and ruptures any "struction" from the order, organization, and coherence implied in the paradigm of construction.[3] This unruliness is only enhanced by the fact that the fragment is shorn of its smooth, form-enhancing coating of plaster or stucco. To disaggregate one of the primary architectonic metaphors invoked through Francis Ponge's description of the mollusk as a "door handle that has secreted its own door," this ruin is a paratactic heap of disparate door fragments.[4] Here the mollusk's "hinge"—a ligament that connects the two valves and articulates the leeway of its opening and closing—has been repeatedly twisted and cracked, and the valves themselves further broken and shattered.

The chaotic deposition in this miniature midden is a "partial education" in what both enlivens and deadens, sustains and decimates.[5] This partiality is diametrically opposed to any totalizing and disciplinary edification that one might draw from these shells whose shaping forces of time, climate, labor, and capitalism have retracted into an autonomous and immanent form, which would then set them free for subsequent acts of dispossession, repossession, and inhabitation. These voided shells do not operate as a "metaphor of metaphor," like an abandoned mollusk shell that is the "borrowed dwelling" occupied by a hermit crab, nor are they simply like those "shells abandoned at the seashore" that Giorgio Agamben uses as an example of what is called *res nullius* in Roman law: "things that are not the property of anyone."[6] This fragment of tabby concrete both attests to and resists the fragmentary record of its sedimented habits and habitats of adaptation, occupation, circulation, possession, and ownership: it is a "marino-ontological inconsistency" formed by breaking waves of multiple traumas and ruptures deposited in their wake.[7]

Rather than the faint murmur of the ocean that supposedly echoes from a shell's voided chamber, this ruined tabby fragment registers the din and noise of the habitat that these oysters are shorn from, and to which they sometimes return to seed further growth in more recent eco-infrastructural practices. It also registers the force and violence of enslaved Black labor that was often used to produce tabby concrete and the many buildings constructed with its materials along the southeastern coast. Just as the mollusk shell's deposition is now a primary witness and attestation to the effects of global warming through its increased vulnerability to ocean acidification, this fragment registers traumaticity in the form of multiple shell-shocks: from exploited and vanishing waterways as they have been depleted by overconsumption of mollusks and the deleterious effects of the many gray infrastructures that encase our waterfronts and shorelines and contribute to vanishing these "keystone" animals, to the waves of settler colonialism and slavery built on the exploitation of Indigenous and Black labor and knowledge. Thus, the echoes clanging forth from these shell fragments are not of the order of a regressive fantasy of oceanic exteriority or a pulsating hematic interiority, but rather the slurping and clattering of (over)consumption and extinction to come. They are the sounds of skilled slave and indentured labor, rather than any instinctual form of "unalienated labor" that the mollusk's extraction of its calciferous sources for the excretion of its shell might suggest. This unassuming fragment is a partial material depositing of the migration, circulation, and exchange of these amalgams of matter, labor, violence, knowledge, technology, and their disciplinary instructions in the forms of cultural techniques, architectures, infrastructures, and institutions.

This example of a mollusk-driven architecture is less about the self-positing of form than about the depositing of an evidentiary extravagance—a *testaceous* testimony—in which signification, meaning, address, and form overflow themselves.[8] It is not by chance that the indeterminate forms and movements of the Odradek-like entities that manifest the "volatility of things" in the horror writer Thomas Ligotti's "Sideshow, and Other Stories" are likened to a "snail" and a "giant bivalved mollusk," as they are witnessed dragging themselves across a dirty concrete floor at the bottom of an empty stairwell. These figures attest to a speculative existence suspended between a deep—and not so deep—past and a future that is a not-yet-arriving.[9] The uncanny fragment of tabby concrete is of a piece with an odd kind of evidencing by which the unconscious manifests. In fact, I am tempted to address this partial example of tabby concrete as a species of "ectopic unconscious," which is to say, an architectural unconscious that is out there in the unsublatable exteriorizations of building stuff that circulates—even when it is stuck in place, like the sessility of adult oysters. In turn, this evidencing demands new forms and techniques of analysis and free-floating attention that would elaborate on the in- and overdeterminations that are secreted from the many mantles that the testaceous fragment generates and deposits.[10] This kind of analysis would serve as a *mantle* that we as writers, historians, and practitioners take upon ourselves. Here I am drawing on another sense of that word (the mantle is a muscular membrane covering the mollusk`s visceral mass that secretes the calcium carbonate that forms its shell, and which often protrudes outward in the form of flaps), signifying an important role or responsibility—one might call it an inheritance in the broadest sense of that term—that is passed on, taken up . . . or disavowed. This fragment transfixes and haunts precisely because this strange mollusk assemblage has no fixed abode or addressee but still speaks to us in the insistent mood of the imperative: "Preserve what I impart!"

Nautilus

Joseph M. Siry

Following his mentor Louis Sullivan, Frank Lloyd Wright throughout his career espoused an ideal of organic architecture. Like Sullivan, Wright often referred to plants as metaphors for this concept, embodied in the living forms of flowers and trees. Yet once, in his seventy-plus years in architecture, Wright referred to an animal as a model of organicism, when he wrote of the spiral form of the Solomon R. Guggenheim Museum: "The paintings themselves are in perfectly air-conditioned, well-lighted chambers, chambers something like those of 'the chambered nautilus.'"[1] For Wright, the spiral, more than any other form, signified spatial and temporal continuity. He proclaimed of the 1946 design for this building: "For the first time in the history of architecture a true logarithmic spiral has been worked out as a complete plastic building: a building in which there is but one continuous floor surface: not one separate floor slab above another floor slab, but one, single, grand, slow wide ramp, widening as it rises for about seven stories—a purely plastic development of organic structure."[2] He later wrote: "the construction of the great ramp like that of a seashell, is clear of interior supports of any kind, the fibrous [i.e., steel-reinforced] floors being carried throughout from the outer walls."[3]

With these remarks, Wright linked to a long tradition of scientific and poetic responses to the chambered nautilus.[4] As is well known, Le Corbusier was also interested in certain seashells as exemplary forms, lessons from which he sought to assimilate into his work.[5] Yet for Wright, the nautilus illustrated the core principle of organic architecture. Secreted by this mollusk throughout its lifetime, the nautilus shell is materially continuous; thus its architecture is formed from the inside out, rather than the outside in. Wright often spoke of his aim of creating a modern architecture that would emerge organically from its inner functional life. For him, this was distinct from the outward application of historical styles as the conventional nonmodernist practice in architecture that had been characteristic of the nineteenth and early twentieth centuries. As Wright wrote: "The building is no longer a block of building material dealt with, artistically, from the outside. The room within is the great fact about building—*the room* to be expressed in the exterior *as space enclosed*."[6] In this spirit, the major retrospective exhibition of Wright's lifework at the Guggenheim Museum in New York in 2009 took as its title *From Within Outward*.[7] Wright presented this ideal as a progressive critique of historicism. In

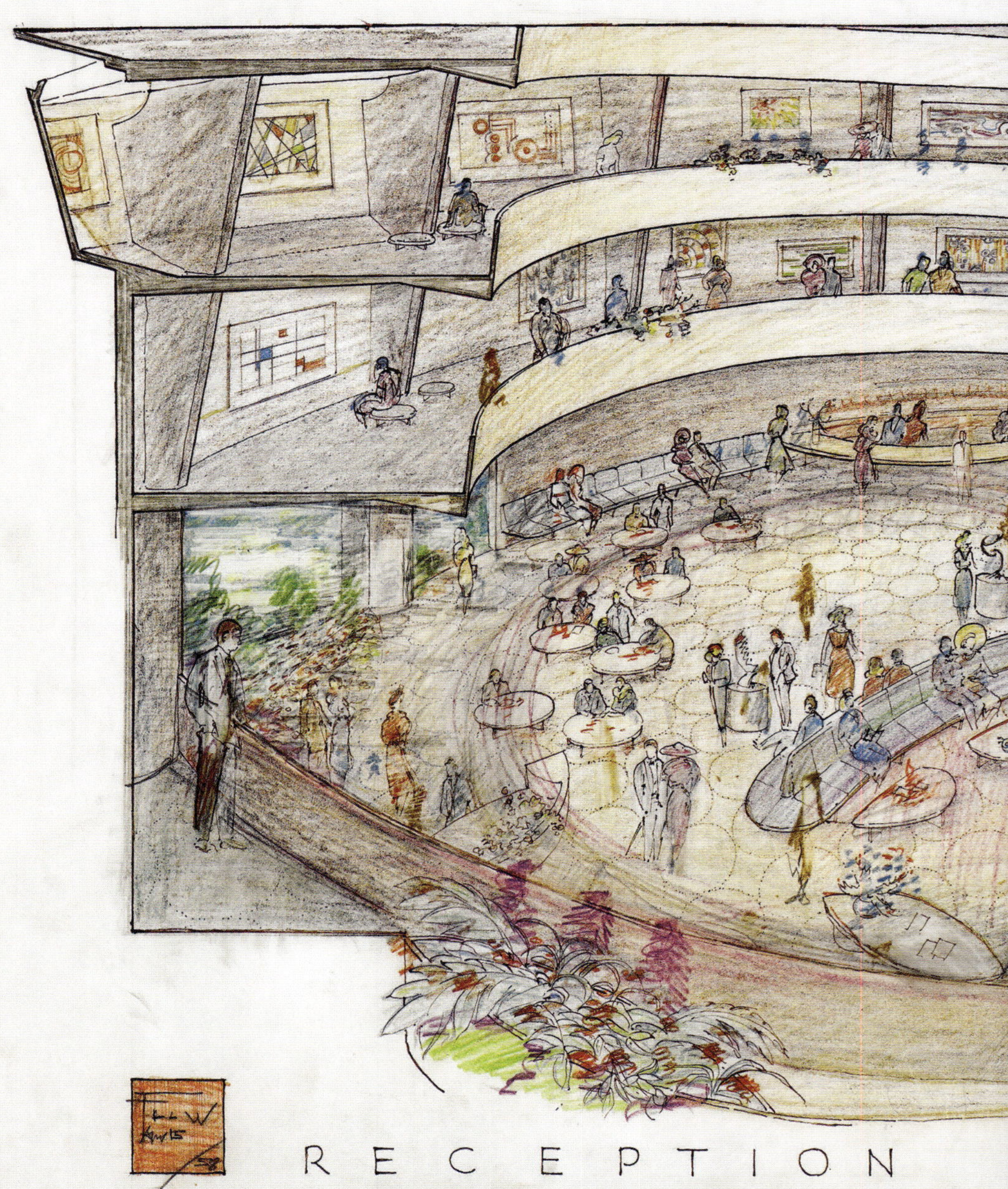
RECEPTION

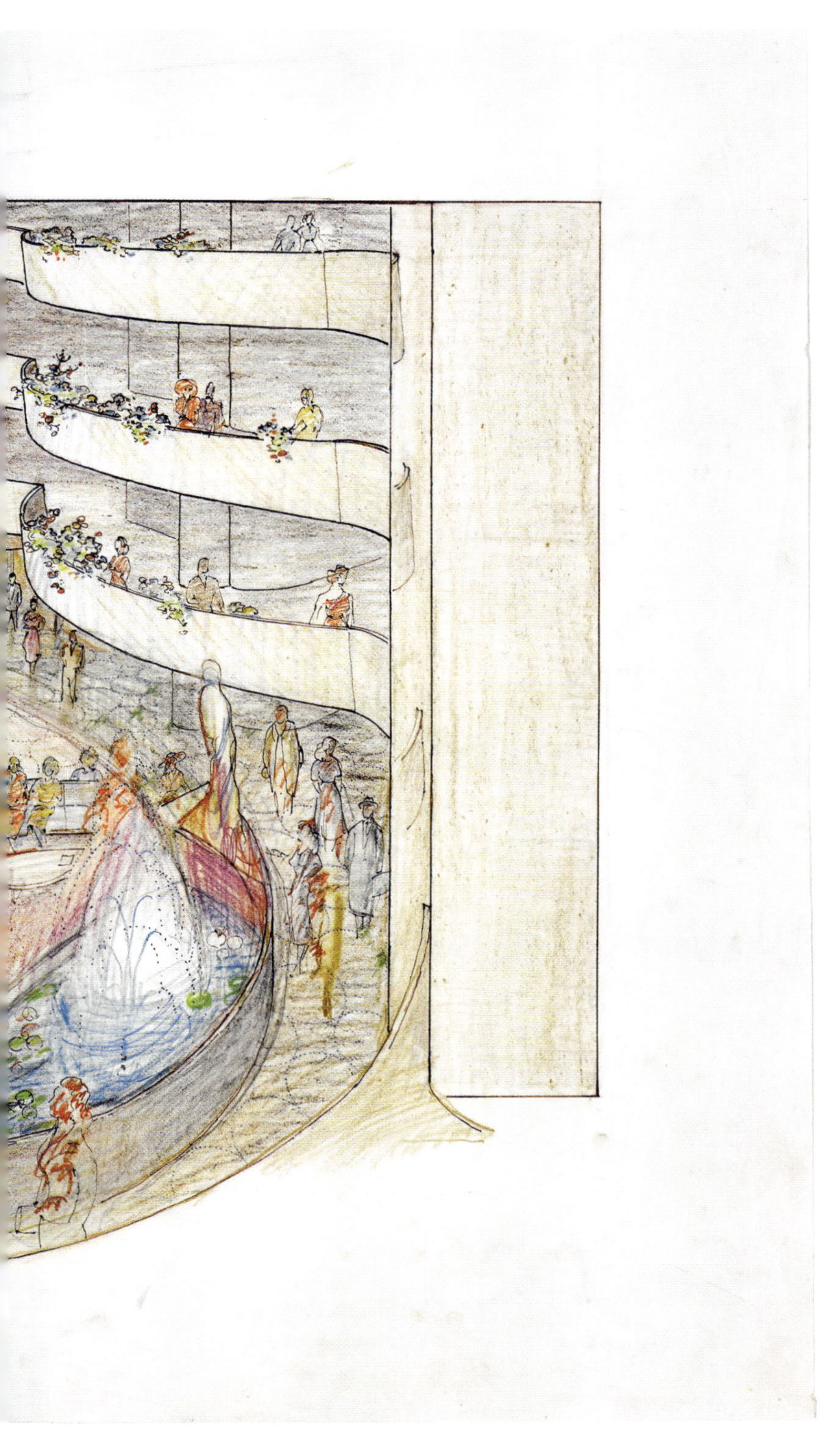

his view, the organic concept was valid because he interpreted it as the way nature created forms. This concept of organic architecture meant that buildings are like natural organisms whose outward forms emerge from their inner life. He wrote: "An organic form grows its structure out of conditions as a plant grows out of soil. . . . Both unfold similarly from within."[8] Citing Lao-Tzu's *Tao Te Ching*, which Wright likely first became aware of through Okakura Kakuzo's *The Book of Tea* (1906), Wright sought that buildings should convey "this new sense-of-the-within naturally unfolding."[9] He saw buildings as ideally responsive to their functions as organisms are, and the animal that for him represented this concept was the chambered nautilus.

The nautilus is celebrated for its shell's perfectly logarithmic spiral, and Wright was pursuing the expressive potential of the spiral most monumentally in the Guggenheim. Actually, in the Guggenheim Wright only evoked the logarithmic spiral, which expands geometrically in diameter out from its central point of origin: his spiral for the museum is not truly logarithmic but arithmetic, because its diameter does not increase geometrically but rather more gradually as it rises.[10] Yet conceptually, the precise geometry of the chambered shell was perhaps for him less important than its embodiment of the ideal of organic form as growing from within outward. Wright believed that the Guggenheim's spiral demonstrated a principle everywhere evident in nature, from the shape of galaxies to the tendrils of the vine leaf. The spiral also recurred in historic architecture from antiquity, and it was susceptible to renewal in modern materials. Yet only in the nautilus did the spiral result in a form of shelter for an animal that was grown from within. Hence it is a distinctly apt metaphor for the ideal of organic architecture as shelter for humans. Wright made this point directly in his most extensive recorded statement on seashells, a talk that he gave to the Taliesin fellows in 1953. He stressed their power of example as outward forms that emerged from inner living processes: "There is but one generic principle here: All these little shell-houses are doing the same thing, but not in the same way. . . . Every ornamentation, that is to say, every *pattern*, you see here, and the exquisite forms of the shells themselves, are tributary to the force that is being exerted by its like upon itself from within, as the growing shell is being made."[11] Wright also highlighted the seashells' variety as another principle of organic form. Referring to a tray filled with shells, he stressed their creative differences: "All these infinitely variable forms are

Figure 14.1 (previous pages)
Frank Lloyd Wright, Solomon R. Guggenheim Museum, New York, "The Reception," 1958. Graphite pencil and colored pencil on paper, 19⅛ × 38¾ inches. The Frank Lloyd Wright Foundation Archives (The Museum of Modern Art | Avery Architectural & Fine Arts Library, Columbia University, New York). FLWA, drawing no. 4305.092.

saying exactly the same thing. No interior change in *idea*, yet here is another and another and another *individual*. . . . Here, for instance, is a beautiful form of *principle at work*."[12]

In addition to embodying ideals of organic form and individual variety, the seashell for Wright represented his abiding principle of plasticity in architecture, which the Guggenheim's construction distinctly embodied. As noted above, to realize plasticity in building was to substitute continuous material structure for discrete posts and beams. As Wright wrote: "If form really followed function—it did by this ideal of plasticity—why not throw away the implications of post or upright and beam or horizontal entirely? . . . Now why not let walls, ceilings, floors become *seen* as component parts of each other, their surfaces flowing into each other to get continuity in the whole."[13] Of seashells he said, "Always, in these forms, in these little poems, there is the ebb and the flow, the plasticity of the elements by way of which, and in which, they came to exist."[14] As Wright wrote in his initial major statement about the Guggenheim in 1946, "Not only is the entire monolithic building plastic in the form of a rising spiral but it is plastic in actual construction also."[15] What completed the analogy of this building to the chambered nautilus was the use of gunite, a sprayed-on concrete, for each curving chamber-like section of the museum's outer spiraling walls.[16] The building literally grew via a process that approximated the liquid secretions of the nautilus, by which this animal created the chambers of its spiraling shell. In this way, this animal was a model for Wright's architecture not only in terms of its form but also in its constructional process of realization. Hence his comparison of the Guggenheim to the chambered nautilus operated simultaneously on philosophical, aesthetic, and material levels.

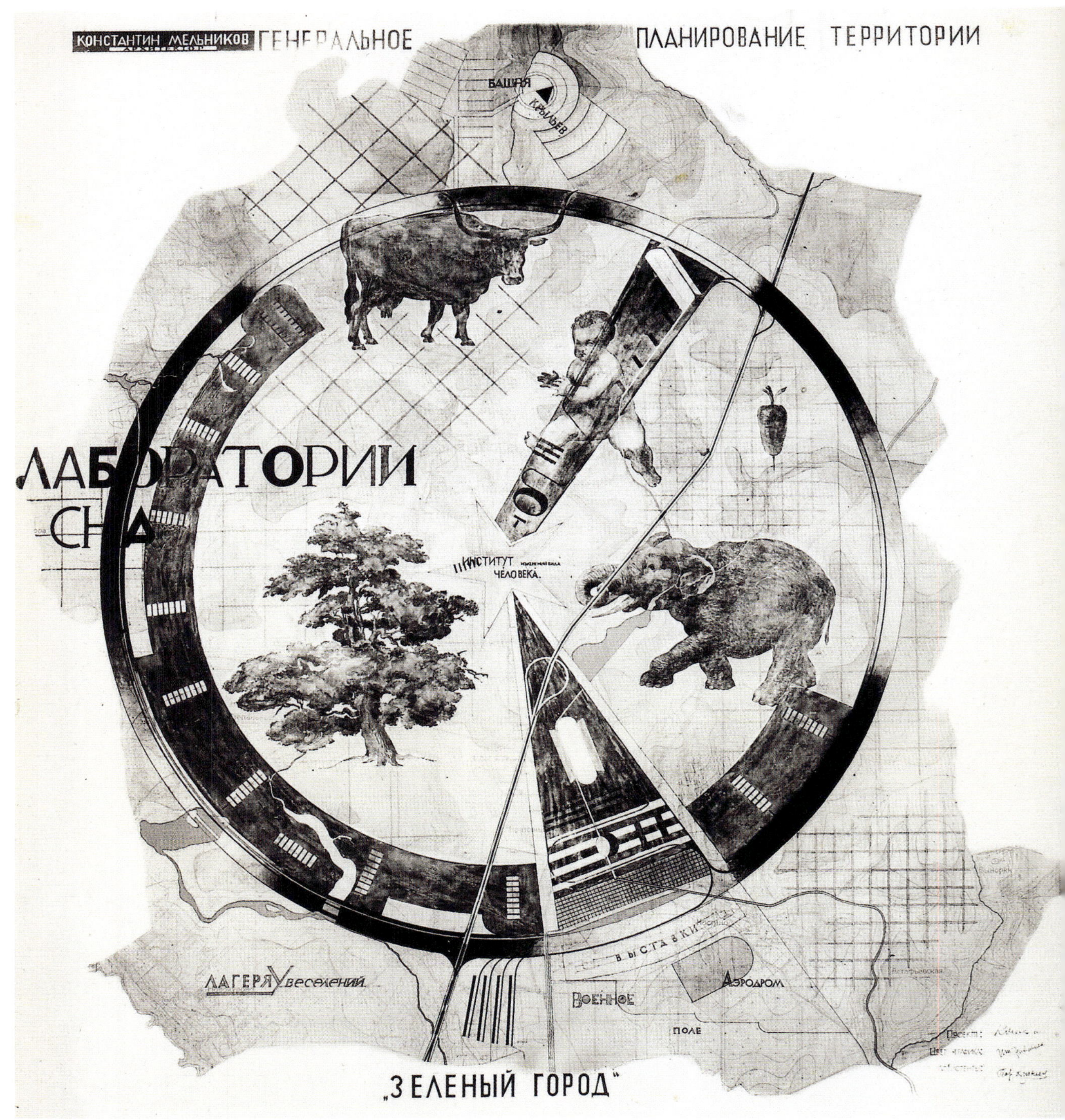

Figure 15.1
Konstantin Melnikov, master plan for the Green City project, 1930. Competition entry. *Stroitelstvo Moskvy* [Construction of Moscow], no. 3 (1930): 21.

Ox

Pavel Kuznetsov

On the main board of the competition entry by Konstantin Melnikov (1890–1974) for the Green City (1930), five objects, realistically represented in big scale, float inside the urban circle: a carrot, an oak, a child, an elephant, and an ox. The never-built Green City was supposed to be a model resort village for the "new Soviet man," northeast of Moscow, the master plan for a kind of a "recreation factory" for the builders of communism.[1] Although the choice of the circle is explained by its optimum geometry (the minimum length of perimeter for a given area), the master plan can also be perceived as a self-sufficient visual form superimposed on the natural landscape. Moreover, the different arrow-shaped sectors have as their reference the view of the land from the sky but also remind us of the famous Russian Civil War propaganda poster by El Lissitzky titled *Beat the Whites with the Red Wedge* (1919). But, more than anything else, the Green City project was Melnikov's one and only opportunity to state what modern design in a rural landscape should be like.

Farm animals were indispensable parts of this rural landscape, especially if we consider Melnikov's early childhood as the son of a peasant family living in a village at the outskirts of Moscow where his parents had a small dairy farm. In practice, young Kostya grew up as a shepherd; and he was still a young shepherd bringing milk to the big city when the engineer and inventor Vladimir Chaplin discovered the boy's talent for drawing, hired him as an errand boy for his firm Chaplin & Zalessky, and became something like a second father by financially supporting his education, first as a painter and then as an architect. But Melnikov never forgot, even when he was at the peak of his career, that the land of rural mother Russia was all about herds of cattle offering their life-giving milk. In his manuscripts written toward the end of his life, Melnikov turns back to his childhood memories of the sunrise in the meadows where herds of oxen and cows represent nature untouched, in contrast to the modern mechanized city with its medical pills, artificial heat, and soulless machines.

Unlike his contemporaries the Soviet constructivists, for Melnikov the animal world, and more broadly the world of nature, was a crucial component of his philosophy of architecture and part of a healthy, sustainable lifestyle and human habitat. While constructivists viewed animals solely functionally, as livestock machines necessary for the rapid growth of the agrarian industry of large collective farms, Melnikov aimed at an integration of human and nonhuman natural forces into a more holistic architecture, one that would be quite low-tech in comparison to the constructivist heroic machinism.[2] While in the case of the Green City competition the constructivists envisioned a total industrial agriculture in the form of a satellite city-farm for 5,000 people, in Melnikov's vision wild and domesticated animals were meant to be an integral part of the human settlement, occupying two-thirds of its extended territory. If, for the constructivists, animals were productive entities like machines, for Melnikov machines were new forms of animated animals, like the British Leyland buses that appeared to him as thoroughbred horses, each one occupying its own place in huge stable-like modern garages.[3] At least, this is how he justified the straight-line traffic system that he invented when designing the giant Bakhmetevsky garage.

A perfect illustration of this contrast between a "scientific" exploitation of nature and a more organic integration of human and other living beings is provided by the famous scene from Eisenstein's 1929 movie *The General Line*, also known as *Staroe i novoe* (The old and the new), where a herd of cows in the foreground is juxtaposed with a white, stylish constructivist cowshed in the background. The alien form of the Corbusian farm—an actual set design created by the architect Andrei Burov especially for this film—hides the forthcoming tragedy of the Russian peasantry which under Stalin went through collectivization, devastation, famine, and a new serfdom in the form of the kolkhozes (collective farms): if the architects' aim is to create a new architecture for people, why not also place all oxen and cows in farms that look like the purist villas of *L'Esprit Nouveau*? But if this is a structure so clearly foreign to animal life, why is it considered ideal for the development of human life?

However, this questioning is eventually not about the form of architecture but about its means and aims. For the constructivists, projects such as the Green City should serve only one purpose: the construction of the new Soviet society from scratch, a new, brave world that would transcend both the restrictions of nature and the conventions of the past. For Melnikov, the aim should be to seek a new balance in a rural environment that could be both modern and humane, reparative and therapeutic, inclusive of certain practices and mentalities and lifeforms of the past. This is why in Melnikov's Green City the guests would be able to come into direct contact with plants and animals, as they would breathe the fresh air in their three-level hotel rooms or enjoy the morning sunshine, catching vitamin D in the solariums of the pavilions. In practice, human, animal, and plant life would harmonically coexist: cattle meadows would seamlessly merge into open zoos in which smaller and bigger animals (even elephants) would live unrestricted; the Gardens Sector and the ZooAgro Sector (forests, farmland, and the zoo) would be close to the Children sector and the Public Sector; mobile cafes, libraries, and sports fields would be available everywhere.[4]

In this effort to rethink architecture as a modern form of well-being in direct contact with nature, Melnikov introduced the concept of "rationalized sleep": sleep not only as a form of rest but also as a therapeutic action, a treatment for all ailments and diseases, even a reconstitution of the person's character. In his theory, sleep is a way for all living beings to recover their energy but also to rejuvenate themselves, as every morning is like a new birth. As he wrote a few decades later: "For one third of their life, a human is asleep. In their sixty years—twenty years of sleep; twenty years of travel in the field of mysterious worlds without consciousness, without guidance, touching unexplored depths, sources of healing mysteries, and maybe—miracles, yes, maybe even miracles."[5] In the Green City, Melnikov designed five types of "sleep concert" (*SONnaya SONata*) units in the form of shared chambers for sleep treatment. Short therapeutic daytime sleep had to take place in different modes: physical (humidity, pressure), chemical (aromas of meadows and fields), mechanical (twisting, tugging, toppling), psychic (noise of leaves, sea breeze, music, nightingales, thunderstorm), and even thermal (heat, cold).

Among the sources of Melnikov's theory about the role of sleep in the rehabilitation and even prolongation of human life were, on the one hand, the religious and philosophical idea of Russian "cosmism" by Nikolai Fedorov (1829–1903), whose book *The Philosophy of the Common Task* (its main theme was the overcoming of death) already had many followers. On the other hand, there were other ideas circulating among Bolshevik intellectuals of the 1920s—like Leonid Krasin (1870–1926), patron of the young Melnikov, first People Commissar of Foreign Trade, and ambassador to France and Great Britain—on how the progress of science could even bring humanity closer to immortality. This idea of a sleep therapy—quite scientific, admittedly—was projected onto the traditional rural world, this world of dreams and childhood memories in which oxen, as symbols of an "innocent" rural past in danger, expressed an inner "resistance" to the ruthless Soviet industrial world.

Utopian and bucolic, open and inclusive, these "dreams" of a non-Soviet architect like Melnikov for an alternative type of multispecies community were eventually realized in his "l'île mystérieuse" (obviously named after Jules Verne): the small, serene garden of his own unique two-cylinder house, a small paradise with fruit trees and vegetable patches, albeit without an ox, in the heart of the Soviet capital.

Ornitorrinco. UBU. | São Paulo 25/5/'85 Lina Bo Bardi

LE POLOCHON "é porco de duas cabeças" recebe o Publico na entrada do Teatro

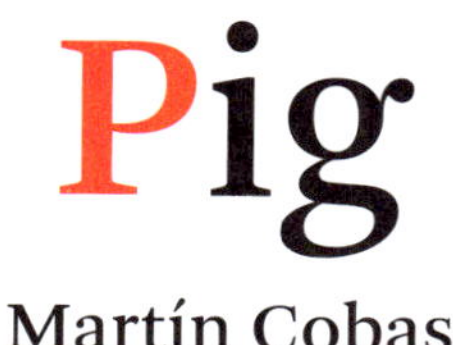

Pig

Martín Cobas

"Tiens, capon, cochon, félon, histrion, fripon, souillon, polochon."[1] Although the *Polochon-as-creature* was Lina Bo Bardi's own invention, the word *Polochon*—neither as noun (i.e., *traversin* or bolster) nor as creature—had been introduced by French absurdist writer Alfred Jarry (1873–1907) near the end of his play *Ubu Roi* (1896) in one of Mère Ubu's inventive wordplay-loaded monologues.

By 1985, when Italian-born Brazilian architect Lina Bo Bardi (1914–1992) created the *Polochon*, she was well acquainted with the experimental theater culture of São Paulo, a "scene" she had embraced since her arrival in Brazil with Pietro Maria Bardi in 1946 that culminated with the design of the Teatro Oficina, completed in 1993.

A bigger-than-life pig-like creature, the *Polochon* was sculpted in papier-mâché—the economic composite material of choice for puppetry and the inventive allegorical figures of Mardi Gras and other carnival-related celebrations, and the material with which the original marionettes for *Ubu Roi*'s first representations were made. An imposing and rather grotesque four-legged creature on wheels and colored pink (seductively tactile when looking at the fragments of paper and textiles composing its "skin"), resembling the large white swine or *Sus scrofa domestica* breed, its playfulness should not be underestimated: for the exhibition *Mil brinquedos para a criança brasileira* (A thousand toys for Brazilian children) held at SESC Pompeia center in 1985, Bo Bardi wrote: "children's play is a serious thing."[2] The *Polochon*'s most distinctive feature is, nonetheless, an anatomical oddity: it is a "porco de duas cabeças" (two-headed pig), or so Bo Bardi declares in one preparatory sketch,[3] not in the fashion of some misfortuned mutations (where the two heads are partially attached) but, awkwardly, one at each end of the creature's body. Two black incrustations as eyes, an intriguing cleavage front and back. The pink pig has two heads and, most importantly, it follows, two mouths. You might wonder, understandably, about the *Polochon*'s digestive tract.[4]

Figure 16.1
Lina Bo Bardi, *Polochon*. Preparatory sketch, 1985.
Ink and watercolor on paper. © Instituto Bardi/Casa de Vidro.

The *Polochon* was designed as part of the set for the play *UBU: folias physicas, pataphysicas e musicaes*, an adaptation of Jarry's *Ubu Roi* made for the Teatro do Ornitorrinco, an experimental theater company in São Paulo working under the direction of Carlos Eduardo "Cacá" Rosset.[5] The play, whose main character is a monstrous and scandalous man, Ubu, is a critique of the bourgeoisie written as a burlesque or parody. Indeed, the *Polochon* barely resembles Ubu's purposefully grotesque physiognomy. Yet its animality or creatureliness (beyond its digestive tract) might have implications well beyond Jarry's avant-gardist absurdism and dramatic innovations.[6]

As odd (and singular) as it is in its anatomical constitution, the *Polochon* is part of a much larger economy and ecology of figures and animals that populated Bo Bardi's world and architecture. Indeed, in Bo Bardi's work, animals and architecture are enigmatically interlocked. First, in her own house, the Casa de Vidro, built in São Paulo in 1951, a puzzling zoological menagerie of creatures local and exotic, real and fantastic: from two Paris-born Birman cats "imported" from France to turtles and parrots or the furtive visit of *macacos* (monkeys), a remembrance of the Mata Atlântica precariously conquered by the city. Then, in her creative work, from drawings to installations and performances. Recall, for instance, *Entre-ato para crianças* (Intermezzo for children, 1985), an installation that transformed the SESC Pompeia center (also a project by Bo Bardi) into a festive parade of animals populated by animal props and, among other taxonomical oddities, an inventory of cockroaches. But also, importantly, the animal played a key role in her ethnographic incursions in the Brazilian northeast, in Amerindian and Afro-Brazilian arts, from imposing *carranças* (figureheads) to *bodes expiatórios* (scapegoats) and beautifully crafted little creatures (elephants, oxen, and the like) famously collected in the exhibition *A mão do povo brasileiro* (The hand of Brazilian people), held at the Museu de Arte de São Paulo (MASP) in 1969.[7] Animals also appeared in Bo Bardi's editorial work—cat photography was proudly displayed in the magazine *Habitat*.[8] And pigs were also portrayed by Pierre Verger, Bo Bardi's dear friend—and a regular guest at the Casa de Vidro—in his ethnographic photography.[9] Creatures were as much collected as they were socialized. Creatures became a tool of translation in a modernizing society in search of a topical idiom. Whether codified in the absurdist tradition of Jarry or the subversive imprint of experimental theater and its carnivalesque undertones, in their pet-like whereabouts, ethnographic reconnaissance, or museum display, animal acts were ubiquitous. There is a good reason for this topical subversive modernity, and it asks for an ethno-zoo-anthropology of the *Polochon* (before returning to its digestive tract).

"Are peccaries human?" Swinology might well be an anthropological matter. In Eduardo Viveiros de Castro's "reverse anthropology," the question is not meant to be deemed real or utterly false but rather to articulate, in the footsteps of "multinaturalism" and "perspectivism"—defining notions of a "Brazilian" anthropological ontology—one of the fundamental dichotomies of Western metaphysics, that of the human-animal divide.[10] Peccaries, the anthropologist argues, "are of enormous interest to those humans who say that peccaries are human," and adds: "What is indeed worth knowing is: what are the Indians saying when they say that peccaries are human?"[11] Peccaries and humans are "inseparable variations of a single concept." Thus, Viveiros de Castro continues, "If we conceive of humans as somehow composed of a cultural clothing that hides and controls an essentially animal nature, Amazonians have it the other way around: animals have a human, sociocultural inner aspect that is 'disguised' by an ostensibly bestial bodily form."[12] Viveiros de Castro discovers in the Amazonians a type of nonhierarchical coexistence of all living beings, an ecology further complicated by the "animality" of man.[13]

Shall we see the *Polochon* as having a human "interiority," as occupying a liminal space between the human and the animal? Bo Bardi's tropical creature operates precisely in this direction: it reflects upon the nonhuman animal as constitutive of our own human ontology, that is, in continuity with us. Bo Bardi presented the *Polochon* or "o porco de duas cabeças" as "le polochon," often nicknamed it "o porquinho" (the piglet), "porco travesseiro" (pillow pig), and, finally, in an effort to name the creature's offspring, as "filhotes" (puppy pigs). The *Polochon* was designed not exclusively as part of the set design for Ubu's *folias* but also as a prop to be displayed at the lobby of the theater; indeed, the *Polochon* played the clerk. It was sketched in the Casa de Vidro, it was built in the Teatro do Ornitorrinco's workshops, it clerked for *Ubu*'s audiences, and then returned to the Casa de Vidro in family fashion (the *filhotes* colonized the house). There is an ecology of the *Polochon*, a sort of virtuous circle of design, atelier-made collective sculpture, performative creature, misplaced animal prop (the pig traveled the world), and *paterfamilias*. This entanglement between humans and nonhumans created a "liminal topography," a malleable and plastic milieu in which Bo Bardi thought to operate and display a social, political, and ethical critical agenda through which to reconcile apparently irreconcilable ethical conundrums between cultures (from Amerindian communities in the Amazonia to Afro-Brazilian cultures of the northeast) and between bodies (human and nonhuman). This, Bo Bardi shows, implied subversive and provocative "animal acts," and the consecration of a reenchanted world (modern *tout court*?) in which there was room for invention, provocation, and magic. In so doing, Bo Bardi triggered unprecedented affective and cognitive responses, delineating a differential modernity.

Entanglement is the *Polochon*'s motto; it dwells in the modernizing frontier, in a liminal topography that includes zoologies and botanies. This space we shall call the "creaturely modern," and the *Polochon* a "liminal creature," an indecisive dweller defined in a relational and therefore provisional way (as perspectivist anthropology suggests). And yet the critical productivity of the

Polochon as the beholder of a human "interiority" becomes relevant only insofar as we explore the creature's digestive tract.

You might wonder, therefore, about the *Polochon*'s digestive tract. Two heads, two mouths: the *porco de duas cabeças* is the only-devouring creature. *Polochon*'s anatomical oddity points, in fact, to Brazil's most enduring modernizing *ur-motif*: anthropophagy.

In a tradition that harkens back to Michel de Montaigne's essay "Des cannibals" (Of cannibals) of 1580 and to the "land of cannibals" introduced in early maps and travel literature alike, Oswald de Andrade's "Manifesto antropófago" (Anthropophagic Manifesto, 1928), published in the first volume of the *Revista de Antropofagia*,[14] defined Brazil's "rule of anthropophagy" and, to paraphrase Haroldo de Campos, placed Europe "under the sign of devoration."[15] Indeed, the consumption of "the other" prophesied an opulent and grandiose universal bacchanal. Shakespeare's line in *Hamlet* was thus rewritten as "Tupi or not Tupi."

At the crossroads of a particular incarnation of a "cannibal metaphysics" (as Viveiros de Castro would have it),[16] "human interiority," and modern devoration (also provocatively antimodern), the *Polochon*'s anatomical oddity encounters a properly architectural twin. Its animality played perilously close to architecture and performance. Remember: animals and architecture are enigmatically interlocked. Roughly contemporaneous to the *Polochon* was Bo Bardi's design for the Teatro Oficina in São Paulo's Bexiga neighborhood.[17] The final project reimagined the "scene" of dramaturgy in the form of a catwalk or street stage,[18] in Bo Bardi's words an "espaço frase" (narrative space).[19] Theater was thus conceived of as an architectural adventure that unfolds *in* time, a devouring (and processing) machine. Architecture itself became a performative organism entangled with the theatrical element. This had, predictably, profound political undertones (as in subverting, masking, carnivalizing, caricaturing, depatronizing). The Teatro Oficina is the architectural (and political) anatomy of the *Polochon*, more specifically its "human interiority": blood, feces, and urine of quite a few performances revealed its digestive machinery. Jose "Zé" Celso Martinez Corrêa, the company's director, recalls: "The magic word for theater is MERDA [shit]. But the guts at 520 Jaceguay do not have an asshole."[20] The anthropophagic machine is excessive and omnivorous; its perennial incorporation makes this rare form of consumption unstoppable, like a recursive carnivalesque parade with its byproducts endlessly recycled (blood, feces, and urine included). The *Polochon* and the Teatro Oficina are anthropophagy at its most radical.

And yet the anatomy of the *Polochon* has been a matter of contention. Whereas its ancestry and humanness offer little or no resistance, the particularities of the creature's digestive tract remain more problematic. Admittedly, and in spite of Bo Bardi's own name for it—the *porco de duas cabeças*—the "heads" resemble buttocks. One is impelled to notice some ambivalence in Bo

Bardi's own drawings of the *Polochon*: note, for instance, that the creature has one and only one pair of eyes. The black incrustations are not repeated in the two heads, which leads one to believe that the second head could be, in fact, a butt. If that is the case, why are the head and butt identically proportioned (the odd cleavage in front and back)? Far from a ludicrous foray into the anatomical reversals of the creature, this makes the *Polochon* dwell in an ambivalent territory of devouring and excreting. Think of the *Polochon* as a two-headed pig and you get the only-devouring creature. Think of it as a two-butted pig and you get the only-excreting one, the anti-cannibal. Think, then, of the *Polochon* as holding dual citizenship: in the kingdom of scarcity and in the kingdom of excess. Such is the moral conveyed by the *Polochon*: animal, human, devourer, excreter.

In the sometimes complementing and sometimes competing realms of representation, architecture, and display, Bo Bardi made the animal (or imaginary creature) "communicate." Even though the worlds of the animal and of the creature are neither symbolic nor linguistic (as we read in Heidegger, Lacan, or Levinas), they are certainly communicative; there is, as Diane Davis suggested, a "creaturely rhetorics."[21] This nonlinguistic status makes the animal simultaneously untranslatable and readily available for "conversation" (in a nonverbal communication). Animals are co-constitutive of the topographies we inhabit, and in this way social relationality is extended to nonhumans. The *Polochon* occupies a place beyond language in the city of all possible languages. The *Polochon* is an urban creature and a *Paulista* one. Remember the *Polochon*.

Queen Bee

Robin Skinner

Sir Basil Spence presented his 1964 expressionist design for "the Beehive," the Executive Wing of the New Zealand Parliament, to the politicians and citizens of New Zealand with magisterial eloquence. Though it was seen as "clearly a stunt" by some,[1] figurative description and convincing rhetoric can sometimes ensure that a flawed design will not only be accepted but championed, despite sound rationale against its adoption. This was the case with Spence's Beehive.

When opened in 1922, the impact of the recent war and limited funds had resulted in only half of New Zealand's Edwardian baroque Parliament building being constructed. Four decades later, moves were made to complete the design. The government's architects were enthusiastic for a tall modern block standing alongside the existing structure, although the politicians and their advisors were unimpressed with this "dog box" proposal. They wanted to see the earlier design completed. With no clear way forward, in August 1963 it was decided that an architect of international standing should provide an opinion. The British designer of the recently completed Coventry Cathedral, Sir Basil Spence O.M. (1907–1976), had coincidentally been asked to deliver lectures in New Zealand the following year, and so—naturally—he was asked to advise. While his brief was only to comment on the style of the addition, he nevertheless took it upon himself to prepare a design.

Some two weeks after his arrival, Spence declared the task to be a "hornets' nest."[2] The following day, he presented a design of a freestanding domed addition in sketches and a model. Arguing that a rectangular building was inappropriate on sloping ground, he told the politicians that the circular form would become a hub for the government center and that it would perform well under seismic loading. Echoing an engineer's practical rhetoric, he declared that like a "peg in the ground" the circular building would stabilize the site.[3]

Figure 17.1 (following pages)
Sir Basil Spence, Beehive sketch, March 1964. 12.7 × 17.8 cm. New Zealand Parliamentary Collection. © New Zealand Parliamentary Collection.

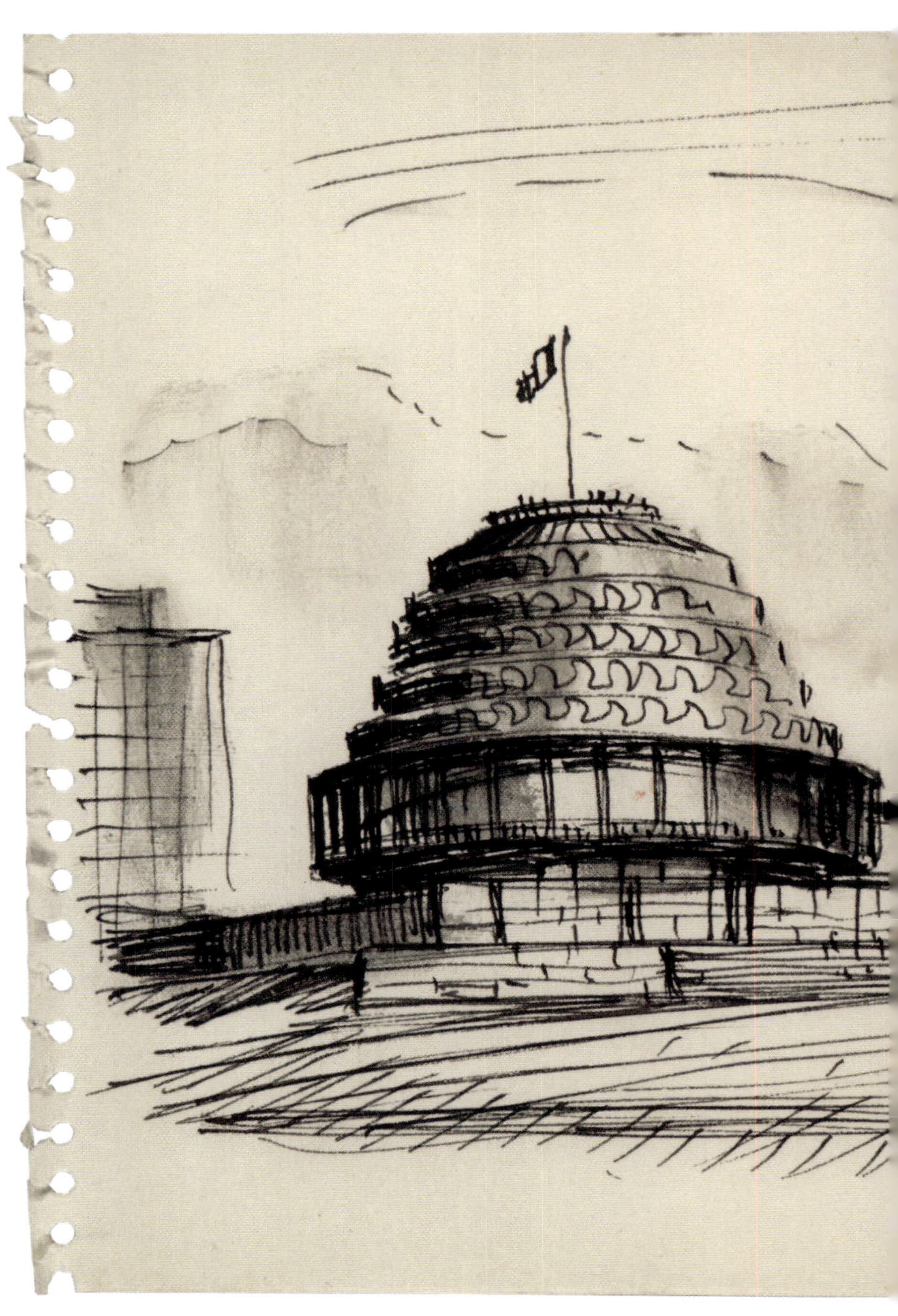

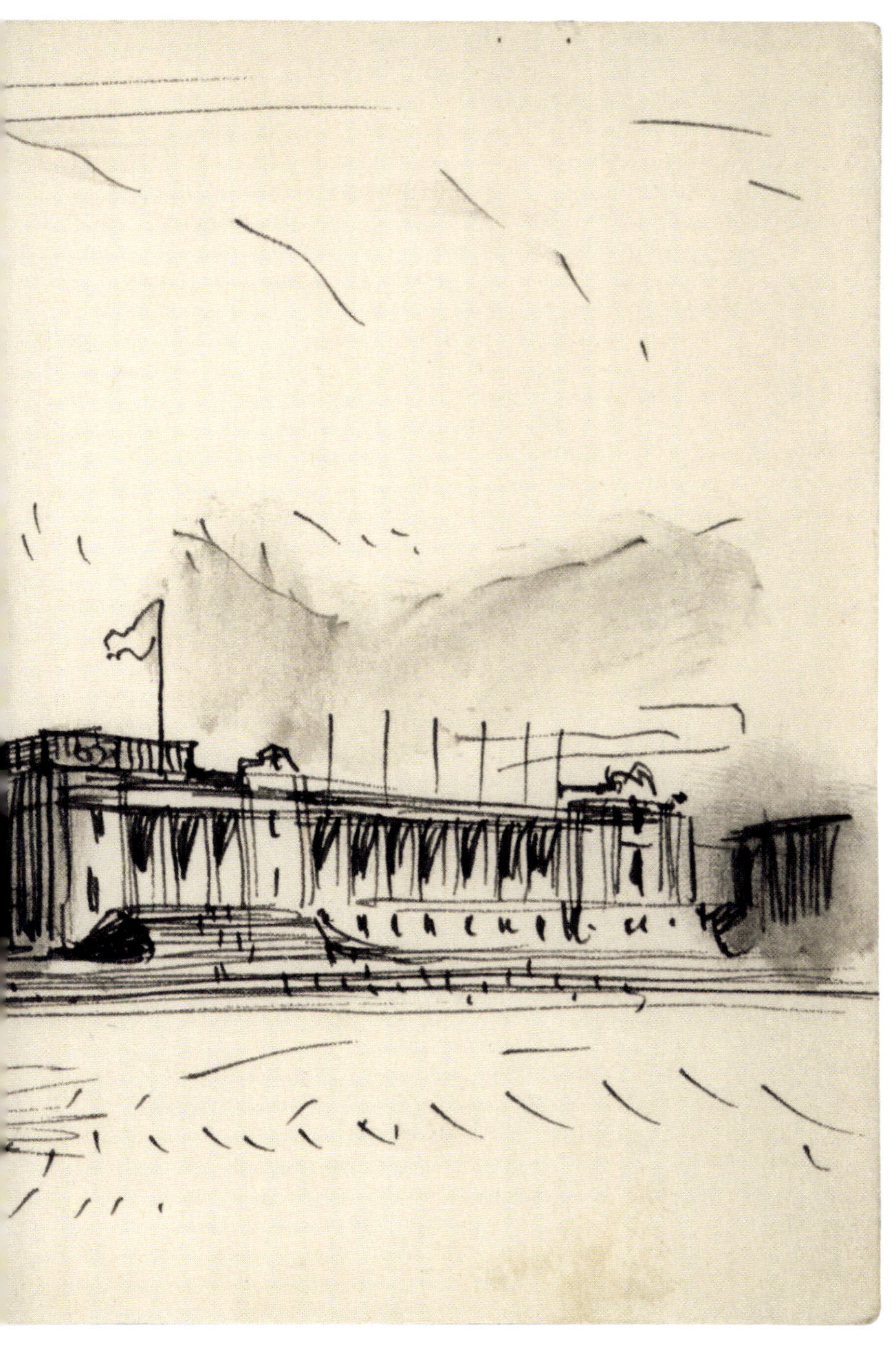

Completing the neo-baroque design, he stated, would be dishonest in these modern times. Nevertheless, with considered thought, he believed the proportions, facade treatment, and materials of a modern addition could echo the adjacent earlier structure.[4] Emphasizing the uniqueness of the design, he quoted Pericles extolling the Athenians: "We don't imitate—we are the model for others."[5] It was, of course, under Pericles' leadership that the ambitious building program on the Acropolis was begun; however, here the Greek politician spoke of democratic government rather than a work of design.[6] This distinction went largely unnoticed. Extending his vespine metaphor from the previous day, Spence described the building as "a beehive," where everyone would work in harmony. Immediately the name caught on.

Anchoring its architecture on well-chosen words, Spence presented the design as new, original, and visionary. This was what the politicians expected for a building of such import. Although this grandiloquence swayed the decision-makers, local architects deplored the design, while Australian critics described it as "looking freshly up-turned out of a neo-classic jelly mold."[7] However, such was the aura of the overseas expert that Spence was kept on as a consultant, partly to help the government architects fend off criticism from their fellow professionals. This was no easy arrangement, with the government architects subsequently gaining total control of the project after the sketch design phase. Nevertheless, the Spence charm had worked its magic. He had convinced the once-reluctant Prime Minister, Keith Holyoake (1904–1983), of the correctness of the radical scheme to the extent that he became its greatest champion, stating that it would be a source of "national pride and international interest."[8] Presumably, Holyoake thought that this would be an architectural equivalent to the opera house then proposed for Sydney Harbour, itself described symbolically as sails of sea vessels.

The beehive metaphor has a rich architectural tradition. As Juan Antonio Ramírez has documented, models from apiculture were studied by Antoni Gaudí, Frank Lloyd Wright, Mies van der Rohe, and Le Corbusier.[9] In secular circles, the beehive was understood as a symbol of an ideal, well-organized society. In New Zealand, Spence's allusion certainly captured people's attention, taking on a life of its own. A rumor emerged that the form was prompted by a beehive logo on matchboxes that are commonly available in that country. Cartoonists illustrated bees circling the building. A humorous poem appeared.[10] It was even suggested that the design recalled Hiona, the earlier circular temple of the Māori prophet Rua Kēnana. As a freemason, Holyoake may have been attracted to the form as an established metaphor for industry and harmony. This interpretation was widely shared; in 1977 when Queen Elizabeth II opened the yet-to-be-completed building, she said, "it is hard to imagine a better image for those who serve the people than the busy and industrious honey bee."[11] Her string of well-worn adjectives, "bold, imaginative, impressive," prompts one to wonder what she really thought.[12]

Although Spence left the project in 1965, as the design developed the proportions he had initially resolved, his sketch plans for each floor, his facade elevations that detailed the shading to be achieved by the radiating fins, and his resolution of the building's crowning cap were faithfully executed with little variation. The government architects remained bound to his visionary sketches, which they reworked and re-presented as their own.

Despite the convincing rhetoric of 1964, the building did not deliver all its creator's promises. The circular floors are not space-efficient, the curved arc of the Banquet Hall lacks spatial unity, and even seasoned incumbents have become disoriented within the encircling corridors. Denied the full commission, Spence later declared the final design to be poorly executed, dissociating himself from it altogether.[13]

Nevertheless, the power of his allusion had captured the imagination of a nation. Today the building is featured on banknotes, stamps, in political cartoons, and on numerous other graphic displays. Politicians aspire to occupy its lofty offices. Now the country's principal site of celebration and protest, it has become an iconic symbol for the capital city of Wellington and, beyond that, a metonym for the nation's government itself.

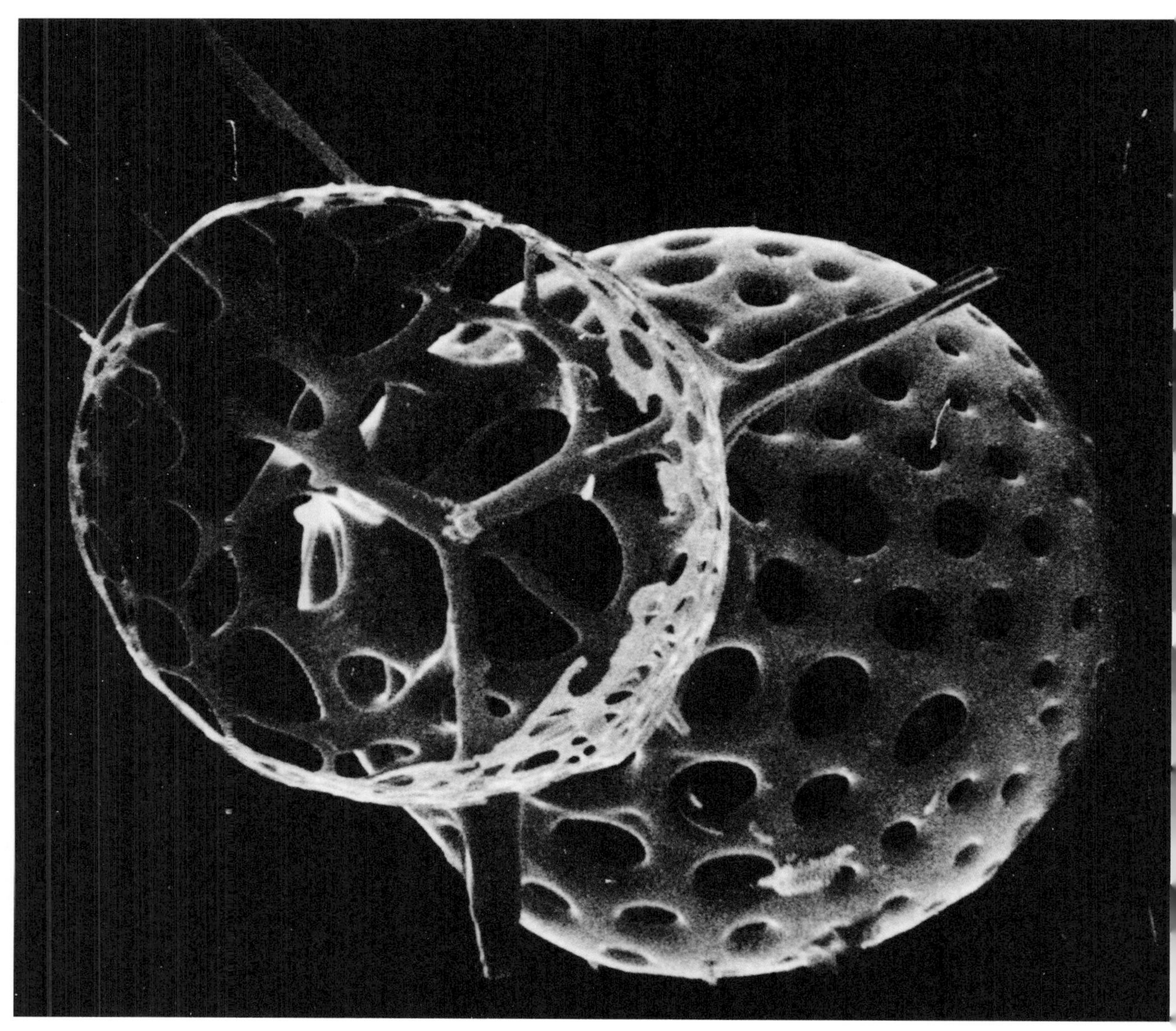

Figure 18.1
Electron micrograph showing a Radiolaria shell, published in Universität Stuttgart, Institut für Leichte Flächentragwerke, "IL 3: Biology and Building, Part I," 1971. Photo: Research Group for Micromorphology, Berlin.

Radiolaria

Daniela Fabricius

What can architecture learn from Radiolaria? Radiolaria are single-cell organisms that typically measure 0.1–0.2 mm in diameter. They have inhabited the earth for 550 million years, but humans only discovered them in the nineteenth century. They are housed within perforated lattice shells made of silica that is drawn from the seawater, forming what are essentially tiny glass enclosures with radial patterns. The soft interior of a radiolarian, in contrast to its shell, is wet, oily, and frothy. Despite being made up of one cell, Radiolaria display an enormous amount of diversity, which results from how their structures respond to differing environmental conditions.

Frei Otto encountered the radiolarians and their protist cousins—diatoms—through his collaboration in the early 1960s with the biologist and anthropologist Johann-Gerhard Helmcke.[1] Helmcke was a specialist in the microstructures of diatoms and radiolarians, and published entire atlases filled with images taken with an electron microscope. Otto describes his encounter with these images as follows: "Helmcke showed me his stereoscopic photographs of diatoms and Radiolaria taken with an electron microscope. In these photos I saw shapes which had formed 'of themselves' in my experiments with pneumatics, i.e., soap bubbles, soap films, rubber membranes and net structures. From then on, I saw only such forms in all living organisms, not only in diatoms."[2]

The experiments Otto is referring to, especially those with soap films, are well known. What is less well known is that by the 1970s they were conducted primarily in service of his search for the *Pneu*, a concept of his own invention that describes self-forming minimal structures of enclosure. The idea of a lightweight structural membrane filled with air or fluid had fascinated Otto early on in his studies of soap films. Helmcke's interest in the concept of the *Pneu* stemmed from his research on Radiolaria, which he believed to have begun as tiny, soft membranes before hardening into filigreed silicon structures.[3]

Otto believed that the *Pneu* was tied to the very origins of life—"Am Anfang war der Pneu" (In the beginning was the *Pneu*), he wrote, and it was "the essential basis of the world of forms of living nature."[4] As a prehistoric form of life, the Radiolaria would have held a prominent place in this genealogy of forms. Otto's theory of the *Pneu* was promiscuous, however: it could describe anything from pig intestines to kernels of corn, salamander eggs, human skin, or clouds. In other words, Radiolaria were by no means the only creatures in his bestiary.[5]

Otto, of course, was hardly the first to see possibilities for architecture in the structures of Radiolaria. The detailed illustrations of Radiolaria in Ernst Haeckel's *Kunstformen der Natur* (1904) closely resembled architectural motifs of his time, and Haeckel even decorated his house in Jena with lamps, furniture, and murals resembling Radiolaria. Haeckel's publications directly influenced art nouveau and *Jugendstil*: Hendrik Petrus Berlage drew from Haeckel's work for his interiors, and René Binet famously constructed the massive entrance gate to the 1900 Paris Universal Exposition according to Haeckel's interpretation of a radiolarian.[6]

It is clear that interpretations of radiolarians' architectural qualities conformed to the historic conditions and desires of the architects who admired them. By the mid-twentieth century, Buckminster Fuller saw the Radiolaria as a model of a universal mathematical order that mirrored that of his geodesic domes.[7] In their first co-published article in 1962, entitled "Living and Technical Constructions: Observations on Shells and Spaceframes in Nature and Technology," Otto and Helmcke compared diatoms to constructions by Fuller and Pier Luigi Nervi. However, their approach was not based on mathematics or even geometry, but on the criterion of structural performance. Helmcke's approach to microstructures was architectural—his stereoscopic photographs were used to create photogrammetric measurements of diatoms and radiolarians that allowed for a "spatially correct impression of the framework of the building elements."[8] This provided the basis for reconstructive drawings, with architectural conventions like plans, sections, and renderings. Similarly, Otto developed elaborate measurement instruments to document material experiments at his Institut für Leichte Flächentragwerke (Institute for Lightweight Structures), rather than relying on a priori mathematical principles.

Otto and Helmcke claimed that the diverse forms exhibited by Radiolaria are not the result of underlying genetic codes but are instead rapid chemical and physical responses to their environment. Just as there is no underlying code, there is similarly no ideal geometry—Radiolaria, as Helmcke's photographs show, display irregularities and deformities that can't be explained through mathematics. Otto also emphasized that the geometries of Radiolaria do not behave as crystals, which would disturb their "process of life," but are essentially liquid—their skeletons, he points out, have qualities that resemble amorphous quartz or window glass.[9] The reference to window glass can't be overlooked; it suggests that, at a material level, Otto saw a kinship between the Radiolaria and modern architecture.

Otto nevertheless insisted that his motivation for looking at the Radiolaria was not to find a model for human construction, but rather, inversely, to identify analogies that would allow structures in nature to be better understood through architectural analysis.[10] In other words, the idea is not for architecture to mimic natural structures, but for it to uncover relationships between different forms that suggest a common principle of structural organization. For Otto, this essentially comes down to the question of self-formation, whether in the pneumatic shapes of soap film, the optimization of path systems, or the lattice structures of the Radiolaria. These are structures that were not predetermined and thus are capable of open-ended flexibility and indeterminacy.

If the interpretation of Radiolaria is historically determined, then Otto's reading of radiolarian form as an adaptive, self-organizing structure should be considered in the context of postwar West Germany. Otto's concern with lightweight, optimized structures originally stemmed from the constraints imposed by the conditions of postwar Germany's economic and material austerity (though, in the more abundant years of Germany's "economic miracle," lightness became less tied to economic need and increasingly became a virtue in itself). For Otto, lightness was also explicitly associated with the historical and political project of rebuilding West Germany, where he believed lightweight, flexible architecture "might bring about a new and open society."[11] Otto became preoccupied with "adaptable" (*anpassungsfähig*) building during his years of independent research in West Berlin in the 1950s, viewing it as clearing the path for "a new way of thinking that departs from the static toward a life that is eternally changing."[12] Architecture should not have a fixed form or dimension, but should be able to respond to shifting needs. These needs were often related to questions of economy: Otto studied different forms of optimization at his research institute, which included not only how structures transfer forces along a path but also the amount of energy (fuel or food) needed to move a truck or a human being, or the cost of shipping or transporting goods. In the context of Germany's energy crisis and the growing environmental movement of the 1970s, Otto's arguments for natural structures were increasingly made in favor of global environmental concerns, and optimization and lightness became a project of ecological risk management.

The search for alternative structures and more ecologically oriented forms of inhabitation led Otto to the tracing and crossing of boundaries between living and nonliving, natural and technological. He produced a variety of elaborate theories (supported by detailed charts) that organized both living and nonliving objects, from the molecular to the planetary scale, according to their structural properties rather than their received taxonomies. Wholeness in architecture, he argued, would come about only through a synthesis of these disparate evolutionary moments in natural history: "We have not yet experienced the fragile, perhaps even ephemeral, architecture of the physical and psychical integration of man into his environment. But we seek the architecture of understanding and of the great vision of a synthesis of all the objects of nature."[13] Thus, the Radiolaria, and other protists, held a particular fascination for Otto in part because of their taxonomic ambiguity, as they appeared to share qualities of animals, vegetables, *and* minerals.[14]

For Otto, prehistoric forms like the Radiolaria suggested the possibilities of such a synthesis of categories for advanced structures: "The first constructions of early humans resemble the holes, nests, and designs of animals, but not at all the inner structure of living beings themselves, which already existed at a high level of perfection in prehistoric time."[15] Otto's idealizing of the prehistoric as a potential new beginning for architecture was in keeping with the "transhistorical consciousness" of the 1960s.[16] Radiolaria can in fact be described as witnesses and documentarians of the earth's history. Upon their deaths, their shells float to the bottom of the ocean, where they amass in the form of a siliceous ooze. The layers of sediment rock formed by countless generations of Radiolaria is a forensic site for micropaleontologists, who are able to read in the carbon imprint of these tiny skeletons the changing temperatures of the earth over its long history.[17]

Otto's placement of the Radiolaria in both an ideal past and an imagined future suggests he saw in radiolarian architecture not simply a model of efficiency or adaptability, but an architecture of potential transformation and becoming. Similarly, the photographic documentation of Radiolaria created by Helmcke, along with the display and publication of these images, was about more than just measuring and studying the structures of Radiolaria. These images reveal the desire for an imaginary, the ability to envision these organisms as built, inhabitable structures.[18] Helmcke's photographs were in fact stereoscopic, presenting two slightly different views of the Radiolaria, which is what allowed for the precise measurements of their structures. But this also allowed for the ability to view the structures three-dimensionally, experiencing them as if they were at human scale. Stereoscopic glasses were included in several of Helmcke's and Otto's publications, and stereoscopic projections of Radiolaria and diatoms were often used during presentations. Otto's desired physical and psychical integration of man into the environment was perhaps partially achieved through these optical illusions, these projections that made the Radiolaria into inhabitable space.

Sea Jelly

Konstantina Kalfa

Over the last decade of the twentieth century and the dawn of the twenty-first, architecture's fascination with animals thrived as an unapologetic zoomorphism. Greg Lynn in a way set the trend when, in 1992, he made the bold—and rather provocative—suggestion to revisit one of the most blatant, if not kitsch, animal architectural references, reconceptualizing Venturi's "duck" as a promising "alien" form of architecture, one that escapes the century-old burdens of structural rationalism and geometric exactitude.[1] In general, Lynn was describing the broader unleashing of possibilities at the exact moment when the figural meets the structural, rather than the duck as an animal to imitate. The duck, with its "classical" symmetry and charming cuteness, could hardly stand as a model in Greg Lynn's new, blobby architectural universe. To critics, the gelatinous, adaptive form of the jellyfish appeared, instead, to be the most prevalent zoomorphic reference in Lynn's animate ecology.[2]

However, looking at Lynn's own descriptions of his work, one would find it rather challenging to locate any reference whatsoever to the jellyfish. Lynn has never portrayed it, despite his numerous illustrations of other animals like D'Arcy Thompson's crustacean carapaces, Johann Caspar Lavater's frog, mites on a hedgehog flea, planarians, Bateson's Coleoptera beetles, or Marey's galloping horse, to name a few. Neither has he ever verbally referred to it in his texts and speeches, despite the fact that he has used a host of other animals as examples and references: birds, ants, crabs, insects, lizards, parrots, hippopotami, and even sea creatures like the whale, fish, devilfish, and barracuda, whose dynamic, interactive movement in the water interested him much more than that of the "floating jellyfish."[3] Even when discussing the Ark of the World, a project which is repeatedly described in the architectural media as having been directly inspired by the jellyfish, Lynn has instead brought up the frog as his inspiration—as his "kind of hero"—for showing the way "of a gradient color and a change in texture as the structure moves across the surface," that is, more for a biological performance than an animal form.[4] In a recent conversation, Lynn made it clear that although he feels no need "to disagree if someone thinks something [he] ha[s] done looks like a jellyfish or another plant or animal," he does not design buildings or industrial products using "stylistic organicism." Besides, as he declared, he does not have "a strong affinity for jellyfish" anyway.[5]

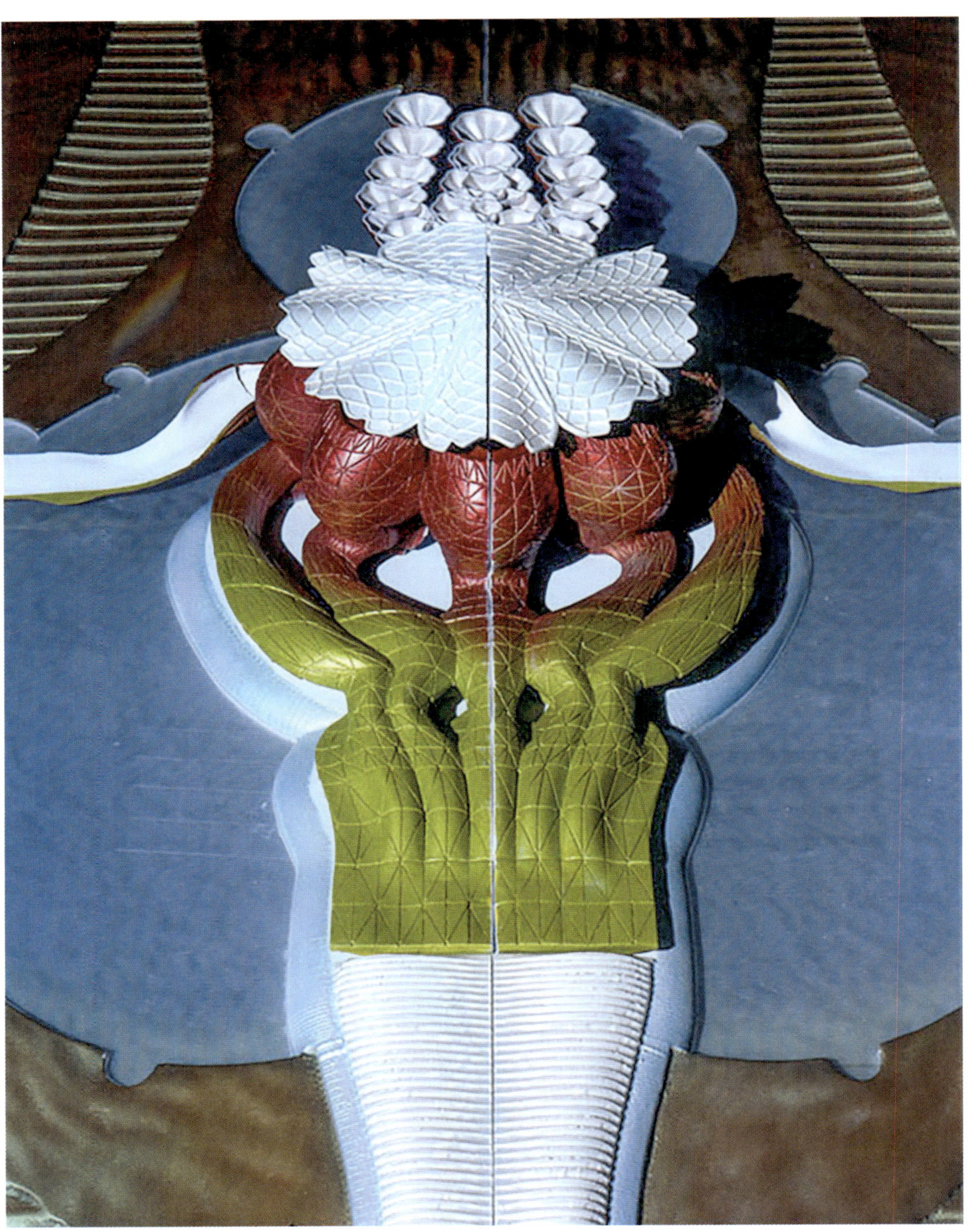

Why, then, are the jellyfish so omnipresent in his work to the eyes of observers? Perhaps there are good reasons for this, which we should seek beyond the similarities in appearance or the architect's own intention. Evidently, regardless of whether animalism, particularly in the form of a jellyfish, was a deliberate effect of Lynn's and his peers' design experiments, new computer software and construction possibilities exposed late twentieth-century architecture to the era's first applications in artificial intelligence and bioengineering. As Lynn recounts, back in the 1990s at the Architectural Association and ANY conferences, "fellows of the Santa Fe Institute" and "economists and political scientists using software modeling [and] biological (often Neo-Darwinian) metaphors," shared with architects the fantasy of bio-inspired automated production.[6] Inasmuch as the eventual passivity of his early projects, like the Ark of the World, makes them a weak version of such a fantasy, Lynn clearly envisioned an architecture whereby primitive forms of life and automata act in synergy under the influence of vital forces. Lynn's architectural universe was created through strange "alien" creatures, "chrysalides," surfaces on which moss grows, forces "allowed to act in free space and interact with one another," "shells," and "membranes." Together with architects like Karl Chu and John Frazer (who are often mentioned in Lynn's texts), Lynn called for a design process produced through self-similarity, mapping "behavior patterns and forces," enabling "decay, acceleration and turbulence," imitating the "awesome creative power of natural evolution" through "symbiotic behavior and metabolic balance" and through using the computer as an "evolutionary accelerator and a generative force." Fueled by this rhetoric, Karl Chu even described capitalism as a whole as "a demiurgic system that is destined to become virtually intelligent and alive." Both Chu and Lynn spoke of computing machines that could be considered as "animate" or as a "global brain" acquiring "an internal will to being: a self-organizing and self-synthesizing monad," reproduced "organically" and leading to forms that could be conceived as having been "bred."[7]

The thread of biological ideas that nourished such fantasies at the time used the jellyfish as a central metaphor or reference. For instance, Lynn and his peers were keen on Alfred North Whitehead's theories, including the idea that not all biological actions rely upon the control of a center and that, therefore, there are alternative forms of perception, such as the "causal relationship with the world" developed in the very-little-centralized way "a jellyfish advances and withdraws."[8] Evolution theorist D'Arcy Thompson, a steady influence for Lynn, illustrated his basic insight that organisms mutate under environmental forces by comparing the form of a jellyfish to that of one liquid dropped

Figure 19.1
Greg Lynn FORM, Ark of the World Visitors Center. Model photograph by Brandon Welling, 2003. © Greg Lynn FORM/Brandon Welling.

into another of lower density. Both Rene Thom's morphogenesis and the concept of self-organization proposed by Stuart Kauffman (a star of the Santa Fe Institute)—again, central references in Lynn's writings—admittedly drew a lot from Thompson's metaphor; and physician Hans Jenny's experiments in cymatics, illustrating *Animate Form* (1999), reversed this imagery, producing jellyfish-like forms through vibrating liquid. In these elaborations, jellyfish reach for a blurring of the boundaries between life and the inorganic, which was a fundamental presupposition for Lynn's and his peers' architecture.

It is therefore not by chance that late twentieth-century animalistic architecture in general, and Lynn's architecture in particular, direct us toward the inexact plasticity of the jellyfish. Uncontaminated as it is by consciousness, history, or culture, the jellyfish stands for an inorganic yet "animate" form that is self-enclosed—an autonomous machine that could replace human labor by reproducing itself, in accordance with what Deleuze and Guattari (another constant reference for Lynn and his peers) had described as a new kind of "machinic surplus value" indispensable to human labor.[9] Perhaps, then, the jellyfish can be described as a formal/visual metaphor for the ideological device that has recurred in capitalism since the invention of the steam engine: the device that relegates life to bare life under the perspective of the development and expansion of machines in every single field of production until they eventually replace human labor.

But then again, the jellyfish can also provide the means to question this utopian perspective: deprived as they are of actual emotions, desires, sensibilities, and that "alien will" on the appropriation of which lies "the presupposition of the master-servant relation" (and therefore the creation of surplus value), they seem to disturb the promise of full automation through laborless production.[10] Under this lens, the jellyfish inevitably takes the discussion on the use of animals in architecture to a whole new level: that of the political economy of architectural products and the ways they stand both for a utopian "wish image" (Walter Benjamin) and the dissolution of this image as a result of the contradictions of the system itself.[11]

Turtle

Rebecca O'Neal

In the beginning
there was a great tortoise
who supported the world.
Upon him
all ultimately
rests.
Without him
nothing will stand.
He is all wise
and can outrun the hare.
In the night
his eyes carry him
to unknown places.
He is your friend.

—WILLIAM CARLOS WILLIAMS,
excerpt from "The Turtle," 1956[1]

A giant turtle frequents the spaces of the paintings and drawings of the late American architect, artist, and educator Samuel Mockbee (1944–2001). In annotated sketchbook drawings from the 1990s, Mockbee labels the recurring turtle as "Chelonian" and occasionally as the "Black Warrior Turtle." Like the Native Americans' mythical turtle—the world-builder who originated the earth by bringing mud up from the bottom of the sea to create *terra firma*[2]—Mockbee's turtle is imbued with significance as protector, capable of burrowing into the dark safety of the earth. Above ground, it signifies nomadic shelter and the potential for internal escape from the world, an earth unto itself. In the water, the turtle is burdened only with the metaphysical weight of yearning for the elusive "shelter for the soul" desired by Mockbee and guiding his philosophy for an architectural pedagogy of social consequence. In the space of Mockbee's picture plane, despite being tied up with ropes or ensnared in a trap, the Black Warrior Turtle serves as a silent and patient witness.

Samuel Mockbee, a fifth-generation Mississippian, grew up in the racially segregated South in Meridian, Mississippi. Benefiting from the societal advantages

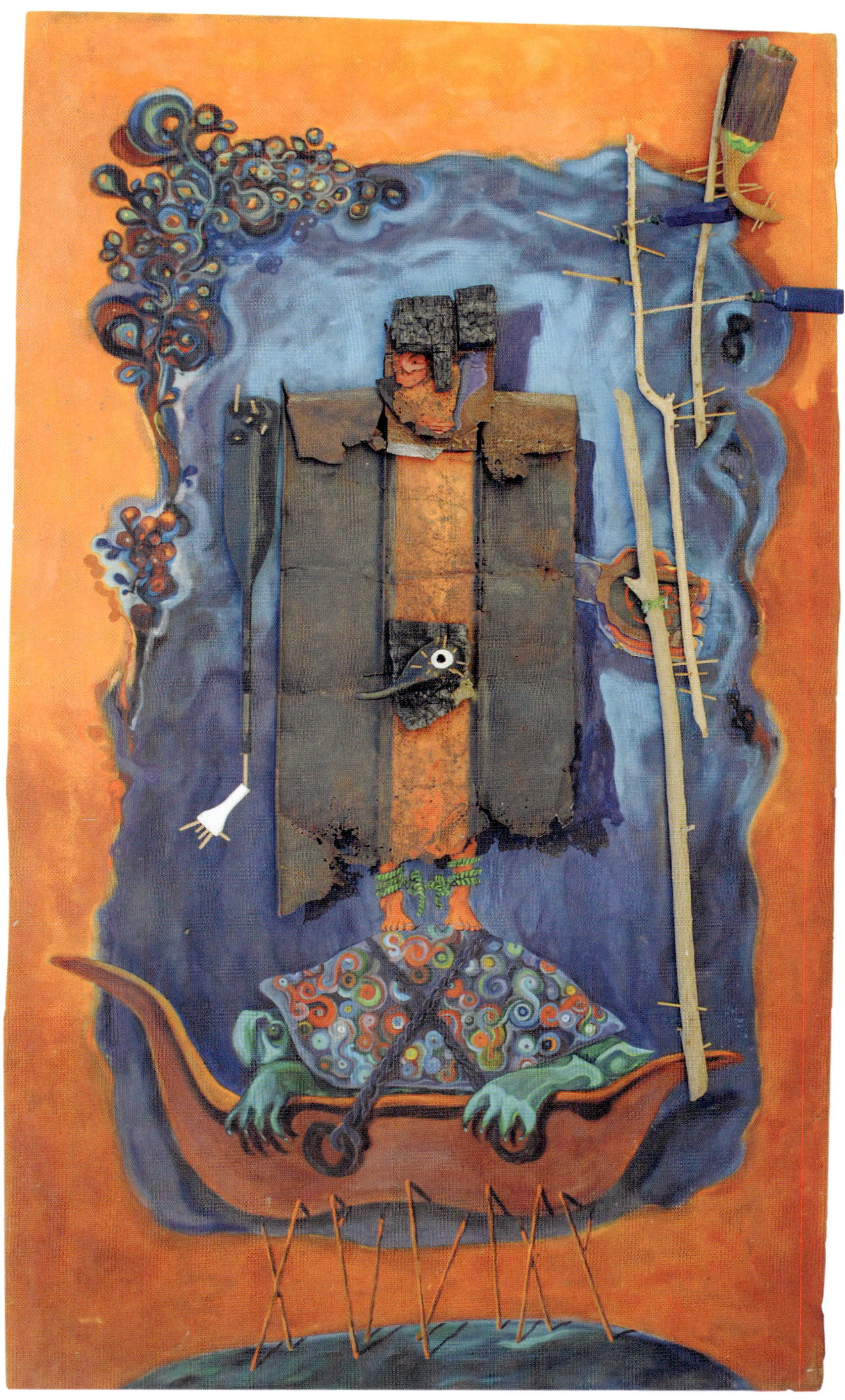

of a southern white male, he came of age during the civil rights movement. An explorer of the Mississippi landscape and natural world during his childhood, he was influenced by formative social interactions with Black Americans and white Americans, and with both the wealthy and the poverty-stricken. Becoming increasingly aware of the inequities around him in the South and of his privileges, Mockbee rejected his childhood indoctrination to admire "heroes" of the Confederacy when he understood the truth of the blood-soaked past of the Civil War in Mississippi and the state's shameful history of racism and bigotry.[3]

In a formative moment of his young adult life, Mockbee was delayed due to road construction near a Meridian cemetery. While waiting, he wandered into the graveyard and happened upon the grave of the slain civil rights activist and Freedom Rider James Earl Chaney, who was violently tortured and murdered at age twenty-four in the summer of 1964 by white Mississippi racists. Mockbee said he was overcome with grief, realizing that they would have been the same age had Chaney lived. Both born in Meridian, Mississippi, in the early 1940s, they were separated only by the cultural framework of race. For the rest of his life, Mockbee carried with him an understanding of Chaney's sacrifice and of the unjust horror of his fate. It spurred him into advocacy for social justice and equality through art and architecture. Mockbee spoke often about James Chaney, saying, "For me he defines who I am and who I am not. He represents the true heroes of the South. He had the courage to risk his own life. His courage was a gift and his presence was felt on earth."[4]

> The Black Warrior drifts, floating among the graves of the innocent.
> SAMUEL MOCKBEE[5]

As the core of his last series of works on paper and paintings, he developed a "semi-fictionalized" mythology of supernatural characters and animals, including his "Chelonian." The protagonists and antagonists in his visual chronicles are chimeras made up of real and fictional people. Individuals occupying the representations are composed of essences of specific Mississippians from his past in Canton, Mississippi (where he and his wife raised their family of four children), combined with aspects and personalities of certain Alabamians from Hale County, home of Rural Studio, the Auburn University architecture program's design-build "Citizen Architect" program that he co-founded.[6]

Figure 20.1
Samuel Mockbee, *Chelonians / Sternotherus Minor (The Loggerhead Musk Turtle) / Black Warrior River*, hand-drawn ink with annotation, 1994. Mockbee Archive, Canton, MS; access courtesy of Jackie Mockbee. Photograph by Rebecca O'Neal, 2016.

Over a period of years, precise details of the recurring chimerical animals and their appearances, roles, and vices are documented across formats. In addition to the recurring Chelonian, Mockbee codified a menagerie of mythical characters such as the "Loan Shark," a "worm seller," "Klansman," the "Fox," and the "Serpent" (of Eden, Mississippi). His images of the serpent represent "vices," while his abstract flowers indicate "virtue." The main cast of the mythical world-changers features "The Black Warrior (earthbound)," "Apple (spiritbound and fertility)," "the Paramour," and the all-powerful "Master Knot of Fate," among others.[7] Often alluded to in the title of a work, the content of the entire backstory is not explained to the viewer. Codified while he was in his battle with cancer, Mockbee's internal world is layered with elements of the supernatural, the darkness, and the afterlife.

Deep in the southern United States, the Black Warrior River has been a constant presence in the Alabama landscape throughout its tumultuous history. Named after the powerful sixteenth-century Native American chief Tuscaloosa, meaning "Black Warrior," the Black Warrior River was a primary Native American travel route between key Indigenous settlements until the area was conquered by the Spanish. The Spanish decimated the first peoples and their cultural systems. The Black Warrior was destroyed, but his river remained. By the nineteenth century, an endless number of enslaved people were forced to supply massive quantities of cotton out of the South. Wealthy white planters lived on "high ground" amassing fortunes from cotton exports at the expense of the subjugated. Born on the backs of slaves and the brutal institution of slavery, the cotton trade in Alabama consumed the agrarian landscape of the fertile Black Belt region.

When the flood waters recede the poor folk along
the river start from scratch.
RICHARD WRIGHT[8]

Samuel Mockbee became fascinated with Alabama's Black Warrior River and the history of the Black Warrior legends after meeting Shepard Bryant. Mr. Bryant was an impoverished elderly African American fisherman who became the first "charity house" client of Rural Studio. Mr. Bryant and his wife, Alberta, lived in a shack on land at Mason's Bend formed by the river. Mr. Bryant caught massive loggerhead turtles in the river as sustenance. Mockbee was fascinated by these beasts, and one of his treasured possessions was a huge turtle shell (at least two feet in length) gifted to him by Shepard Bryant.[9]

For *The Black Warrior*, a massive painting from 1996, Mockbee casts the turtle as both foundational and captive.[10] The painting is canvas on wood construction measuring thirteen feet tall, a work of architecture in itself. The viewer is immersed by the scale of the painting, becoming part of the scene. Rusted metal sheets plucked from the Rural Studio's Red Barn form the warrior's cape. Collaged elements include a phallic gourd, knotted ropes, and a beaver stick "spirit tree" staff.[11] In the full tableau, the Chelonian occupies a liminal space, elevated out of the water and above ground. Either a digger or a swimmer, in the confines of the composition the turtle is out of both its earth element and its water element, having neither land nor river. Standing atop its shell, surprisingly, the Black Warrior is also lashed by rope at the ankles. The two entities are bound together in the boat, out of water.

Symbolically, Mockbee's turtle possesses compounded identities across artworks. Despite the complexities of origins and references, the animal consistently remains a steady signifier of the unresolved and the passing of time. Visually, the turtle is a conduit for the observer's own perceptions. Chthonian in nature, the aquatic earth dweller exists as an oscillating metaphor. Earthbound, it is an excavator, captive, life-giver, and revealer of truths. Throughout the body of work, the turtle holds gravitas, supporting critical portions of Mockbee's imagined world. In his artistic beast fable, "The Black Warrior" and "Chelonian" are lashed to the "Master Knot of Fate," who is Mockbee's all-powerful source, the decider of life and death.

Samuel Mockbee's efforts to capture and lay bare the anguished realities of the indignity of poverty remain with us after his death through his art. His artworks are evidence of his lamentations on southern culture and its tumultuous history of social injustice and racism. Vestiges of this history and its cultural heritage continue to have generational repercussions.

American poet William Carlos Williams wrote the poem "The Turtle" for his young grandson in 1956. It is not known whether Samuel Mockbee (also a young boy at the time) read the poem then; however, Mockbee called Williams his favorite poet. Similar to Williams's turtle, Mockbee's turtle is a seer, a wise savior. Interchangeably signifying shelter and protection, vulnerability and innocence, even when it is confined this turtle has the strength to stay alive. Its beaked face appears imperturbable despite the turtle's being restrained by ropes and notwithstanding the disquieting context of the painted environments that it inhabits.

At moments in the illustrations the turtle represents Mockbee himself, who was stricken with aggressive leukemia in 1998. At ease being a leader in all situations, he was at the mercy of a brutal treatment regimen, including a bone marrow transplant from his sister. For his mythic and resilient turtle, the protective chelonian carapace was on the exterior. Conversely, Mockbee's protection originated in the interior, deep in his bones with the new marrow which gave him several more years. He fought valiantly but was still tied and bound to the "Master Knot of Fate."

Mockbee's drawings of his last architecture project, Subrosa Pantheon, reveal only two occupants. Built on the grounds of Rural Studio's Chantilly site, Subrosa was constructed by Carol Mockbee in honor of her late father while she was an Auburn University student.[12] It is a heavy cave-like cenotaph and earthwork, a place to connect with the earth and to whisper secrets. In Mockbee's Subrosa drawings, underneath the abstract rose arbor (which grows wildly above the oculus), there is a pair of loggerhead turtles, together at a circular pond.[13] Unbound and eternal in the drawing, his chelonian sentinels keep watch from below.

The turtle lives in the mud
but is not mud-like,
you can tell it by his eyes
which are clear.
When he shall escape
his present confinement
he will stride about the world
destroying all
with his sharp beak.
Whatever opposes him
in the streets of the city
shall go down.
Cars will be overturned.

—WILLIAM CARLOS WILLIAMS,
excerpt from "The Turtle," 1956[14]

Unicorn

Manuel Orazi

Something of the mystery of man flows in the symbols:
his very existence asks a concrete expression. The great symbols
are for expressing the unity of his world.

GERSHOM SCHOLEM, "The Star of David: History of a Symbol" (1949)

Friedman's birth name was Janos-Antal (John-Anthony). He changed it to Yona when he joined a small Zionist group of resistance during the Nazi occupation of Budapest in 1944. It is the name of a special prophet, Jonah, the only one who dared to disobey God. Nevertheless, the choice of the name Yona was not at odds with his surname. The meaning of Yona in Hebrew is "dove," a universal animal and symbol of peace that goes along well with his surname, which in German/Yiddish means "man of peace." Animals are very much present in the medieval manuscripts of European Jewry. The Haggadah, the Talmud, and the Torah are full of real and imaginary animals taken as symbols, like the Leviathan, the Behemoth, the Ziz, and, at least since the fifteenth century, the unicorn.

Even though it is also present in the Chinese, Vietnamese, and Japanese traditions, the unicorn is more widespread in European cultures, particularly in Jewish culture. The combativeness of the unicorn is typical of Jewish symbolism. In fact, the *Re'em*—"unicorn" in Hebrew—has a single horn that represents right intention opposed to the untamed emotions and wild desires of the wolf or the lion. In several old synagogues of Eastern Europe, there were representations of a wolf (or a lion) that is gored by a unicorn. A reproduction of this scene is still exhibited in the Magyar Nemzeti Galeria in Budapest. It is also possible to find unicorns printed on the title page of significant cabbalistic books published in France and Lithuania.

Penned in 1281 by Isaac ben Solomon abi Sahula, a Jewish scholar living in Spain, the *Meshal ha-Kadmoni* (Fable of the ancients) presents opinions on various subjects as voiced by animals. It was first printed as a modern book by Gershom Soncino in Brescia in 1491, including an anonymous woodcut representing a unicorn and a ram discussing the wickedness of hunters. As a biblical animal, the unicorn was interpreted allegorically in the early Christian church. Thus, some medieval writers likened it to Christ, who raised a horn of salvation for mankind and dwelt in the womb of the Virgin Mary. This is why

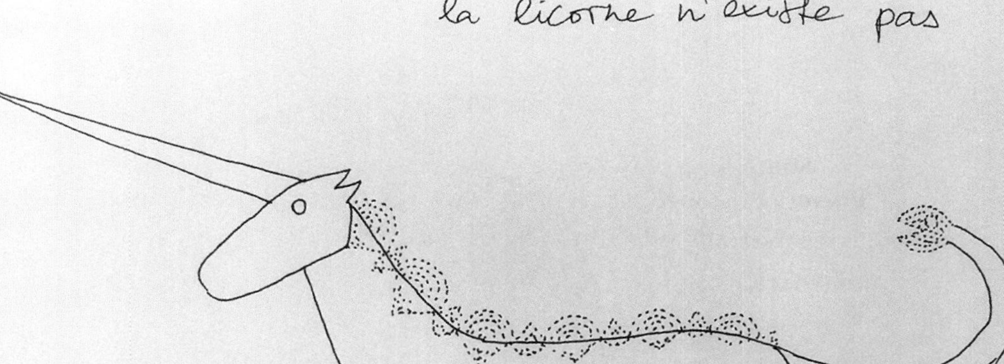

Figure 21.1
Yona Friedman, "The unicorn doesn't exist," 1962,
in Yona Friedman, *Petit bestiaire 1962–81*, Paris ENSBA, 2009.
Courtesy of Fond Denise et Yona Friedman.

we find the unicorn in many works of art, like *The Hunt of the Unicorn*, a French or Flemish millefleur tapestry of the late fifteenth–early sixteenth century, or in Raphael's painting *Young Woman with Unicorn* (1505–1506), in an etching by Albrecht Dürer, *A Woman Abducted by a Man on a Unicorn* (1516), and again in some sketches by Leonardo da Vinci. From the time of Marco Polo's *Milione*, it was a common belief that only a virgin could calm down a unicorn. At the end of the sixteenth century, a unicorn was put in the royal coat of arms of the United Kingdom, symbolizing Scotland as a quadruped rebel so wild that it has to be chained. That's why there are several historical British naval vessels and even submarines called "unicorn." More recently, unicorns entered popular culture through Japanese manga series (*Yuniko* by Osamu Tezuka, 1976–1979), animated fantasy films (*The Last Unicorn*, 1982, directed by Arthur Rankin Jr. and Jules Bass), films about desire and the end of childhood (*Unicorn Store*, 2017, directed by Brie Larson), and even finance: in the last decade privately held start-up companies valued at over US$1 billion are called unicorns because of the statistical rarity of such successful ventures.

The unicorn first appeared in a series of simple drawings by Friedman under the title *Petit bestiaire* (Small bestiary) in 1962, which was published again afterward.[1] Its naïve style might make it seem like a book for children, but actually there is a certain irony in the way the animals are presented. For example, a depiction of the lion says, "the lion is vegetarian by brokerage," as it clearly has a smaller animal inside its stomach. If the peacock "invented the wheel" and the elephant is "specialized in defense," the last animal is the unicorn, "the one that doesn't exist." The inexistence of the unicorn thus indirectly symbolizes utopia, a term that Friedman detested.[2] But, as he explained frequently, every utopia starts from a sense of dissatisfaction and consequently from something that is missing.

After his participation at Documenta 11 in 2002, and in several Venice Biennales, Friedman started an intense collaboration with the contemporary art world. In 2009, the Centre International d'Art et du Paysage on Lac de Vassivière, not far from Limoges, asked him to realize an art installation. He chose to draw a giant *Unicorn Eiffel*, a flat sculpture that occupies the entire field in front of the museum, drawn on the ground and visible in its totality only from a drone or from Aldo Rossi's lighthouse building, which dominates the island.

Finally, in 2017, Friedman published a book for children, *A Trip to Unicornia*, "a beautiful world of harmony and peace where everyone would love to live"; in a nutshell, a utopia.[3] Unicorns are therefore symbols of what architecture is still missing: not high tech or neofuturist devices as in the high-tech megastructures of the 1960s but, once again, mobile architecture or, in one word, improvisation that is a poor technique, purely low-tech: "We are not accustomed to the idea. There is a mind-set problem. Improvisation is a key adaptive strategy, however. All animals use it, and we do too, though we don't realize it, through mimicry and hand movements for instance—all unplanned gestures."[4]

In the long life and career of Yona Friedman, animals have played a major role as symbols embedded in all his extremely varied life experiences—such as the dog.[5] Symbols are tools for expressing ideas. It is not a coincidence that unicorns were described poetically by great authors of the last century such as Rainer Maria Rilke in *The Sonnets to Orpheus* (1923) or Jorge Luis Borges in *The Book of Imaginary Beings* (1957–1969).

When I was writing my PhD thesis on Friedman's work, I went regularly to visit him in his unique apartment in Boulevard Garibaldi in Paris, where he moved in 1968 with his second wife, Denise Charvein. During those memorable encounters in his Merzbau-like apartment, with the dog Balkis walking around from room to room, Yona gave me the drafts of *L'ordre compliqué* (The complicated order), the last of his collections of theoretical essays.[6] He wanted to give it an alternative title, "How to Build an Image," because he was returning to his youthful interest in physics and mythology, the disciplines of Werner Heisenberg and Károly Kérenyi, two extradisciplinary masters who helped him outline an image of the world if not scientifically at least aesthetically. On the title page of the book, there's a unicorn: "The unicorn, pure and virginal, doesn't know grammar. His thoughts are difficult to define, but it is really he who embodies spontaneous and perfect order." Inside the drawing, the author added the following text: "The order of the Unicorn resembles a disorder / it's the complicated order." Thus the disorder is an order that we can't see yet.

The first lesson that Friedman received as a student in Budapest was when attending a public lecture by Heisenberg about Goethe: poets can be truer than scientists. The second lesson was given to him by Kérenyi in a public course in 1944: mythology can be truer than science:

> I got more and more into the idea that mythology is essentially a protoscience, because it gives a complete description of the world. This was Kerényi's influence, although he was presenting it as an image of the Greek world. At the same time, I realized that official science is somewhat questionable. Heisenberg was talking about Goethe's *Farbenlehre* [theory of colors]: it's not scientific and it doesn't fit with science, but at the same time it fits. For me it was quite important to realize that you can build up a system. I am calling it *the image of the world*.[7]

A system is something that you cannot see but that surely lives and operates autonomously, or at least something in which you could believe, just like a unicorn. In this sense, it is also a symbol of the search for truth. Moreover, using symbols to express difficult ideas enhanced the communication of Friedman's ideas in opposition to the majority of academic architects. As Bernard Tschumi first remarked: "He's not a dreamer, but often a poet who says very simple and clear things while everybody else tries to make them very complicated and obscure."[8] This is why Yona Friedman loved repeating the following phrase: "the unicorns are always real friends of mine" while caressing his faithful Balkis.

Vulture

Kostas Tsiambaos

Animals are everywhere in Pikionis's Acropolis Works (1954–1957), both on the built constructions and in the dozens of pencil sketches and drawings that he did. Horses, snakes, vultures, fish, owls, doves, deer, lions, and other animals were used by Pikionis as multivalent symbols referring to a cultural tradition that transcends space and time by being both ancient and modern, indigenous and global. A comparison of the drawings for the northern pediment of the temple of St. Demetrius—the middle-Byzantine-era temple standing at the foot of Philopappos hill that Pikionis reconstructed and extended—shows that the only ornamental elements that remained true to the architect's original drawings are two spolia-like marble plates, one at the center of the tympanum and one at its right corner. The central plate, measuring approximately 80 × 80 cm, depicts a vulture in front view standing with its wings outspread, and a deer in side view galloping at the front; the second plate, a triangle with its perpendicular sides measuring approximately 25 × 100 cm, depicts a snake in side view slithering toward the left with its head standing straight.

The vulture and similar birds had always been represented as a symbol of strength, pride, and freedom, from the sacred Egyptian vulture and the Roman *aquila* to the Mayan king vulture and the bald eagle, symbol of the United States of America (sculptures of eagles are found on the pediments of the east central entrance to the US Capitol and of the east entrance to the Senate wing).[1] In the case of the temple of St. Demetrius, the vulture at the center of the tympanum is not something that refers to any specific architectural tradition, Byzantine or other. However, in the mind of Pikionis, the eagle could find a central place among other spolia on the walls of the temple since it was both a mythical personification of sky god Zeus and heraldic symbol of the Byzantine Empire. It was this double reference, to both ancient Greek mythology and Byzantine art and culture, that made the vulture such a seminal figure: the fact that it endured for millennia as a meaningful form in different geographies, environments, and contexts. What the figure of the vulture does, like the deer, the snake, and other symbolic figures—animalistic or not—is that it becomes a character of a pictorial writing that transfers a lost, transhistorical language. Those animal figures represented in the form of carvings or bas-reliefs perform as "hieroglyphics" of a forgotten story that could transfer the viewer back to a lost world. Pikionis used to say that he wanted through his work to be

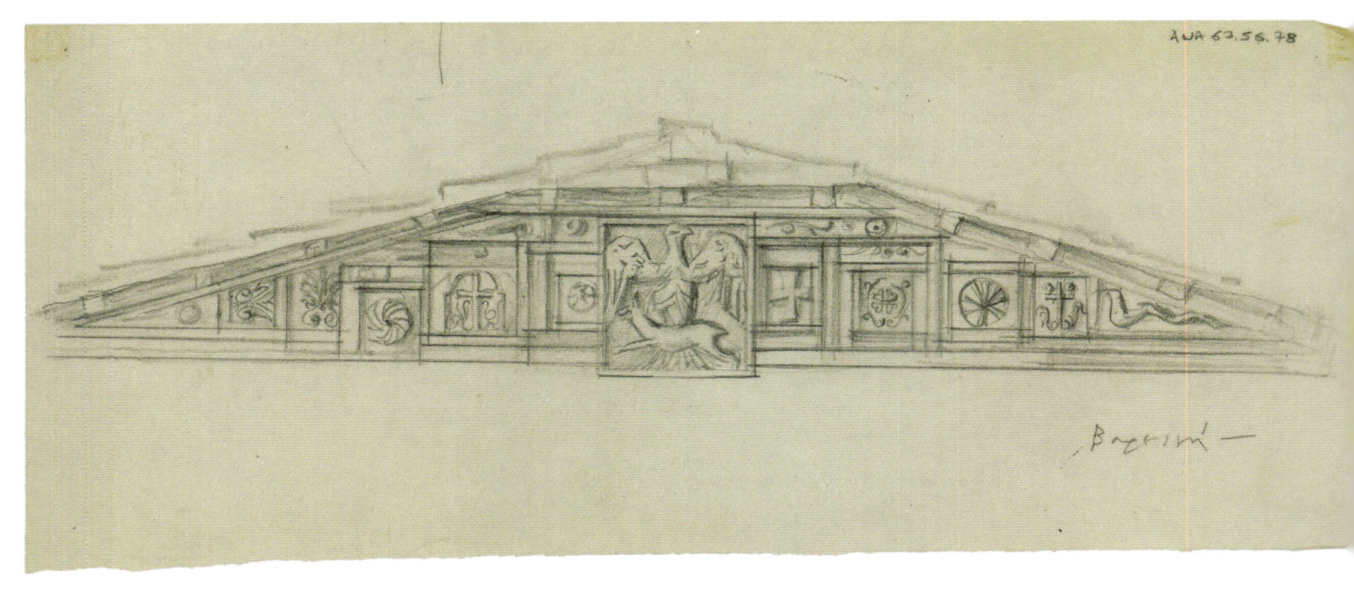

Figure 22.1
Dimitris Pikionis, Acropolis Works, temple of St. Demetrius, drawing of the northern pediment (1954–1957). © Modern Greek Architecture Archives, Benaki Museum.

able to immerse himself in this "indivisible tradition of the world" and "swim across it like a trout."[2] By this he meant that he wanted to be able to return to a primitive origin (*arché*), the primordial cultural cradle which designates a starting point, namely a reversal of time, and at the same time a movement toward an almost prehistoric matrix, the return to an ancient maternal *chora*.[3]

Aesthetically speaking, animals were important for Pikionis for their pure visual and physical attributes. And, like the vulture that devours dead things, Pikionis "devoured" ancient animal symbols as an act of aesthetic relating. In Pikionis's words: "A secret mystery ties this hour and its Light with the golden skin of the wild beast, with the spirals of the horns and the fleece of those sheep that pass by, having the yellowish color of the aged marble or being black like the shadow of the dark rock."[4] The architect should be able to "see" the harmony that is everywhere in nature, to feel, in an empathetic way, the "law" according to which all things natural are composed, and convey this law through silent, inanimate architectural forms. In this creative process, the ways animals are aesthetically articulated as geometric forms and material appearances, always in harmony with nature, is the biggest lesson on how architectural constructions of high standards should be similarly composed within their natural environment. Lively and earthy, daring and wise, powerful and ethereal, wild and serene; this is how a noble architectural work should look, almost like an animal in its natural environment.

Yet what makes this reference to the vulture significant, beyond its symbolic content and formal configuration, is the fact that it refers to the origins of architecture itself. By putting the marble plate with the vulture at the very center of the pediment, Pikionis reminds us that the Greek word for "pediment," which is *aétōma*, originates etymologically from the Greek word for eagle (*aetós*). The logic behind this metaphor is that the form of the gable resembles the form of the eagle with its wings spread at the moment it either lands or takes off. And it is not by coincidence that the few studies of vultures that Pikionis did were part of a series of sketches and drawings titled "elements of pediments" (*stoicheía aetomáton*). What animal could more fittingly be placed at an *aétōma* than an *aetós*? All this may sound too formalistic, but, certainly, it is not a kind of hermeneutic formality that Pikionis was after. On the contrary, the architect insisted on studying the vulture as an appropriate form but also as an appropriate "word," a word that had transferred its meaning to one of the constitutional elements of architecture, as the gable is.

Eventually, it is this early architectural reference to animation that is lost in the various succeeding architectural terms of Latin origin (fastigium, gable, fronton, tympanum, etc.) which, having "forgotten" the winged analogy, rationally describe the pediment as the apex of a building, something that stands at the top or at the front, a fixed and stable construction, abstractly geometrical and tectonic. Why was the Greek reference to the freedom of flight abandoned? What happened to the vital motion and brute force that the etymology of the word *aetós* refers to? How did the gable, from a winged construction ready to soar into the air, end up being a "tamed" triangular roof covering a space?

In 1888, parts of the sculptures of the pediments of the archaic temple called Hekatompedon (570–550 BCE) were found buried on the Acropolis, southeast of the Parthenon. In contrast to the classical sculptures of the Parthenon's pediments that represent human-like figures (gods, demigods, and even mortal Athenians), the sculptures on the pediments of Hekatompedon display wild animals and other animal-like figures fighting each other: two lions attacking a bull, a snake-bodied Demon, a lioness devouring a calf, gigantic snakes, a Triton, a panther, an owl. It is no secret that Pikionis reinterpreted, if not just copied, these archaic sculptures in order to use them as sculpted symbols in his Acropolis Works. It was not the rhythmical beauty and balanced anthropocentrism of the Periclean Parthenon (447–438 BCE), standing across from the temple of St. Demetrius, but the dramatic animalism, the awe toward the greatness and power of the natural, wild, and irrational elements that attracted Pikionis. His quest was for a "rewilding" of architecture, the reconceptualization of architectural construction and form as rough and raw, vibrant and multifaceted, volatile and audacious.

For Pikionis, this animated tension was lacking both from the disciplined classicism of the fifth century BCE and the rational modernism of the twentieth century. The vulture on the pediment condenses Pikionis's drive to "fly" away in order to find again this forgotten, furious, and fertile architectural world.

Wild Boar

Deborah Ascher Barnstone

Hermann Finsterlin's 1922 aquarelle *Boar Hunt* is a dreamlike splash of sinuous, brightly colored lines and images dancing across the page. As in many of his watercolors, his title alludes to a subject that is barely recognizable in the painting. In this case, three splotches of black represent the boar, while the swirling colors and combinations of realistic human faces and abstract forms juxtaposed in a surrealistic manner suggest the dynamic energy of a hunt. The boar was one of numerous animals, real and mythical, that were subjects of Finsterlin's art alongside his idiosyncratic, but equally dreamlike, visionary architecture; the techniques he used to portray the hunt parallel those in his architectural imaginary.

Finsterlin was an unusual figure in the 1920s German avant-garde. Although he hailed from a family replete with artists, including a grandfather who was chief court painter and intimate of King Ludwig I of Bavaria, Finsterlin did not set out to be an artist or architect. Instead, he claimed to have studied a spate of other subjects at university including chemistry, physics, natural sciences, medicine, mythology, philosophy, and Indology, although it is impossible to confirm whether this is a true account or a mythological biography made from partial truths.[1] When he did decide to attend art school, he struggled to pass his subjects because his work did not conform to contemporary expectations.[2] Finsterlin retreated from Munich to the family estate in Berchtesgaden after disillusionment with art school set in. There, while climbing Watzmann mountain, the majestic landscape supposedly inspired a "cosmic" artistic epiphany after which he began to write mystical poetry.[3] If many biographical details are unclear or fabricated, Finsterlin's aesthetic interests are indisputable. He was fascinated with myth, distorted reality, unconventional form, and the surreal.

Finsterlin's university studies of mythology informed a continued interest in such subjects in his art: his paintings depict characters or stories from a wide range of literary traditions, including Pandora, Phrixus and Helle, Orpheus, and the god Hermes from Greek mythology; Saint George and the Dragon from Christian lore; and Snow White from German folktales. The topics that Finsterlin worked with demonstrate his deep understanding of many allegorical traditions, while the images he made evince serious efforts to develop a visual language that could effectively represent both the substance and essence of these tales.

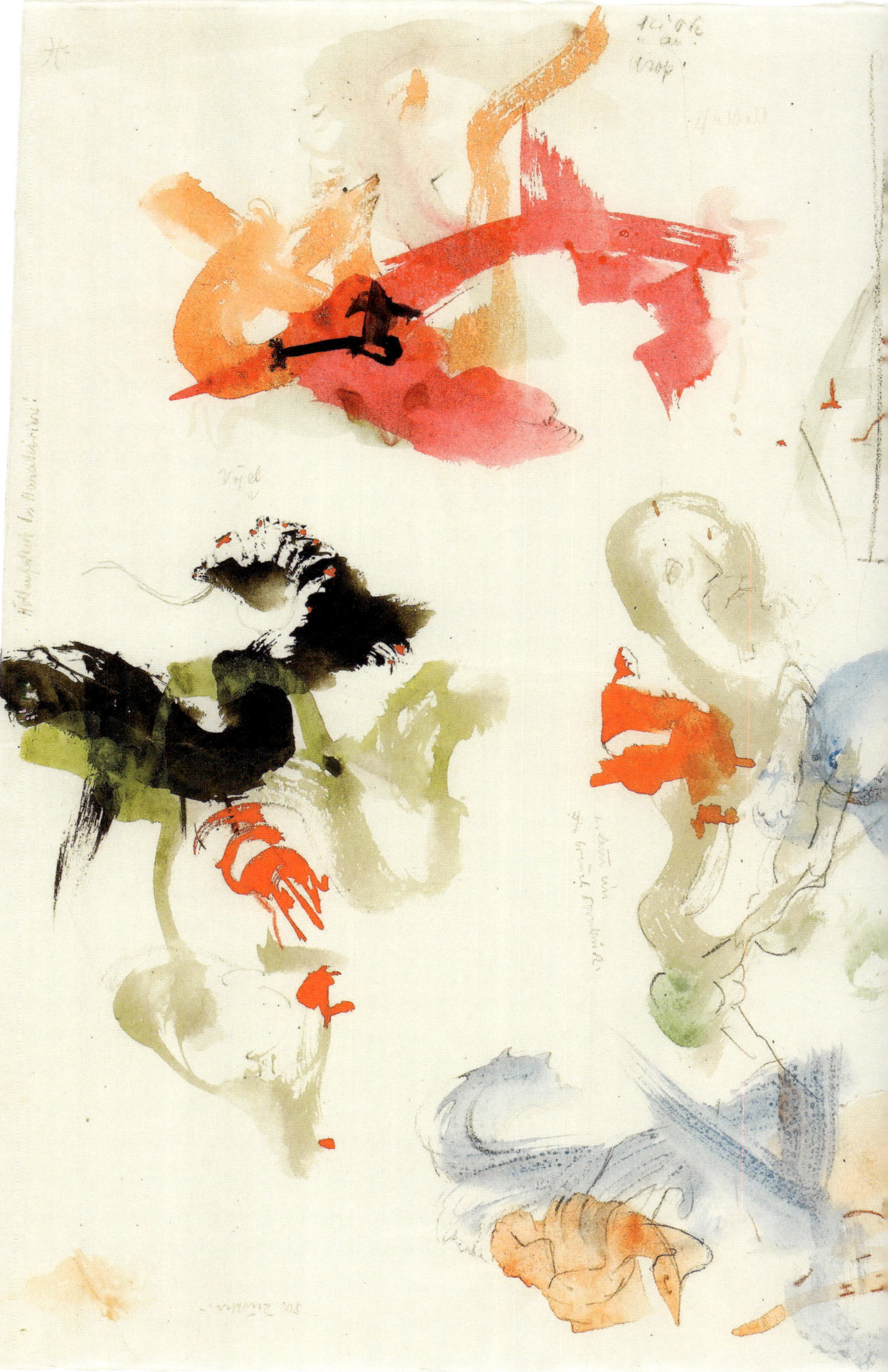

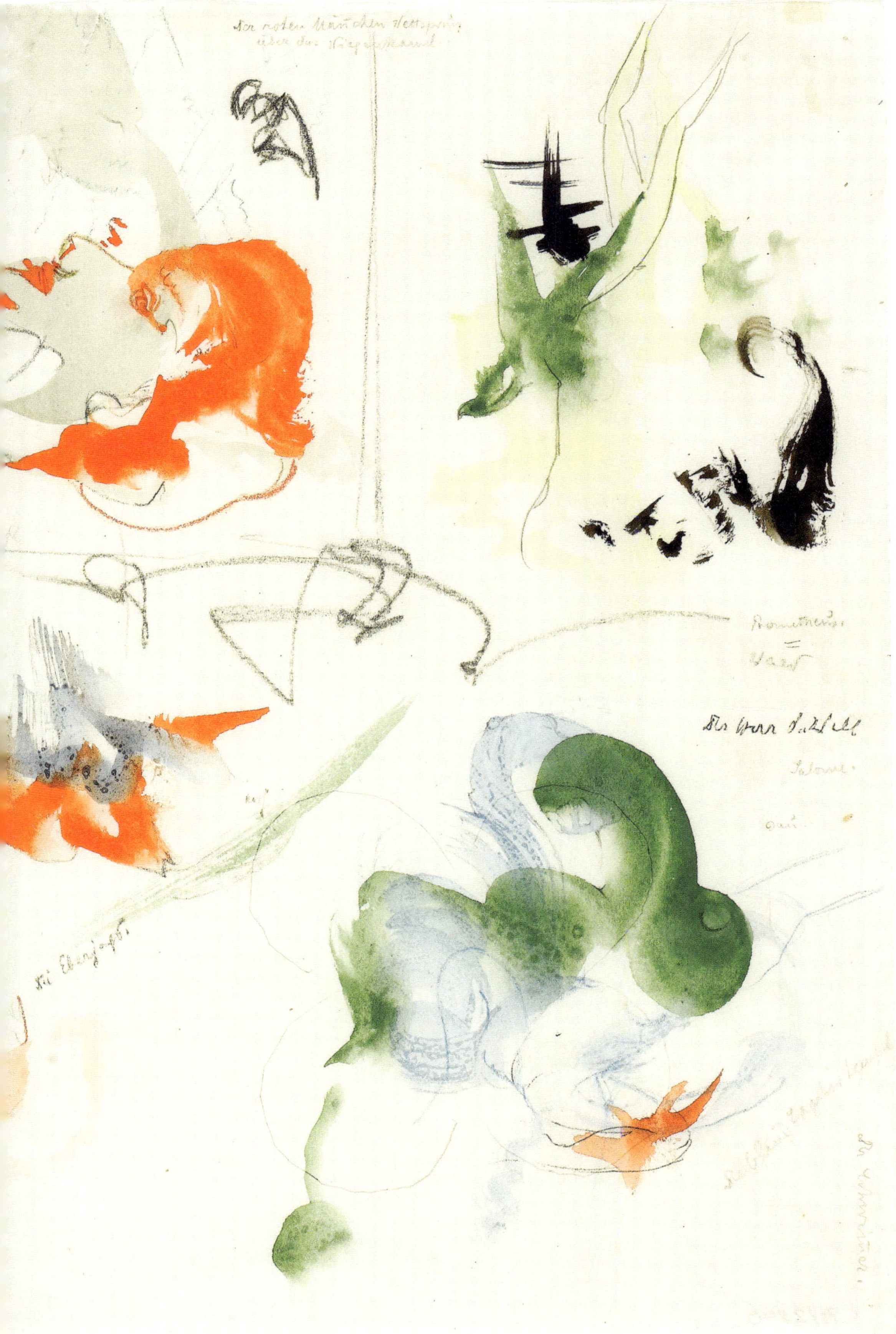

Boar hunts were an allegorical subject of traditional painting dating back as far as the Babylonian and Assyrian civilizations.[4] They typically feature a group of hunters armed with spears with their pack of dogs surrounding the wounded boar. In Christian iconography, the boar hunt symbolized the human struggle with evil and with Satan; in secular iconography, the boar hunt represented the constant human engagement with natural threats. The boar was considered a particularly ferocious animal, with insatiable appetites. It stood for "great sexual prowess" as well as "bravery and strength."[5] While not a part of the original *Physiologus*, the wild boar was a common entry by the late twelfth century, and the beast figured in many widely read medieval texts such as Chaucer's *Canterbury Tales*, Gottfried von Straßburg's *Tristan und Isolde*, and Thüring von Ringoltinen's *Melusine*. The boar in *Melusine* is even associated with the supernatural, which would have appealed to Finsterlin's interests. The hunt itself was an important aristocratic pastime by the twelfth century and a sign of social status—Finsterlin was raised in a family that would have hunted, possibly even wild boar.

The *Boar Hunt* embodies many of the aesthetic principles that Finsterlin pursued in his artistic and architectural fantasies: flowing shapes reminiscent of natural forms, situated between abstraction and reality, and saturated in color.[6] The watercolors pushed the boundaries of conventional painting at the time by combining abstraction with representation, using a traditional subject in an unusual composition, dispensing with perspectival space, and employing color without regard to nature. Many critics refer to the work as "surreal" because of its unexpected juxtapositions and contradictory conditions of real and unreal. Finsterlin wrote that his work attempted to encompass "line and color" rather than form—another departure from painting conventions. He called his paintings "event pictures" and "objectless line and color inspirations," descriptions that accurately convey the essence of his work.[7] Indeed, *Boar Hunt* is an event on more than one level: it portrays an event, the hunt, while the painterly style, with its swirling motion, is a visual event.

Although a prolific painter all his life, Finsterlin is best known for his utopian architecture. His first experiments in imaginary form date to the period just after the First World War when he responded to Walter Gropius's call for revolutionary designs for the 1919 *Ausstellung der unbekannte Architekten* (exhibition of unknown architects) at the J. B. Neumann Graphic Cabinet in Berlin.[8] The exhibition was sponsored by the newly formed avant-garde group the Arbeitsrat für Kunst (Working Council for Art), modeled on the revolutionary workers' and soldiers' councils established in Russia after the political events of 1917. The group called for a complete renewal of art and arts institutions in Germany; their hope was to begin this effort by showing futuristic architecture to the German public.

Figure 23.1 (previous pages)
Hermann Finsterlin, *Die Eberjagd* (The Boar Hunt), 1922. © bpk-Bildagentur.

The architecture that Finsterlin showed in the exhibition was unlike anything seen before. The buildings had strange biomorphic forms, often several stacked atop one another or collaged together in hybrid compositions.[9] These were sometimes reminiscent of familiar plants or animals, like *Konzerthaus 1919* with its sea-urchin-like bulbous red forms on the top; others had plant-like appendages similar to mushrooms or fungi or shapes that vaguely recall rock outcroppings. When included, the usual markers of buildings, like stairs, doors, and windows, are oddly shaped to conform to the overall building contours. Signs of building structure like columns and beams are nonexistent. Any relationship to gravity and gravitational force is also absent. Finsterlin's use of color in this first series is another departure from architectural norms; structures are green, yellow, blue, or any other color without relationship to usual building materials and their physical properties. All these aesthetic strategies contribute to the dreamlike impression the buildings leave with any viewer.

In the four years or so following the exhibition Finsterlin continued to paint architectural fantasies. These often used saturated colors, rather than the muted colors of the 1919 work, articulated line, and more aggressive forms. Bright yellow, green, blue, red, and pink are typical of Finsterlin's palette at the time. The watercolors are composed with contour lines, often in bright colors, in keeping with his ambition to create using "line and color." In addition, the building forms are increasingly fluid, flowing shapes akin to his abstract paintings or semiabstract compositions like *Boar Hunt*. Finsterlin intentionally rejected the hard geometries typical of most buildings in favor of forms that might derive from the natural world: mountains, molehills, dunes, rock formations, plants, and clouds as well as microscopic organisms like the amoeba, clearly influenced by what he had learned in his university studies. Finsterlin wrote: "Form is only a relatively surprising, uninterrupted, enclosing moving system of forces that develops relatively closely in four-dimensional space: its material, peculiar manifestation is the result of self-tempo and variety and the respective combat games with the objects of space, with light pressure and all the waves of the finest spirits; a gradient of alternate motions, forward and backward, surrounding or penetrating densities."[10] Finsterlin's form-making and image-making privileged what he called the "organic" and "spiritual."[11]

By 1924, any vestige of real building disappeared from his work, so that the images are pure fantasy—strange, dreamlike and animated figures similar to the inscrutable scribbles in *Boar Hunt*. Finsterlin signals the truth about his visions when he begins to label them "Cloud Cuckoo Land," a synonym for "absurdly over-optimistic fantasy." As such, the designs are expressions of his desire for an alternate reality.

The 1919 "unknown architects" exhibition brought Finsterlin's work its first public attention and critical acclaim, as well as ridicule. Importantly for Finsterlin, it connected the reclusive artist to a likeminded group. The architect Bruno Taut, who also participated in the exhibition, soon organized the Gläserne Kette (Crystal Chain) correspondence, which provided another outlet for Finsterlin's creativity and an audience of sympathetic artists who were struggling with similar challenges. Finsterlin's pseudonym was Prometheus, the mythical Greek god who gave man fire and hope, tools humans needed to navigate the forces of nature. By assuming this name, Finsterlin suggests his own role as artist, one who mediates between myth and reality, nature and humankind. But also, one who gives people something they need—in this case, a new architecture that had not yet been conceived or understood but that will change humankind's being in the world. Sadly, the Crystal Chain dissolved by 1921.

Over time, Finsterlin has metamorphosed into a mythological figure—not Prometheus but certainly a figure of mystery, since neither the man nor his art, conform to any accepted norms. The famous German art historian Hans Hildebrandt remains the first and only scholar to attempt to situate Finsterlin's oeuvre in the canon of art history in his 1924 book *Art of the 19th and 20th Centuries*; more recent retrospectives present the artist as an enigma and anomaly.[12] Although Finsterlin continued to enjoy notoriety and success throughout the 1920s and 1930s, with exhibitions around Germany and in the Netherlands, he never managed to realize any of the building proposals. They remained with the wild boar in the dream-world realm of the fantastic.

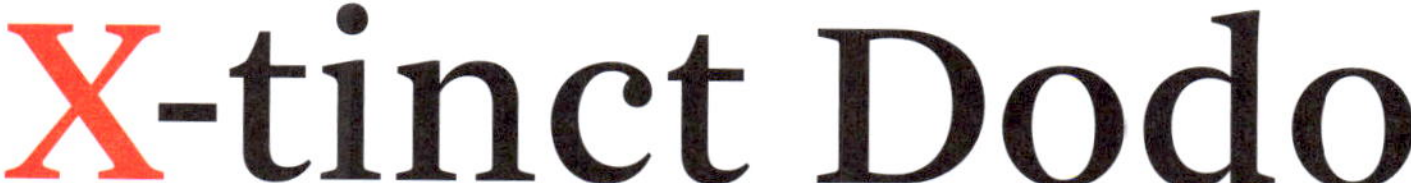

X-tinct Dodo

Nicholas Olsberg

Death is a law of Nature in the Species as well as in the Individual; but this internal tendency to extinction is in both cases liable to be anticipated by violent or accidental causes. Numerous external agents have affected the distribution of organic life at various periods, and one of these has operated exclusively during the existing epoch, viz. the agency of Man.

H. E. STRICKLAND AND J. G. MELVILLE, *The Dodo and Its Kindred; Or the History, Affinities, and Osteology of the Dodo, Solitaire and Other Extinct Birds of the Islands Mauritius, Rodrigues, and Bourbon* (London: Reeve, Benham, and Reeve, 1848), iii

The proposal in 1859 to move the collections of natural history from their crowded basement in the British Museum to a separate facility came from their superintendent, the paleozoologist Richard Owen, seeking what was described as a library for the growth of knowledge of the natural world through the examination of specimens. By 1863, a competition was announced for designs for a museum on the site of the Royal Engineer Francis Fowke's halls for the International Exhibition of 1862, which, lying just below Kensington Gardens, were almost universally decried as the ugliest sheds in London. The competition was won by Fowke himself, for a more or less Renaissance design following Owen's recommended *parti* of a central hall flanked by two wings—one for the living world and the other for the dead—with the central hall serving like the catalogue room of a library as a taxonomical "index hall," in which the entire collection was first introduced through acknowledgment of the human agency by which nature was classified, named, and managed. Fowke died suddenly late in 1865, and the commission passed the following year to the young Manchester architect Alfred Waterhouse, who, having just completed the extraordinary Venetian Gothic Assize Courts there, had moved his practice to London. With the museum, and the rows of mansion block that followed, South Kensington began to complete the conversion of "a dreary cabbage garden in a deserted suburb"[1] into Albertopolis, the great west London complex of art, music, learning, and science conceived by the Prince Consort and to some extent built in his memory.

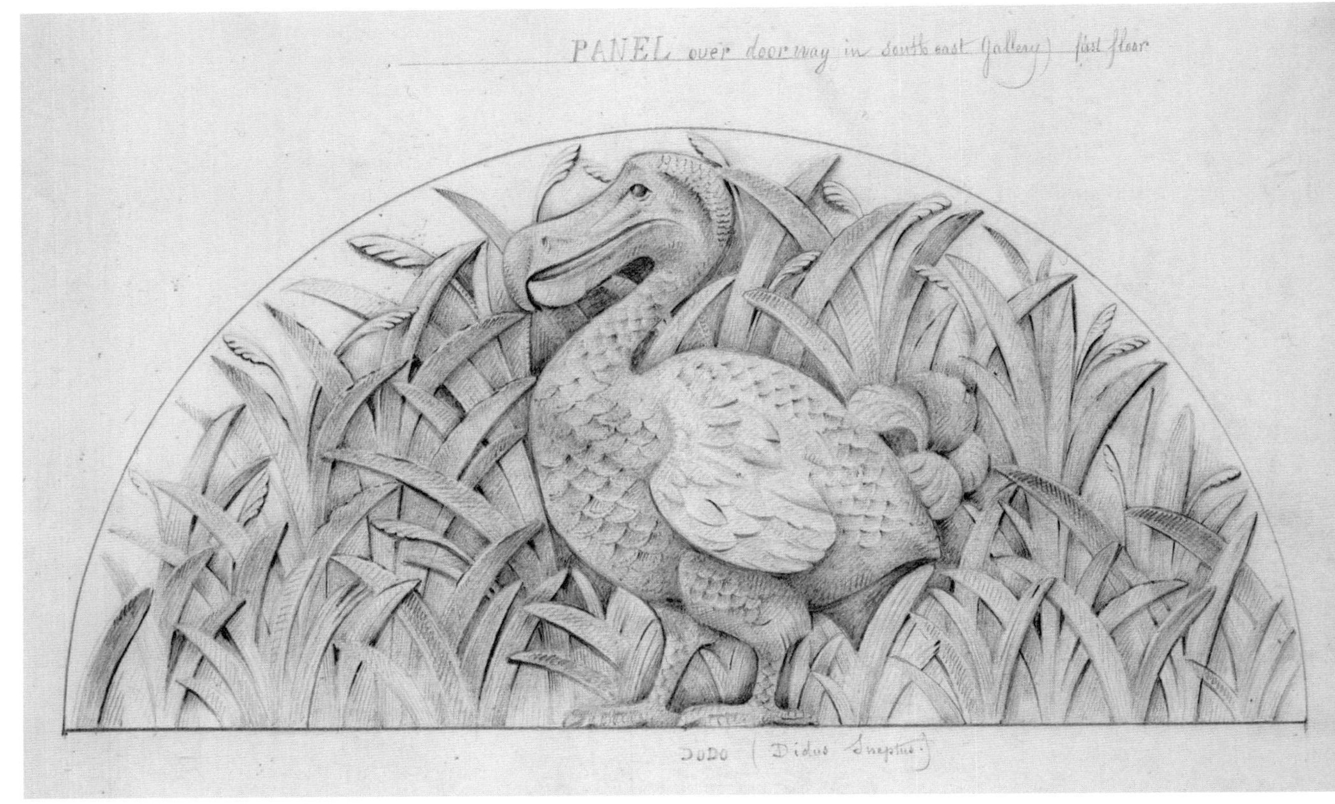

Figure 24.1
Design for a dodo decorative panel for use over a doorway in the southeastern first-floor gallery, Natural History Museum, London, 1878. © Natural History Museum, London/Bridgeman Images.

Waterhouse agreed to work within Fowke's general plan, though he slowly adapted it into coherence, and he embraced enthusiastically one of the demands of the scheme, which was to celebrate the infinite variety of nature by decorating the structure with a riot of gargoyles, finials, and reliefs from the animal world. In separating prehistoric from living forms, Owen displayed his discomfort with the fundamental principles of evolution and adaptation, implicitly denying the progression from the lost world of the fossil to the tissue of the epoch of mankind, reserving a separate almost anti-taxonomical place for the human form, and encouraging Waterhouse to place above the entrance to the index hall the quite distinct figure of Adam opening his arms to the wonders of a lowly creation of which he was not perhaps a part. As London's skies grew murkier and its fabric dirtier, architects turned increasingly to the washable durable and vivid surface of terracotta, especially for the ornamental features of work in brick (as Charles Barry had done at Dulwich College and Fowke himself at the Royal Albert Hall), and Waterhouse now turned to terracotta brick and tile not only for the incidental decoration but for the entire surface of his great museum.

Waterhouse's travel drawings of the 1860s—they are full-fledged studies rather than sketches—show a fascination with the relative imprecision of Romanesque ornament and decoration. By uniting these two ideas—a material (clay) that was quick and efficient to mold, and a historical vocabulary of depiction and form in which simplification rather than elaboration ruled—he could produce a rich and flamboyant *architecture parlante*. A viable fundamental design completed, the building works could begin. The museum did not open until Easter 1881, but by January 1876 work was sufficiently advanced for Waterhouse to welcome a tour of the Architectural Association, showing them examples of ornamentation "entirely based on the extinct and living species of birds, beasts, fishes, reptiles, and insects of which examples will be found in the museum."[2] This terracotta work was entrusted to Charles Dujardin, a French sculptor working with the architectural sculpture firm of Farmer & Brindley, with whom Waterhouse had been engaged on the Manchester Town Hall. The terracotta forms were made by a pipe manufacturer in Staffordshire. Blocks and repeated, mostly geometric, figures were cast from molds and fired in multiples. But Dujardin's singular figurative elements—with which Waterhouse was "singularly happy"—were modeled directly in the terracotta clay after the architect's drawings and simply sent up to be fired.

Surviving drawings for this great bestiary begin to appear at the start of construction and continue for a full four years: first for the predatory mammals, live and extinct, that guard the parapets of the main facade, then for the monkeys that climb the volutes of the arches in the index hall and the woodland creatures that peer from the spandrels above; then for medallions of paired cormorants, herons, and the other long-necked birds so central to the aesthetic of the era; and seemingly last, toward the end of 1878, for a demilune above the double doors of one of the middle galleries within the eastern wing of extinguished life, the almost farcical figure of a bird from Mauritius that had disappeared little more than 200 years before, but whose habits, colors, tissue, and very shape remained uncertain: the dodo.

"Big Birds," in *The Cornhill Magazine* for Christmas 1890, recounts the disappearance of the largest avians and tells the tale that "every schoolboy knows": that these great birds were simply pigeons who, having the great wooded isle of Mauritius to themselves, "found the field so entirely their own that they increased and multiplied and replenished the earth till they overran the whole place with their numerous descendants. But having no need to fly, and no enemies to fear, they waxed fat and kicked, and grew careless in the process. Their wings atrophied from disuse, and they waddled about awkwardly on the ground . . . till they developed into pigeons of truly obese and aldermanic proportions." But "one fine morning a cannon boomed," and men arrived, who simply knocked them over to cook them, while their cats and dogs and pigs ate their eggs and young. So rapid was their extinction that "hardly a skeleton of the dodo now remains in any of our museums to give systematic naturalists a passing clue to the nature and affinities of the extinct pigeon."[3]

The defining image of the dodo in the nineteenth century was that of the naturalist George Edwards's "The Dodo." Edwards prepared his plate, which showed the dodo beside a guinea pig for scale, in 1757, rendered slightly more scientific, less bulky and more erect, more feathery, and in a more feasible posture than in an image captured by Roelandt Savery in a large oil painting of about 1626, then in Edwards's own collection, where a dark and scaly dodo with golden wing tips and an almost heraldic version of an ostrich tail occupies the center ground of a tropical scene.[4] Savery's painting was believed to have been made from observations of a plump and overfed living specimen in a menagerie in Holland. Edwards deposited the oil in the British Museum two years later, and it eventually moved with the Natural History collection to Waterhouse's museum, where it hung for fifty years in the Bird Gallery.

Fragments of dodo bone and tissue existed, most famously in the head held by Oxford University's Museum of Natural History, and Owen had, in fact, recently and very famously exploited the discovery of a full skeleton, from which he constructed a new image of the dodo—more erect, more feasible, and leaner than Waterhouse and Dujardin would have it. But the squatter image of the bird, though faulty, could not be erased, so deeply ingrained was the imagined dodo in everyday culture: as a memento mori; as a cautionary tale of gluttony and ease in which mental acuity, unneeded for defense or sustenance, dissipates as surely as the power to take wing; and finally, as an affectionate simile for anyone stupid or hopelessly out of date. Dodo was already, as it remains, both real and myth, creature and metaphor, a bird equally of legend and of science, and, like the phoenix and the roc, the improbable contours of the mythic version could not be erased by science.

Waterhouse's drawing is closest to the bulky morphology and posture seen by Savery, and it is in some ways a portrait of what could not have been, balancing the bird in an unfeasible stance with his weight leaning backward on the single short rear toe. Indeed, such fancy and naivete in the museum's terracotta menagerie was soon found wearing. One critic in the opening year could revel in a hall where "in the archivolts the squirrel, the lizard, and the newt twine themselves through the reticulations of the floral enrichments; monkeys 'squeak and jibber' at the spectator from the recesses of the floral friezes; birds alight on the apex of each smaller gable, . . . sing on every spray, and hide in the bosky umbrage of the capitals."[5] But it took only five more years for another writer to realize that the animals were not only childish in their representation but illogically portrayed in action, as if in "mockery of the very zoological science with which the specimens have been gathered and classified." It is stuff fit for children's stories rather than a library of solemn knowledge.[6]

Savery and Edwards gave their dodo a lucid human eye that Waterhouse captures in the drawing. It is that hint of the anthropomorphic that must have caught John Tenniel's and Lewis Carroll's eye when they based Alice's enormous dodo of 1865 (a characterization of the author himself, so Carroll said) on the Edwards print, and then slipped human hands and a walking stick under its wings. That human cast persists, but as if every type of human could inhabit the dodo's form. Blanche McManus's illustrations in 1899 show the dodo as an old lady in a bonnet, Peter Newell's in 1901 show one redundant wing evolving a human finger at its tip, and Arthur Rackham's in 1907 presents a forbidding figure looming whose claws have become wizened human hands. Disney's first dodo in 1951 unaccountably inhabits the dress and persona of a jaunty seafarer with a pipe, but Norman McLeod's magically real *Alice in Wonderland* of 1933 places the human back into the dodo's supposed real condition, finding a woman's voice in a body mask of feathers and beak as faithful to the Savery painting as the stuffed replicas of natural history museums throughout the world. And from the defunct dodo's mouth comes the tedious history that Carroll had the mouse recite, on the conquest of England by the Normans, so that the extinction of a particular human culture on one island by human agency is remembered by a creature so rapidly conquered and extinguished by the same terrible human force upon another.[7]

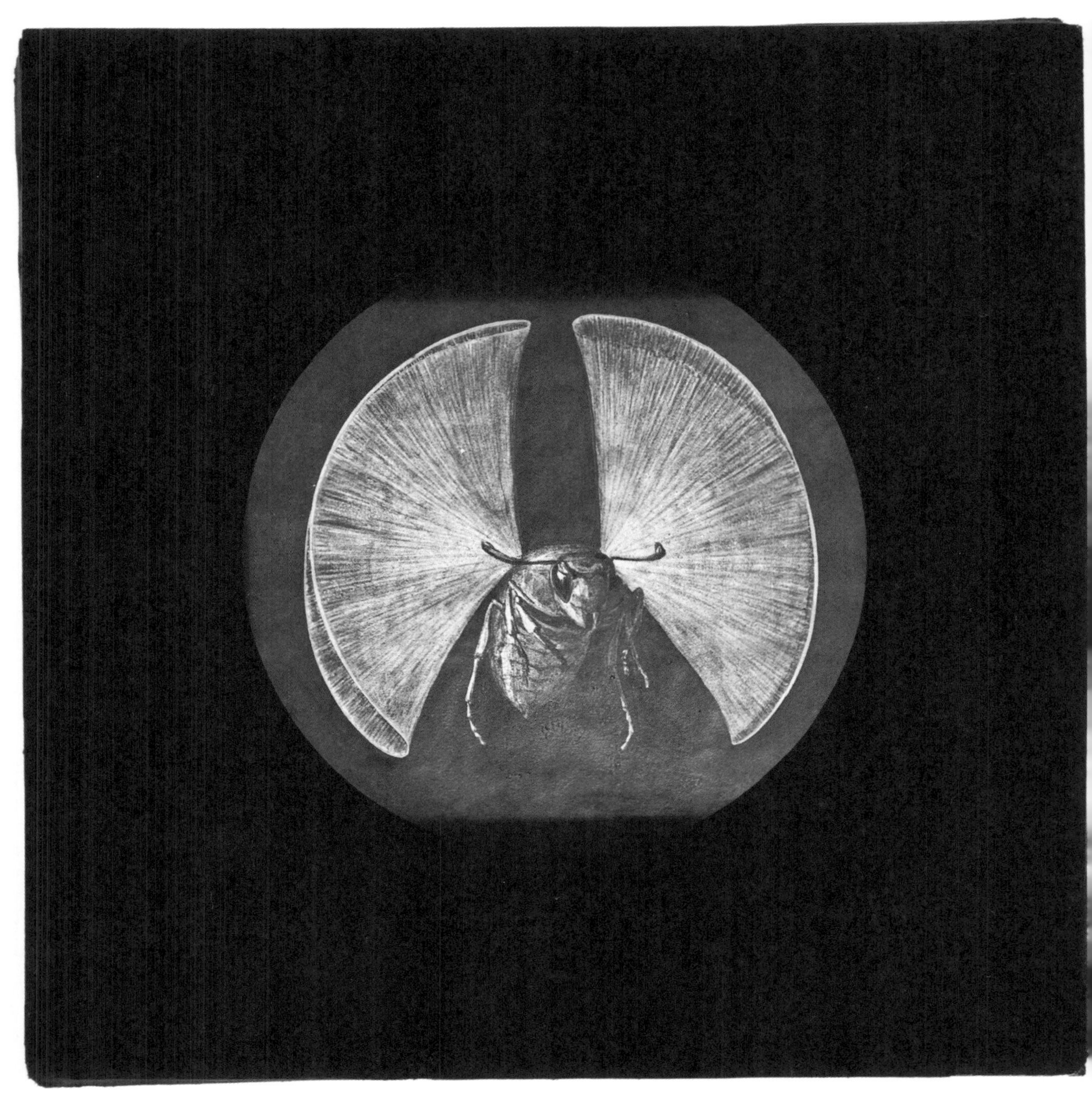

Figure 25.1
Étienne-Jules Marey, "Aspect d'une guêpe volant," n.d. Gelatin-silver bromide on glass, 8.5 × 8.5 cm (support). In *Locomotion animale III C*. Fonds Marey, Archives, Collège de France. © Collège de France.

Yellowjacket

Enrique Ramirez

Listen! There's that sound again, a menacing, middle-pitched thrum. It comes in at about 125 Hz or so, supposedly the same frequency as a male baritone's singing. But there are no voices, only a discordant, furious *arco* tuned to the key of B flat. It comes from a phalanx of violins, violas, cellos, and an occasional double bass, all tucked in a small orchestra pit glowing with limelight. It is November 26, 1909. Here, inside the New Theatre, on St. Andrews Street, Cambridge, the audience prepares for tonight's entertainment: a Greek-language production of Aristophanes' *The Wasps*. The lights dim and a warm, incandescent glow descends upon the horseshoe-shaped auditorium. The overture swells, ensnaring an audience now deeply engrossed as the music changes in tone and color. The relentless, plodding *archi* from before give way to a strident theme. Brimming with joy in these final moments, the music is carried away as winds, brass, and strings play an ascending motif that hovers in the air inside. In the audience, one man gives the stage a studied glance. Ralph Vaughan Williams rests his chin on his knuckles and closes his eyes as he imagines the sounds as clusters of eighth and sixteenth notes splattered in lampblack across the treble staves on a blank page. This is his music, his first commission, and a moment that comes back to him in 1914 when, as if following in the footsteps of his tutor, the composer Maurice Ravel, Vaughan Williams too finds himself an ambulance driver, evading enemy fire while ferrying the mortally wounded across the barbed-wired and mine-laden ground. Above, Batignolles and Krupp shells hiss along their noisy arcs in a sky that glows with fire, and he pauses then to think about his overture to *The Wasps*, laughing at the fatal irony. Those artillery shells, in those moments before committing to the end of their trajectories, also hummed to a pitch that approximated the tonic of *The Wasps*, B flat, the only musical key signature that calls to mind a crushed insect. *Bee . . . flat*.

What then of the actor, standing now, reciting his lines? He is the leader of a chorus of litigants, all dressed in dark tunics and leather sandals. As he recites his stuttering iambic trimeter, the audience cannot help but laugh at his headdress with two antennae, the taffeta wings, gauzy and iridescent, attached to the back and catching the ambient light, or even the segmented papier-mâché abdomen attached to his rear waistline. But this is a calculated spectacle, a kind of inside joke, if you will, for the yearly Cambridge Greek Play is a lark. It began in 1882 thanks to John Willis Clark, a member of Cambridge's esteemed Faculty of Zoology whose intellectual curiosities ranged from Greek verse to the stones of Cambridge itself. (The latter passion led him to complete one of the most daunting archival projects of the day: the 1886 publication of Robert Willis's incomplete *The Architectural History of the University of Cambridge*. A true polymath, Willis wrote about numerous disciplines, from natural philosophy to mechanics, and even counted Karl Marx among his students.)

With his zoologist's gaze Clark might have appreciated the chorus leader's resemblance to *Vespula germanica*, the common European wasp. A most sociable insect, the wasp joined the ranks of other animals exhibiting what the French zoologist Henri Milne-Edwards called "an instinct directing all toward some common labor." This describes the bustling activity in the theater as well, for here in this building actors, directors, stage managers, dramaturges, choruses, musicians—all part of a larger movement of organized bodies in space—rehearsed and ritualized. And Milne-Edwards saw something similar while examining the bodies of dissected invertebrates. In them he saw an intricately arranged "domestic economy," a "workshop where each worker would be employed to perform similar work and where, consequently, their number would affect the amount but not the nature of products, each of their body parts contributing to the maintenance of life."[1] For the sociologist Émile Durkheim, this description of a body organized into different kinds of specialized tasks was nothing short of revelatory—it was the basis for an understanding of the ways societies work, an inspiration for his own writings about the division of labor.[2]

Beyond its role as a *dispositif* illustrating the organization of labor, *Vespula germanica* would emerge as a cipher for the modernity of vision itself. One of the most fascinating afterlives of the common wasp—and the most visually arresting—comes from Étienne-Jules Marey's *station physiologique* of the 1870s. It is a drawing of a flying wasp (*guêpe volant*), arrested in mid-flight by dint of the artist's deft pencil. In bold, confident strokes, we see the insect up close. With eyes resembling obsidian orbs, extended mandibles, and coiled abdomen, the wasp looks dangerous, ready to strike. And yet its flight is only illusory. If we are to understand that this wasp is flying, it is only because the movement of the wings appears as rapid vertical flutterings. The image, which first appeared in Marey's *La machine animale, locomotion terrestre et aérienne* (1873), is an intervention with aesthetic consequences. That is, it portrays an image of insect flight that was only perceptible because Marey had daubed the tips of a wasp's wings with gilded paint; when illuminated by sunlight, the insect appeared to carve fiery figure eights in the air.

Like the chorus leader's recitations at Cambridge, the wasp's gilt-winged flight is a performance that suspends its audience between wonder and disbelief. As they watch an actor in a wasp costume, the audience revels in the music and the prosody, captivated by the same kind of aural delight that transports listeners to a world otherwise inaccessible. Encountering Marey's wasp, a viewer is also held in a state of suspended disbelief. The gilded figure eights appear as incandescent ribbons, which, for a moment, cause us to wonder whether they are actually seen, or a best guess of what may happen when the wasp beats its wings. This was a concern of Marey's, and, dogged researcher that he was, he had not been able to capture that moment when an insect's wing appeared as an appendage paralyzed in the middle of a dihedral or anhedral. This was still a couple of years before Eadweard Muybridge presented his first images of galloping horses at Leland Stanford's ranch in Palo Alto, California. Using a series of cameras rigged with trip wires that captured the galloping horse at an astonishing one-thousandth of a second, these images shattered the illusion of motion into constitutive segments, decomposing the elusive gallop into successive microepisodes that revealed animal motion as temporal movement.

It was around this time that the spell was cast on Marey. Inspired by Jules Janssen and Francisco Antônio de Almeida's photographic apparatus for capturing the transit of Venus in 1874, he envisioned a portable version that could be aimed like a gun at birds and insects and, with the squeezing of a trigger, freeze its quarry in space and time—much like Muybridge's multiple cameras, but condensed into a single instrument. Each click of the shutter was a kind of *petit mort*, suspending life itself in the amber of the photographic plate, forever changing our idea of what it meant to have a modern eye. In his photograph of a wasp arrested in midflight, any distinctions between science and art, or for that matter between technics and aesthetics, are momentarily elided in service of an image that captivates our attention. Like slack-jawed spectators at a midway, we too stare at this image of something that is otherwise unseen, made recognizable only because of its sheer beauty. It is nothing short of beguiling.

Marey's wasp made a final, fluttering appearance at the beginning of a great conflagration about to consume the world. It was in a book by Marey's former assistant, Pierre Nogués, published in 1933 as *Recherches expérimentales de Marey sur le mouvement dans l'air et dans l'eau* for the French Air Ministry, a comprehensive volume that presented, for the first time, the entirety of Marey's work as a kind of discourse with air. It seems rather quaint, however, as the gilt-winged wasp gave way to the stunning wind-tunnel chronophotographic plates showing lambent trails of smoke flowing over objects. The ghostly scrim is an eerie visitant, a foretelling of a near future when phalanxes of bombers would leave their own cloudy hexagrams over Europe and Asia. *Vespula germanica* continued through its transformations, the imago of a flying insect now embedded in the language of a world at war. We see it in 1940, at the Fore River Shipyards as the *Essex*-class carrier USS *Wasp*, later sunk during the Solomon Islands campaign in 1942. We see it in the thousands of enlisted United States Navy Construction Battalions, known first by their acronym, "CB," and popularized by the now famous portmanteau "Seabees." And we see it in cadres of fearless women ferrying bombers and fighter planes in hazardous conditions across land and ocean as part of the Women Airforce Service Pilots, or WASP.

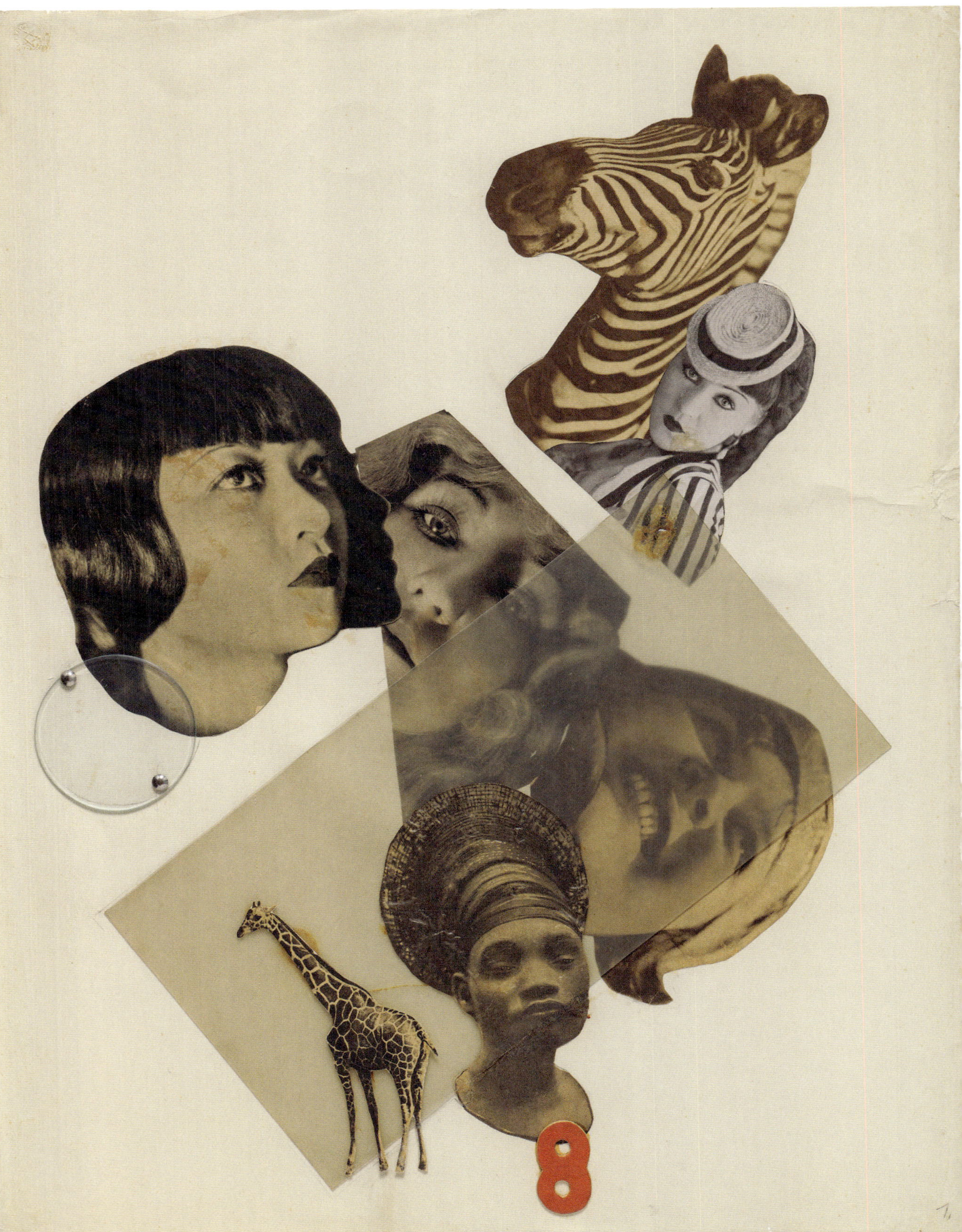

Zebra

Brett M. Van Hoesen

In July 1923, the female American adventurer Osa Johnson, wife of the filmmaker Martin Johnson, was featured riding a zebra in a cover photograph for the German illustrated weekly *Berliner Illustrirte Zeitung* (*BIZ*).[1] The image was part of a strategic advertisement campaign to help promote the filmic works of the Johnsons, who captured the curiosity and attention of American and European audiences alike thanks to their well-documented travels to Africa and the South Seas. Exotic, playful, and wittingly out-of-context, the zebra's appearance on the cover of *BIZ* resonates with uses of the animal in our own time, including the recent album cover for popular German jazz cabaret singer Max Raabe's *Wer hat hier schlechte Laune* (Who is in a bad mood here).[2] In both scenarios, the zebra's unique striped pattern creates visual allure. For Raabe, the invocation of the zebra is an intriguing juxtaposition to modern urban space and also pointedly echoes the signature, vintage black-and-white formal attire of the singer and his band.

In the 1920s, the zebra's unique stripes not only functioned as a fashionable design aesthetic, but also served as a symbol for travel well beyond the geographic bounds of North America and Europe. The German artist Marianne Brandt's 1929 assemblage *Untitled [With Anna May Wong]* captures this duality. For Brandt's generation, the zebra's black-and-white stripes connected with Bauhaus methodologies that scrutinized form and color relationships as a means to create increasingly effective modes of visual communication. More than simply a design tactic, however, the zebra in Brandt's work also refers to complicated discourses during the interwar period in Germany that connected

Figure 26.1
Marianne Brandt, *Untitled [With Anna May Wong]*, 1929. Harvard Art Museums/Busch-Reisinger Museum, Purchase through the generosity of the Friends of the Busch-Reisinger Museum and their Acquisitions Committee, Richard and Priscilla Hunt, Elizabeth C. Lyman, Mildred Rendl-Marcus, and Sylvia de Cuevas. © Artists Rights Society (ARS), NY, Photo © President and Fellows of Harvard College.

the idea of the New Woman to colonial histories inherent to the development of European modernism.

While Marianne Brandt was not an architect in the conventional sense, starting in 1924 she was a notable student at the Bauhaus of the Hungarian artist, designer, and educator László Moholy-Nagy. Brandt's achievements in product design, painting, and photography ultimately led to her status as the acting director of the metal workshop at the Bauhaus in 1928. A year later, she worked in the architectural offices of Walter Gropius in Berlin, the same year that she created the assemblage *Untitled [With Anna May Wong]*. During her tenure at the Bauhaus, Brandt was educated in the foundational elements of design, which included her mentor's teachings and writings on aspects of visual communication. Moholy-Nagy's seminal book *Painting, Photography, Film* (1925) documents these pedagogical teachings through a combination of short, topical essays and a wide range of black-and-white images that span a rich array of image-making technologies including x-rays, reprinted negatives, wireless telegraphed photography, animated cartoons, film stills, photomontages, reprinted documentary photographs from the popular press, and much more. The images are often paired with captions that instruct the reader, as art historian Pepper Stetler has analyzed, "to experience the photographs in a new way."[3] Moholy-Nagy was particularly interested in the viewer's biological response to imagery. This included what he identified as static versus kinetic optical compositions and the role that color values played in illustrating spatial configurations.[4] Patterns, including stripes, as well as the "lightness and weight of colors," including black-and-white content, embodied the formal characteristics of kinetic compositions and visual dynamism.[5] Therefore, stripes, like those of the zebra, served as a visual tool that Moholy-Nagy illustrated in *Painting, Photography, Film*. In fact, he used a *BIZ* reprint of Martin Johnson's 1923 photograph of zebras and gnus drinking from a water hole, taken during the photographer's travels to East Africa. Like the comparative format used in popular illustrated journals such as *Der Querschnitt*, Moholy-Nagy juxtaposed this photograph with one of a Bavarian fishing station, a bird's-eye view of consecutive rows of fish breeding ponds that create a pattern of light and dark striations, echoing the zebras' stripes on the opposite page. Without additional written explanation for this pairing, Brandt's mentor implied the visual intrigue of striped patterning at a time when black-and-white patterns were in fashion in other popular culture arenas including fashion, film, and advertisements.

The visual grammar of black-and-white stripes, which contemporary designer Christian Leborg refers to as the interplay between visible and active structures, also relates to the strategic mechanisms that prompted the invention of World War I dazzle camouflage.[6] Based on a principle similar to the optical illusions of zebras' stripes when in motion or in a herd that confuse their predator, dazzle camouflage consisting of broadly painted black-and-white stripes helped to disguise World War I battleships and deter an accurate read of their physical location. Indeed, the biology of seeing color relationships, including black and white, can be manipulated depending upon form and pattern, what neurobiologist Margaret Livingstone calls "surround effects."[7] Brandt, as a student of Moholy-Nagy, likely learned these principles of creating visual intrigue explicitly linked to the employment of compositional elements such as black and white striations. An example of kinetic optical composition, Brandt's assemblage included not only an intriguing collection of clipped *illustrirte* imagery and preprinted materials, but also a flat glass sphere and a rectangular sheet of celluloid, modern materials that attract the eye and create transparent layers. In this way, the zebra and the design principles it implies inspired a self-conscious attention to the act of seeing.

If the image of Osa Johnson riding a zebra served as visual intrigue for armchair travelers during the 1920s, Brandt's incorporation of a zebra and its connection to the black-and-white-striped bodice of the adjacent female actress Katherine Hessling facilitated an easy visual parity between trendy female fashion and exotic animals.[8] Zebras fascinate us because each one possesses its own unique pattern.

It is worth noting that the zebra incorporated in Brandt's work was not just any zebra. Indeed, this particular animal was an urban icon used to advertise the Budapest Zoo (Budapesti Állatkert) in a poster dating to 1928. In this way, both actress and zebra are identifiable commodities for a contemporary audience. This connection between female fashion and zebra hide was not simply bound to Europe in the 1920s; quite the contrary, black-and-white striped European female fashions inspired by zebra print date as far back as the early eighteenth century.[9] This was in part due to an extensive history of European colonization in Africa including the establishment of the Dutch Cape Colony in 1652 by the Dutch East India Company. During this time, the Dutch presented the Abyssinian zebra to the then shogun of Japan, and later the quagga species was exhibited at The Hague in the 1740s.[10] As writers Christopher Plumb and Samuel Shaw wonderfully document, the complex geographic history of zebras spans two thousand years across disparate cities and sites such as Cairo, Alexandria, Constantinople, Mogadishu, and royal courts in Afghanistan, China, India, and beyond. Germane to this particular case study, the export of actual zebras to various points across Europe from the eighteenth century until the early twentieth century was undeniably linked to European imperialism. Thus, while the zebra in Brandt's assemblage presents a seemingly playful disposition, it is a symbol for the underlying violence and appropriation integral to European colonial practices in Africa that culminated in zoos, cabinets of curiosities, natural history museums, and a host of visual arts exhibition venues.

Relatedly, Brandt's assemblage points to the increasingly fashionable culture of internationalism in the popular press that involved the construct of the New Woman. Art historian Elizabeth Otto has emphasized in her groundbreaking work on Brandt's photomontages that the artist's selection of "five varied but universally beautiful female heads" in *Untitled [With Anna May Wong]* was an attempt to celebrate global variations of the New Woman.[11] With this diversity, however, there was also the underlying legacy of German colonialism, which officially ended during World War I, but lived on in what I have dubbed "postcolonial cosmopolitanism." In short, the representation of modern women from a wide array of cultural backgrounds, geographies, and races, including Anna May Wong, the popular Chinese American actress, became a trope of European modernism that had its roots in colonialist comparative modalities that often amplified difference. Linked to this construct was a long-established paradigm of modern women pictured with exotic animals during the interwar period, such as Josephine Baker and her pet leopard Chiquita and German film producer Lola Kreutzberg pictured with a cheetah during travels to what was then the Dutch colony of Indonesia.[12] Brandt explores this popular phenomenon in *Untitled [With Anna May Wong]* by invoking two signature African animals—the zebra as well as the giraffe.

In 1978, the zoo enthusiast and eventual mammal curator Kenhelm W. Stott Jr. published a short, richly illustrated guide to his travels with Martin and Osa Johnson that included excerpts from the adventurers' letters and journal entries. In one letter from 1922, paired with a photograph of roughly two dozen zebras taken in northern Kenya, Martin Johnson explained that "the common zebra (Grant's) come in herds of twenty to two hundred."[13] This seemingly mundane, factual anecdote bespoke the visual magnetism of this intriguing animal in both film and photographs during the interwar period. What must it have been like to experience their presence, expanded from a small herd of zebras to the blurring effect of hundreds?

Between Brandt and Moholy-Nagy, we get the sense of a keen interest in learning from the animal and its unique hide as a visual tool to better understand and interrogate how we see. The well-known British art critic John Berger described visibility as a "form of growth." He writes, "It is very possible that visibility *is* the truth and that what lies outside visibility are only the 'traces' of what has been or will become visible."[14] Berger argues that visibility is not simply about light and scale, but about recognizing and receiving. As a signifier for complex aesthetic and cultural codes, the zebra in Brandt's assemblage is far from a silent presence. Rather, the zebra is an instigator promoting the tenets of visual dynamism and, at the same time, imprinting tropes of colonialist legacies on European modernism.

Acknowledgments

As this book project initiated from my research on animals in modern Greek architecture while a Visiting Research Fellow at Princeton University's Seeger Center for Hellenic Studies in 2019, I cannot but thank all the people at Princeton who supported this endeavor from the very start. Dimitri Gondicas, director of the Seeger Center, together with M. Christine Boyer (School of Architecture) and Esther da Costa Meyer (Department of Art and Archaeology) were always present and active during my stay at Princeton, guiding and challenging me at every step so that this abstruse topic could become something simultaneously open and specific. I am also grateful to Anne Anlin Cheng (Department of English), Sylvia Lavin (School of Architecture), Effie Rentzou and André Benhaim (Department of French and Italian), Basile Baudez (Department of Art and Archaeology), Peter Singer (Department of Philosophy), and Aaron Shkuda (Princeton-Mellon Initiative in Architecture, Urbanism, and the Humanities), who gave me the opportunity to discuss my work with them or even present its first findings to small audiences. I was also honored to have Spyros Papapetros, Cameron Wu, and Marshall Brown (School of Architecture) participate as respondents in the workshop entitled "The Architect and the Animal: 20th Century Encounters" organized by the Princeton Athens Center on April 9 and 10, 2021. I would also like to warmly thank Marina Lathouri, who had been kind enough to invite me to present and discuss my research at the AA School, and Fabian Reiner, who organized a postseminar discussion that helped me better reflect on my work. Anne Simon (CNRS) was also kind to share her work for the *Animots* network with me, providing valuable insight.

I cannot stress enough the contribution of Thomas Weaver to the final outcome. As the former acquisitions editor for art and architecture at the MIT Press, his boldness and perceptiveness were decisive for the initial book project to become something special both in content and as an object in itself. Most of the book's playful "animality" is owed to him. Of course, the idea for what this book should be like in its form, graphic design, and printing quality would not have been realized without the generous support of Christos Ioannou (chairman of AVAX and member of the MIT Sloan Executive Board), who unreservedly embraced the project from the start. To him and to Yorgos Tzirtzilakis I feel grateful. Finally, I warmly thank MIT Press senior acquisitions editor Victoria Hindley, who received an almost final manuscript but rather adeptly guided me through the last editing phases, contributing a lot to the clarity, exactness, and balance of the content.

This book is dedicated to my children. Because it is when I first became a father that, for some reason, animals started to have a new effect in my mind.

Notes

Ass

1. Jill Bough, *Donkey* (London: Reaktion Books, 2011), 19.
2. Le Corbusier, *The Final Testament of Père Corbu: A Translation and Interpretation of Mise au Point by Ivan Žaknić* (New Haven: Yale University Press, 1997), 91.
3. Le Corbusier, *The Final Testament of Père Corbu*, 88.
4. Giedion wrote: "Et comme chez lui tout s'exprimait toujours de façon plastique, il m'envoya de Chandigarh une lettre accompagnée d'un dessin (fig. 339). Il y évoquait une conversation avec Ernesto N. Rogers architecte bien connu et éditeur de 'Casabella': 'Rogers prétendait que je suis un génie et moi je certifiais être un âne. J'ai alors représenté la question par ce croquis.' En dessous de son dessin, Le Corbusier avait écrit 'Le génie porte-t'il l'âne, ou l'âne porte-t-il le génie?'" Sigfried Giedion, *Espace, temps, architecture* (Brussels: La Connaissance, 1968), 348; illustration, 339. For information on this sketch, see Viveca Bosson, "Le Corbusier—the Painter Who Became an Architect," in *Le Corbusier Painter and Architect* (Copenhagen: Fonden til Udgivelse af Arkitekturtidsskrift, 1995), 21.
5. A slightly different rendition of this story appears in Stanislaus von Moos, "Voyages en Zigzag," in Stanislaus von Moss and Arthur Rűegg, eds., *Le Corbusier before Le Corbusier* (New Haven: Yale University Press, 2002), 23–44, 283–285.
6. Charles-Édouard Jeanneret [Le Corbusier], *La construction des villes*, ed. Marc E. Albert Emery (Paris: L'Âge d'Homme, 1992), 94–95.

Bull

1. John Berger, *About Looking* (New York: Vintage International, 1991), 5.
2. Peter and Alison Smithson, *The Space Between* (Cologne: Walther König, 2017), 212, 217.
3. José Ortega y Gasset, *The Revolt of the Masses* (New York: W. W. Norton, 1957), 152.
4. Antonio Bonet Correa, *Fiesta poder y arquitectura* (Madrid: Ediciones Akal, 1990).
5. Rosa Perales Piqueres, "El proyecto de la plaza de toros de Picasso y su relación con la arquitectura de masas," *Quintana*, no. 13 (2014): 267–281.

Cetus

1. For more details on the building, see Gregorio Astengo, "White Whale: The Aquarium and Reptile House at the Turin Zoo and the Architecture of Enzo Venturelli (1955–1965)," *Architectural Histories* 7, no. 1 (2019): 1–27.

2. “Acuario y Reptilario,” *Informes de la Construcción* 17, no. 167 (1965): 21–32; Giulio Morgan, “Moby Dick a Torino: L’Acquario-Rettilario di Enzo Venturelli,” *L’Architettura. Cronache e Storia* 9, no. 22 (1961): 810–815.
3. John K. Papadopoulos and Deborah Ruscillo, “A Ketos in Early Athens: An Archaeology of Whales and Sea Monsters in the Greek World,” *American Journal of Archaeology* 106, no. 2 (2002): 215–221; K. M. Coleman, “Manilius’ Monster,” *Hermes* 111, no. 2 (1983): 226–232.
4. Archivio Enzo Venturelli, B.14/f.5.
5. Reyner Banham, “Neoliberty: The Italian Retreat from Modern Architecture,” *Architectural Review* 125 (1959): 230–235.
6. “Un pomeriggio allo Zoo,” *La Stampa*, October 8, 1965, 11.

Dog

1. Superstudio, “Description of the Microevent/Microenvironment,” in *Italy: The New Domestic Landscape. Achievements and Problems of Italian Design*, ed. Emilio Ambasz (New York: Museum of Modern Art, in collaboration with Centro Di, Florence, 1972), 242.
2. Superstudio, “Cerimonia,” *Casabella* 374 (February 1973), 34.
3. Superstudio, “Cerimonia,” 34.
4. Superstudio, “Cerimonia,” 36–37.

Earthworm

1. For Tafuri, in the housing-cum-motorway of the Algiers project, Le Corbusier combines the time of chronography of the elevated roof-motorway—“the time of acceleration, the time that does not leave time, . . . the time of advertising . . . the time of a time that cannot afford to rethink time”—with the time of consumerism of the modular residential cells nested under the motorway, a solution in which constant change produces disposable objects. Manfredo Tafuri, *La dignità dell’attimo. Trascrizione multimediale di ‘Le forme del tempo: Venezia e la modernità’* (Venice: IUAV and Grafiche Veneziane, 1994), unpaginated. I discuss this in “Architecture after Utopia: The Times of the Historical ‘Project,’” in *On Power in Architecture*, ed. Mateja Kurir (Abingdon: Routledge, 2024).
2. For Manfredo Tafuri, Daneri’s Forte Quezzi housing is “a structure that sets into tension, one against the other, the finitude of the development and its frustrated aspiration to become a part of the city.” Manfredo Tafuri, *Storia dell’architettura italiana 1944–1985* (Turin: Einaudi, 1986), 61. In “Worm Architecture,” Riccardo Cozzi has analyzed the Daneri team’s project and intentionally mistranslated *Biscione* as “worm,” in order to appropriate it for his manifesto: “The Biscione of Genoa is a manifesto, / a declaration of war on pure formalism, a detachment from the institutionality of Building. / You called it a worm / But be aware, / this represents the very end for you. / Will you stop biting into nature / you’re your formalist pretensions / . . . / Your inefficiency will be exposed / Your failure will be clear to all / . . . / The Biscione of Genoa is a Worm, / a Worm that has no creator, / It configures itself and settles into the soil / as only worms can do. / . . . / Architecture becomes a worm / nature configures its form / and the power of the architect collapses / stripped of its formal pretensions.” Riccardo Cozzi, “Worm Architecture” (Architectural Association School of Architecture, 2022, unpublished).
3. Georges Bataille, “Formless,” in Georges Bataille, Michel Leiris, Marcel Griaule, Robert Desnos, et al., *Encyclopaedia Acephalica, Critical Dictionary* (London: Atlas Press, 1995), 51–52, translated and quoted by Yve-Alain Bois in Yve-Alain Bois

and Rosalind E. Krauss, *Formless: A User's Guide* (New York: Zone Books, 1997), 5.

4. Yve-Alain Bois, "Figure," in Bois and Krauss, *Formless*, 79.
5. Bois, "Figure," 79.
6. Cited in Bois, "Figure," 80.
7. Bois, "Figure," 80, 79.
8. Jakob von Uexküll, *A Foray into the Worlds of Animals and Humans* (1934; Minneapolis: University of Minnesota Press, 2010), 84, 180, 206.
9. Forensic Architecture, *The Nebelivka Hypothesis*, accessed November 10, 2023, https://forensic-architecture.org/investigation/the-nebelivka-hypothesis.
10. Forensic Architecture with David Wengrow, *The Nebelivka Hypothesis*, 7. Catalogue of the exhibition at the Venice Biennale 2023, 18th International Architecture Exhibition, accessed November 12, 2023, https://content.forensic-architecture.org/wp-content/uploads/2023/04/The-Nebelivka-Hypothesis_FA-Wengrow_Book.pdf.
11. Forensic Architecture with Wengrow, *The Nebelivka Hypothesis*, 17.
12. Chernozem: "a fertile black soil rich in humus and with a lighter lime-rich layer beneath, typically occurring in the temperate grasslands of the Russian steppes and North American prairies." *Oxford English Dictionary* (Oxford: Oxford University Press, 2023).
13. Forensic Architecture with Wengrow, *The Nebelivka Hypothesis*, 47.
14. I borrowed the term from Donna Haraway, who explains: "Critters is an American everyday idiom for varmints of all sorts. Scientists talk of their 'critters' all the time; and so do ordinary people all over the U.S., but perhaps especially in the South. The taint of 'creatures' and 'creation' does not stick to 'critters.' . . . In this book, 'critters' refers promiscuously to microbes, plants, animals, humans and nonhumans, and sometimes even to machines." Donna J. Haraway, *Staying with the Trouble: Making Kin in the Chthulucene* (Durham: Duke University, Press, 2016), 169 n1.
15. Catherine Ingraham sees the "detour" in Hejduk's work as "the construction/devastation of an urban interstice, a hidden space and hidden house." Catherine Ingraham, "Errand, Detour, and the Wilderness Urbanism of John Hejduk," in *Hejduk's Chronotope*, ed. K. Michael Hays (New York: Princeton Architectural Press, 1996), 132.
16. Joseph Jacobs, *Aesop's Fables,* illustrated by John Hejduk (New York: Rizzoli, 1991), unpaginated.

Fish

1. A reference to his work features in José Manuel Fernandes, *Arquitectura e indústria em Portugal no século XX* (Lisbon: Sécil, 2003), 171–173. Iglésias self-published a curious autobiographical monograph. See Eduardo Iglésias, *Um olhar: Um percurso* (n.p. [Porto], 2011).
2. Archives of Faculty of Architecture of the University of Porto, FAUP/CDUA/EI/ARQ/051-pd.04-06. Eduardo Iglésias, *Um stand para os Frigoríficos de Matosinhos*, undated.
3. FAUP/CDUA, EI/ARQ/051-A. Eduardo Iglésias, Posto Gelmar, Praça Gomes Teixeira, Porto, undated [1973].

Giraffe

1. Rem Koolhaas, OMA, and Bruce Mau, *S,M,L,XL* (Rotterdam: 010 Publishers; New York: Monacelli Press, 1995).
2. Koolhaas and Mau, *S,M,L,XL*, 130–194.
3. Hans Werlemann, lecture at the Berlage Institute in Rotterdam, December 16, 2008.

4. This reading was, for instance, suggested by Roberto Gargiani, in *Rem Koolhaas/OMA: The Construction of Merveilles* (Lausanne: EPFL Press, 2008), 141.
5. See Rem Koolhaas, "Worrying Kindness and Ultimate Wisdom," in *The World of Madelon Vriesendorp*, ed. Shumon Basar and Stephan Trüby (London: AA Publications, 2008), 258.
6. Koolhaas and Mau, *S,M,L,XL*, xxii.
7. So far as I know, only two of these animal novellas exist in English: "Baldur D Quorg, spider," published in the collection *The Dedalus Book of Dutch Fantasy*, edited and translated by Richard Huijing (Sawtry, Cambridgeshire: Dedalus, 1993), and "Fame, Fortune and the Ant," in *Nice People: A Collection of Dutch Short Stories*, ed. Gerrit Bussink (Montreal: Guernica Editions, 1992).
8. See also Luis Buñuel, "Une girafe," in *Le Surréalisme au service de la révolution*, no. 6 (May 15, 1933): 34–36. The Marx Brothers film would have had giraffes stuffed with dynamite exploding in Manhattan. See Matthew Galev, ed., *Dali and Film* (London: Tate Publishing, 2007).
9. Salvador Dalí, "Art Nouveau Architecture's Terrifying and Edible Beauty," *Minotaure*, no. 3–4 (1933).
10. Rem Koolhaas, "Europeans: Biuer! Dali and Le Corbusier Conquer New York," in *Delirious New York: A Retrospective Manifesto for Manhattan* (1978; Rotterdam: 010 Publishers, 1994), 235.
11. For a detailed analysis of this particular aspect of the architecture of the villa, see Françoise Fromonot, "The House of Doctor Koolhaas," *AA Files*, no. 68 (2014): 69–87.
12. Le Corbusier, *Quand les cathédrales étaient blanches. Voyage au pays des timides* (Paris: Librairie Plon, 1937); quoted by Rem Koolhaas, *Delirious New York*, 251.
13. Gargiani, *Rem Koolhaas/OMA*, 141.

Horse

1. "Al contrario i cavalli di Palazzo del Te, i cavalli del Mantegna, ricercati nelle fotografie di Luigi Ghirri rappresentano qui la fantasia: anche essi sono bianchi, e sembrano bianchi non per razza ma puittosto pallidi di questo pallore di cui ci parla Virgilio, e questo pallore contrasta con la potente struttura anatomica, terrestre, con cui vengono rappresentati. Nel Palazzo del Te l''interno' diventa un 'esterno'; e i cavalli che ritornano sempre a Mantova sono gli abitanti di un Progetto per Scuderia, da me mai compiuto o solo iniziato, che presentiamo in questo piccolo volume." Aldo Rossi and Luigi Ghirri, *Architetture padane* (Modena: Edizioni Panini, [1984]), 13.
2. "Un interesse principalmente clinico per le ossa e la loro patologia, patologia che ogni Lombardo riporta all'umidità della nostra terra, che probabilmente è vero, ma che forse è anche il risultato di antiche e interne deformazioni. Così lo studio di questi cavalli si confondeva con lo studio di sedie e mobile come strutture portanti." Rossi and Ghirri, *Architetture padane*, 13.
3. Aldo Rossi, *A Scientific Autobiography* (Cambridge, MA: MIT Press, 1981), 11.

Ibis

1. W. M. Crosby and H. P. Nichols, *The illustrated Alphabet of Birds* (Boston: W. M. Crosby & H. P. Nichols, 1851).
2. The ibis belongs to the order Ciconiiformes. It is nomadic, moves in flocks, and inhabits the banks of rivers and lakes, coastlines, and marshy areas. Its appearance is defined by long legs, a curved pointed beak, wide wings, and thick plumage.
3. On the topic, see S. S. D. Damluji and V. Bertini, *Hassan Fathy: Earth and Utopia* (London: Laurence King Publishing, 2018).

4. On the New Gourna Village project, see Hassan Fathy, *Architecture for the Poor: An Experiment in Rural Egypt* (Chicago: University of Chicago Press, 1973).
5. Hassan Fathy, *Nubian Architecture* (Cairo: Social Research Center, American University in Cairo, 1964; unpublished and conserved at the Rare Book and Special Collections Library of the American University in Cairo, Hassan Fathy Archives).
6. Andrew D. Wade et al., "Food Placement in Ibis Mummies and the Role of Viscera in Embalming," *Journal of Archaeological Science* 39, no. 5 (2012): 1642–1647.
7. Kazimierz Michalowski, *Art of Ancient Egypt* (New York: Abrams, 1968).
8. Margaret Bunson, *A Dictionary of Ancient Egypt* (New York: Oxford University Press, 1991).
9. Renisa Mawani, "I Is for Ibis," in *Animalia: An Anti-Imperial Bestiary for Our Times*, ed. Antoinette Burton and Renisa Mawani (Durham: Duke University Press, 2020).
10. Louis Charbonneau-Lassay, *Il bestiario del Cristo*, vol. 2 (Rome: Edizioni Arkeios, 1994).
11. Plutarch, *Iside e Osiride*, in Charbonneau-Lassay, *Il bestiario del Cristo*, 143.
12. Giuseppe Ungaretti, *Vita d'un uomo. Tutte le poesie* (Milan: Mondadori, 1969), 498.

Japanese Dragon (*Ryū*)

1. A reference to William Butler Yeats, "The Second Coming": "A shape with lion body and the head of a man, / A gaze blank and pitiless as the sun, / Is moving its slow thighs, while all about it / Reel shadows of the indignant desert birds."
2. "Sōtō no Dragon" [Double-headed dragon], in *Shin Takamatsu: Space and Concept*, Contemporary Architecture in Drawings, vol. 13 (Kyoto: Dohosha, 1986), 30–33.
3. An insight I owe to an essay by Patrice Goulet, "The Outsider," in *Shin Takamatsu: Architectural Works 1981/1989* (Paris: Electa Moniteur, 1989).
4. "The Amphisbaena has a twin head, that is one at its tail-end as well, as though it were not enough for poison to be poured out of one mouth." From Pliny the Elder, *Natural History*, vol. 3, trans. Harris Rackham (Cambridge, MA: Harvard University Press, 1947), 63.

King Cobra

1. Interview with Balkrishna Doshi by Vera Simone Bader in *Balkrishna Doshi: Writings on Architecture and Identity*, ed. Vera Simone Bader (Berlin: ArchiTangle, 2019), 18.
2. Balkrishna Doshi, "Hans Ulrich Obrist in Conversation with Balkrishna Doshi," in *Balkrishna Doshi: Architecture for the People*, ed. Mateo Kries, Khushnu Panthaki Hoof, and Jolanthe Kugler (Weil am Rhein: Vitra Design Museum, 2019), 14.
3. Doshi, "Hans Ulrich Obrist in Conversation," 14.
4. Balkrishna Doshi, "Die Offenbarung," in *Balkrishna Doshi: Architecture for the People*, 277.
5. Doshi, "Die Offenbarung," 277.

Lion

1. Joseph Jacobs, *Aesop's Fables*, illustrated by John Hejduk (New York: Rizzoli, 1991), unpaginated.
2. John Hejduk in Hejduk and David Shapiro, "John Hejduk, or The Architect Who Drew Angels," *Architecture and Urbanism* 471 (2009): 75.
3. John Hejduk, *Mask of Medusa* (New York: Rizzoli, 1985), 156.

4. John Hejduk, *Soundings*, ed. Kim Shkapich (New York: Rizzoli, 1993), 153.
5. K. Michael Hays, *Architecture's Desire: Reading the Late Avant-Garde* (Cambridge, MA: MIT Press, 2010), 89–90.

Mollusk

1. Conchology is primarily concerned with the study of mollusk shells, while malacology is the study of mollusks that includes the soft body and the shell secreted by its mantle.
2. Of course there is chirality to the formation and coiling of mollusk shells.
3. Jean-Luc Nancy, "Of Struction," translated by Travis Holloway and Flor Méchain, *Parrhesia*, no. 17 (2013): 4–6.
4. Francis Ponge, "The Mollusk," in *Selected Poems*, trans. C. K. Williams, John Montague, and Margaret Guiton, ed. Margaret Guiton (Winston-Salem, NC: Wake Forest University Press, 1994), 37. "Le mollusque" is one of thirty-two prose poems from Ponge's *Le parti pris des choses* (1942).
5. I take the term "partial education" from Stefano Harney and Fred Moten's book *All Incomplete* (New York: Minor Compositions, 2021), 61–77.
6. On the "metaphor of metaphor" and "borrowed dwellings," see Jacques Derrida, "White Mythology," in *Margins of Philosophy*, trans. Alan Bass (Chicago: University of Chicago Press, 1982), 253. On the notion of *res nullius* (things that belong to no one) and "shells abandoned at the sea shore," see Giorgio Agamben, *The Highest Poverty: Monastic Rules and Form-of-Life*, trans. Adam Kotsko (Stanford: Stanford University Press, 2013), 139.
7. Thangam Ravindranathan, *Behold an Animal: Four Exorbitant Readings* (Evanston: Northwestern University Press, 2020), 182. Here I am twisting a passage from this book that reads as "marino-ontological consistency." Ravindranathan's chapter 4 and the epilogue offer some compelling readings of the mollusk and hermit crab in modern and contemporary literature and philosophy.
8. "Testaceous" is an adjective that means "relating to or derived from shells."
9. Thomas Ligotti, "Sideshow, and Other Stories," in *Teatro Grottesco* (London: Virgin Books, 2008), 40–42. It is evident that Ligotti is deliberately drawing on Franz Kafka's figure of Odradek from the short story "The Cares of a Family Man" (1919) in this section, which invokes the snail and the bivalved mollusk.
10. See Thomas Moynihan's elaboration of the "ectopic unconscious" in his intriguing book *Spinal Catastrophism: A Secret History* (Falmouth, UK: Urbanomic Media, 2019), 76, 81, 148.

Nautilus

1. Frank Lloyd Wright, in "Frank Lloyd Wright's Masterwork," *Architectural Forum* 96, no. 4 (April 1952): 144. See William Jordy, "The Encompassing Environment of Free-Form Architecture: Frank Lloyd Wright's Guggenheim Museum," in *American Buildings and Their Architects*, vol. 5: *The Impact of European Modernism in the Mid-Twentieth Century* (New York: Oxford University Press, 1976), 342–343.
2. Frank Lloyd Wright, "The Modern Gallery" (1946), in *Frank Lloyd Wright: Collected Writings*, vol. 4: *1939–1949*, ed. Bruce Brooks Pfeiffer (New York: Rizzoli, 1994), 281.
3. Frank Lloyd Wright, "Frank Lloyd Wright," *Architectural Forum* 84, no. 1 (January 1946): 136.
4. Laurel Joy Waycott, "The Pattern Seekers: The Science of Discernment, 1850–1920," Ph.D. dissertation, Yale University, 2019; chapter 3, "Tracing the Spiral Path of the Nautilus Shell."

5. Niklas Maak, *Le Corbusier: The Architect on the Beach* (Munich: Hanser/Kirmer Verlag, 2012).
6. Frank Lloyd Wright, "In the Cause of Architecture II: What 'Styles' Mean to the Architect" (1928), in *The Essential Frank Lloyd Wright: Critical Writings on Architecture*, ed. Bruce Brooks Pfeiffer (Princeton, NJ: Princeton University Press, 2008), 118; italics in original.
7. Richard Cleary et al., *Frank Lloyd Wright: From Within Outward* (New York: Skira, Rizzoli; Guggenheim Museum Publications, 2009).
8. Frank Lloyd Wright, "Modern Concepts Concerning Architecture," in *Modern Architecture: Being the Kahn Lectures for 1930* (1931; Princeton, NJ: Princeton University Press, 2008), frontispiece.
9. Frank Lloyd Wright, "The Living City" (1958), in *Frank Lloyd Wright: Collected Writings*, vol. 5: *1949–1959*, 261.
10. Joseph M. Siry, "Seamless Continuity versus the Nature of Materials: Gunite and Frank Lloyd Wright's Guggenheim Museum," *Journal of the Society of Architectural Historians* 71, no. 1 (March 2012): 87.
11. Frank Lloyd Wright, "Faith in Your Own Individuality" (1955), in *Frank Lloyd Wright: Collected Writings*, vol. 5, 132; italics in original.
12. Wright, "Faith in Your Own Individuality," 132; italics in original.
13. Frank Lloyd Wright, *An Autobiography* (1932), in *Frank Lloyd Wright: Collected Writings*, vol. 2: *1930–1932* (New York: Rizzoli, 1991), 206; italics in original.
14. Wright, "Faith in Your Own Individuality," 132.
15. Wright, "The Modern Gallery," 283.
16. Siry, "Seamless Continuity versus the Nature of Materials," 83–108.

Ox

1. See, for example, *Stoitelstvo Moskvy* [Construction of Moscow], no. 3 (1930): 9–31.
2. Catherine Cooke was the first to note Melnikov's "low-tech" approach that was intended to be an alternative to "high-tech" constructivism. Cooke, *Russian Avant-Garde: Theories of Art, Architecture and the City* (London: Academy Editions, 1995), 136.
3. K. Melnikov, "Arkhitektura moyey zhizni" [The architecture of my life], in *Konstantin Stepanovich Melnikov*, ed. A. A. Strigalyov and I. V. Kokkinaki (Moscow: Iskusstvo, 1985), 80.
4. *Stoitelstvo Moskvy*, no. 3 (1930): 20.
5. Melnikov, "Arkhitektura moyey zhizni," 82.

Pig

1. Alfred Jarry, *Ubu Roi* (New York: New Directions Books, 1961).
2. Lina Bo Bardi, *Mil brinquedos para a criança brasileira*, exhibition catalogue (São Paulo: SESC Pompéia, 1982), 10.
3. See Lina Bo Bardi, preparatory sketches of the *Polochon* (1985), Instituto Bardi/Casa de Vidro, São Paulo.
4. This essay is an invitation to think *with* the *Polochon*, to borrow from Lorraine Daston. See Lorraine Daston and Gregg Mitman, eds., *Thinking with Animals: New Perspectives on Anthropomorphism* (New York: Columbia University Press, 2006).
5. On the Teatro do Ornitorrinco, see Christiane Tricerri, ed., *Teatro do Ornitorrinco, 1977–2007* (São Paulo: Imprensa Oficial, 2009).
6. See, in this respect, Alastair Brotchie, "Who Wrote *Ubu Roi*, and Why?," in *Alfred Jarry: A Pataphysical Life* (Cambridge, MA: MIT Press, 2015), 171–178.

7. In 2016 the Museu de Arte de São Paulo (MASP) reedited the exhibition and catalogue, originally curated by Lina Bo Bardi in collaboration with Martim Gonçalves, Glauber Rocha, and Pietro M. Bardi in 1969. See *A mão do povo brasileiro 1969/2016*, exhibition catalogue, ed. Adriano Pedrosa and Tomás Toledo (São Paulo: Museu de Arte de São Paulo Assis Chateaubriand, 2016).
8. The first issue of the magazine *Habitat, Revista das Artes no Brasil*, directed by Bo Bardi, appeared in 1950. *Habitat* was part of MASP's cultural programs.
9. Indeed, Verger's work touches on a topic that exceeds the scope of this essay: the domestication of pigs. From wild creatures to transitional categories to livestock husbandry, pigs—along with other animals—played a crucial role in European colonization and the "taming" of the "New World," not to mention their critical importance in economic matters. For a "portrait" of the pig and a general history of its relationship with humans, see, for instance, Thomas Macho, *Cerdos, un retrato*, trans. Nicolás Gelormini (Buenos Aires: Adriana Hidalgo Editora, 2021). For an in-depth study of the evolving relationship between people and animals in the Atlantic world, see Marcy Norton, *The Tame and the Wild: People and Animals after 1492* (Cambridge, MA: Harvard University Press, 2024).
10. For an introduction to the ontological turn in anthropology see Eduardo Kohn, "Anthropology of Ontologies," *Annual Review of Anthropology* 44 (2015): 311–327. The turn to ontology in anthropology is both symptomatic and diagnostic of the exhaustion of numerous dichotomies (e.g., nature-culture, mind-body, and, of course, human-animal) and seeks to overturn them through a fundamental revision of the concept of difference.
11. Eduardo Viveiros de Castro, "The Relative Native," in *The Relative Native: Essays on Indigenous Conceptual Worlds*, trans. Julia Sauma and Martin Holbraad (Chicago: Hua Books, 2015), 31.
12. Eduardo Viveiros de Castro, "Exchanging Perspectives: The Transformation of Objects into Subjects in Amerindian Ontologies," *Common Knowledge* 25, nos. 1–3 (April 2019): 23.
13. Consider, for instance, Giorgio Agamben's affirmation: "the decisive political conflict, which governs every other conflict, is that between the animality and the humanity of man." Agamben's *The Open* constitutes one of the most crucial contributions on this topic. Giorgio Agamben, *The Open: Man and Animal*, trans. Kevin Attell (Stanford: Stanford University Press, 2004), 80.
14. Oswald de Andrade, *Manifesto antropófago e outros textos*, ed. Jorge Schwartz and Gênese Andrade (São Paulo: Companhia das Letras, 2017), 43–60. Originally published in *Revista de Antropofagia*, no. 1 (May 1928): 3, 7.
15. Haroldo de Campos, "The Rule of Anthropophagy: Europe under the Sign of Devoration," trans. María Tai Wolff, in "Brazilian Literature," special issue of *Latin American Literary Review* 14, no. 27 (January–June 1986): 48.
16. See Eduardo Viveiros de Castro, *Métaphysiques cannibales* (Paris: Presses Universitaires de France, 2009).
17. The Teatro Oficina, later renamed Teat(r)o Oficina Uzyna Uzona, is one of Brazil's most respected independent theater companies. It was founded in 1958 by a group of students of the School of Law of the University of São Paulo, among them José "Zé" Celso Martinez Corrêa, who directed the company until his death in 2023.
18. The design for the Teatro Oficina was a collective project undertaken by Zé Celso, Lina Bo Bardi, Marcelo Suzuki (in the early stages), and Edson Elito.

19. Bo Bardi used the term to refer to the narrative character of the exhibition *Caipiras, capiaus: pau a pique*, designed for the SESC Pompeia Center in 1984. The exhibition was aimed at raising awareness about rural architectures, in particular the *casa de pau a pique* (wattle and daub house). See Lina Bo Bardi, *Caipiras, capiaus: pau a pique*, catalogue (São Paulo: SESC Pompeia, 1984), n.p.
20. José Celso Martinez Corrêa, in José Gustavo Bonomi, *Teatro Oficina, 1958–1964: Indícios fotográficos da constituição de um grupo de vanguardia* (São Paulo: Paco Editorial, 2014), 33.
21. See Diane Davis, "Creaturely Rhetorics," *Philosophy and Rhetoric* 44, no. 1 (2011): 88–94.

Queen Bee

1. "The Hive 'It's a Stunt' . . . 'A Fine Conception,'" *Auckland Star* [New Zealand], April 3, 1964.
2. "Architect on Parliament Buildings," *Evening Post* [Wellington, New Zealand], March 24, 1964.
3. Robin Skinner, "A Hive of Controversy: Extending New Zealand's Parliament Buildings," in *Basil Spence: Buildings and Projects*, ed. L. Campbell, M. Glendinning, and J. Thomas (London: RIBA, 2012), 228.
4. He would later write, "How do we get unity? It comes from internal rhythm, the buildings and materials, and a sensitive appreciation of the site, of using ground in a proper way." Sir Basil Spence, "University of Sussex," in *University Planning and Design: A Symposium*, ed. Michael Brawne (London: Architectural Association and Lund Humphries, 1967), 27.
5. "Named Already: The Beehive," *Press* [Christchurch, New Zealand], April 2, 1964.
6. Pericles, funeral oration from Thucydides, *History of the Peloponnesian War*, book 2, chapter 37.
7. "Comment on Beehive," *Dominion* [Wellington], April 4, 1964; *Cross-Section: University of Melbourne Department of Architecture Newsletter*, no. 140 (April 1968): 1.
8. "Dramatic Design for Parliament," *Press*, April 2, 1964.
9. Juan Antonio Ramírez, *The Beehive Metaphor: From Gaudí to Le Corbusier* (London: Reaktion, 1988).
10. Whim Wham [Allan Curnow], "A Round of Applause," *New Zealand Herald* [Auckland], April 4, 1964.
11. Cedric Mentiplay, "'Queen of N.Z.' Opens 'Impressive, Bold' Beehive," *Press*, March 1, 1977.
12. "The Beehive—Concept and Function" (short film, 1979), *NZ On Screen Iwi Whitiāhua*, https://www.nzonscreen.com/title/the-beehive-concept-and-function-1979.
13. Basil Spence, "The Beehive: 'A Hotel in Place of a Parliament,'" *New Zealand News* [London], no. 1248 (November 10, 1971): 7–8.

Radiolaria

1. See Daniela Fabricius, "Architecture before Architecture: Frei Otto's 'Deep History,'" *Journal of Architecture* 21, no. 8 (2016).
2. Universität Stuttgart, Institut für Leichte Flächentragwerke, *IL 38: Shells in Nature and Technics III; Information of the Institute for Lightweight Structures* (Stuttgart, 2004), 141.
3. This process is described in detail in Universität Stuttgart, Institut für Leichte Flächentragwerke, *IL 33: Radiolaria. Shells in Nature and Technics II; Information of the Institute for Lightweight Structures* (Stuttgart, 1990).
4. Universität Stuttgart, Institut für Leichte Flächentragwerke, *IL 9: Pneus in Nature and Technics; Information of the Institute for Lightweight Structures* (Stuttgart, 1977), 5.

5. Helmcke eventually became skeptical of Otto's theory of the *Pneu*.
6. See, for example, H. P. Berlage, *Thoughts on Style 1886–1909* (Santa Monica, CA: Getty Center for the History of Art and the Humanities, 1996), and Robert Proctor, "Architecture from the Cell-Soul: René Binet and Ernst Haeckel," *Journal of Architecture* 11, no. 4 (2006).
7. See Detlef Mertins, "Bioconstructivisms," in *Modernity Unbound* (London: AA Publications, 2011).
8. J. G. Helmcke and W. Krieger, *Diatomeenschalen im elektronenmikroskopischen Bild*, vol. 1 (1961; Weinheim: J. Cramer, 1962), 3; my translation. Helmcke even included a pair of stereoscopic glasses with the original edition of the book.
9. *IL 33*, 10.
10. *IL 33*, 10.
11. Quoted in Winfried Nerdinger, "Frei Otto: Working for a Better 'Earth for Mankind,'" in *Frei Otto: Complete Works—Lightweight Construction, Natural Design*, ed. Nerdinger (Basel: Birkhäuser, 2005), 9.
12. Frei Otto and Entwicklungsstätte für den Leichtbau, *Mitteilung: Anpassungsfähig Bauen*, Mitteilung 6 (Berlin: 1959), 4; my translation.
13. Otto and Entwicklungsstätte für den Leichtbau, *Mitteilung: Anpassungsfähig Bauen*, 25.
14. In 1860, this dilemma led the British biologist John Hogg to propose that they belong to a fourth kingdom—the Protoctista—which refers to their status as "the first" (proto) forms of life. Ernst Haeckel similarly named them Protista in 1866. Radiolaria were commonly considered animals due to their behavior, but by the 1970s were not officially considered so. Today they are often described as Protozoa (protists that exhibit animal-like behavior), and they continue to occupy shifting taxonomic territory. They are currently ordered with animals and plants in the domain of the Eukaryota.
15. J. G. Helmcke and Frei Otto, "Lebende und technische Konstruktionen: Bemerkungen zu Schalen und Raumtragwerken in Natur und Technik," *Deutsche Bauzeitung* 11 (1962): 856; my translation.
16. Fabricius, "Architecture before Architecture: Frei Otto's 'Deep History.'"
17. A leap in human understanding of the Radiolaria took place following the expedition of the HMS *Challenger*, a decommissioned British warship that circumnavigated the globe from 1872 to 1876 collecting deep sea samples. Haeckel published influential reports on Radiolaria found during this expedition as part of the *Report on the Scientific Results of the Voyage of H.M.S. Challenger During the Years 1873–76* (1887).
18. Otto describes a similar visit to Berlin by Buckminster Fuller, during which Helmcke showed him stereoscopic images of diatoms that resembled his domes. When he saw them, Fuller "stood up and wanted to reach into the stereoscopic images." Frei Otto, "Die Forschungsgruppe Biologie und Bauen," in Frei Otto, *Schriften und Reden 1951–1983*, ed. Berthold Burkhardt (Braunschweig: Vieweg, 1984), 171.

Sea Jelly

1. Greg Lynn, "Multiplicitous and Inorganic Bodies," *Assemblage* 19 (1992): 33–49.
2. See, for instance, Anthony Vidler, "Architecture's Expanded Field," *Artforum* 42, no. 8 (2004): 142–147.
3. "The computer-generated designs of Greg Lynn, Lars Spuybroek, and Jeff Kipnis follow a 'blob-grammar' which resembles the amorphous forms and viscous transformations of natural organisms one sees in floating jellyfish." Petra Gruber, Dietmar Bruckner, Christian Hellmich, et al., eds., *Biomimetics: Materials, Structures and Processes* (London: Springer, 2011), 153.

4. Greg Lynn, "Organic Algorithms in Architecture," *TED*, February 2005, https://www.ted.com/talks/greg_lynn_organic_algorithms_in_architecture. See also Mark Rappolt, ed., *Greg Lynn Form* (New York: Random House, 2008), 121.
5. Greg Lynn, unpublished interview with the author, March 11, 2022.
6. Lynn, unpublished interview with the author, September 16, 2014.
7. All quotations are from the following, respectively: Greg Lynn, *Animate Form* (New York: Princeton Architectural Press, 1999), 9, 41, 83, 94, and 134; John Frazer, *An Evolutionary Architecture* (London: Architectural Association, 1995), 9–10; Karl Chu, "The Metaphysics of Genetic Architecture and Computation," *Perspecta* 35 (2004): 74–97, 95; Greg Lynn, ed., *AD: Folding in Architecture*, rev. ed. (London: Wiley Academy, 2004), 12.
8. Greg Lynn, "The Renewed Novelty of Symmetry," *Assemblage* 26 (1995): 11–25; Donald W. Sherburne, *A Key to Whitehead's Process and Reality* (Chicago: University of Chicago Press, 1981), 96 and 125.
9. Keith Ansell-Pearson, *Germinal Life: The Difference and Repetition of Deleuze* (London: Routledge, 1999), 218–219.
10. Karl Marx, *Grundrisse: Foundations of the Critique of Political Economy*, trans. Martin Nicolaus (Harmondsworth: Penguin, 1993), 500–501.
11. Duy Lap Nguyen, *Walter Benjamin and the Critique of Political Economy: A New Historical Materialism* (London: Bloomsbury, 2022), 152–156.

Turtle

1. William Carlos Williams, "The Turtle," originally published in *The Atlantic*, September 1956, 89; reprinted by Annika Neklason, in "From the Archives: William Carlos Williams's Poem for His Grandson," www.theatlantic.com (April 20, 2019).
2. Larry J. Zimmerman, *The Wisdom of the Native Americans* (New York: Chartwell Books, 2011), 146–149.
3. Samuel Mockbee, Bruce Goff Lecture Series (lecture, Gibbs College of Architecture, University of Oklahoma, October 11, 1995). Mockbee references this rejection in his traveling lectures from 1994–2000.
4. Mockbee, Bruce Goff lecture. Mockbee references James Earl Chaney's grave in his traveling lectures from 1994–2000.
5. Samuel Mockbee, "The Black Warrior," in "Strath Brown" (1998); documented by Rebecca O'Neal, 2016 (Mockbee Archive, Canton, MS; access courtesy of Jackie Mockbee). The quotation is an opening line of his poem "The Black Warrior," of which there are multiple variations including the following in the same sketchbook:

   The Black Warrior drifts
   Bound by the Master Knot of Fate
   Floating among the graves of
   the abused
   Drifting past the dreams of the
   neglected.
   Embracing an eddy of a Butterfly's
   Psyche
   flooding a delta of goodness, happiness
   + good fortune
   The Black Warrior drifts
   Its ancient liquid light walking
   on water
   to the horizon line where angels
   like to dream
   Before evaporating toward a Sunrise
   Unknown
   returning with earth bound eggs and
   spirit bound sperm drifting deep into
   the heart of Dixie

6. "Citizen Architect" is taken from the film *Citizen Architect: Samuel Mockbee and the Spirit of the Rural Studio*, directed by Sam Wainwright Douglas (Austin: Big Beard Films, 2010), DVD. For more information on Rural Studio or Rural Studio architecture projects, visit Auburn University architecture program's website, www.ruralstudio.com.

7. Samuel Mockbee, *The Marriage of Life and Death*, 1990, ink drawing, 14 × 17 inches; documented by Rebecca O'Neal in 2016 (Mockbee Archive, Canton, MS; access courtesy of Jackie Mockbee).
8. This and other quotations from Richard Wright were collected and transcribed by Samuel Mockbee into his "Literary Bible" notebook; documented by Rebecca O'Neal in 2016 (Mockbee Archive, Canton, MS; access courtesy of Jackie Mockbee).
9. Jackie Mockbee (Samuel Mockbee's wife) in discussion with the author, June 2016. Item documented by Rebecca O'Neal in the Mockbee Archive in 2016 (Mockbee Archive, Canton, MS; access courtesy of Jackie Mockbee).
10. Samuel Mockbee, *The Black Warrior*, 1996, acrylic and oil paint, canvas, wood, found objects, 14 feet × 8 feet × 10 inches, photo documentation by Rebecca O'Neal in 2016 (Mockbee Archive, Canton, MS; access courtesy of Jackie Mockbee).
11. In the author's 2017 process of documenting and reorganizing the Mockbee large painting archive with Jackie Mockbee, *The Black Warrior* was uncrated by the author and a team of assistants. There was a light-green spotted lizard crawling around sanguinely on the painted surface. Dirt-dauber wasps had built an intricate mud nest underneath the memorable gourd. The piece was documented carefully.
12. Carol Mockbee (Samuel Mockbee's daughter) in discussion with the author, June 2017.
13. Samuel Mockbee, Subrosa Pantheon sketches and works on paper, 2001; documented by Rebecca O'Neal in 2017 (Mockbee Archive, Canton, MS; access courtesy of Jackie Mockbee.)
14. Williams, "The Turtle," in Neklason, "From the Archives."

Unicorn

1. Yona Friedman, *Petit bestiaire 1962–81* (Paris: Cneai/ ENSBA, 2009).
2. "I do not feel like a utopian, nor an architect, nor a writer, but rather all these things together as they complete each other and it is impossible to separate them." Yona Friedman and Manuel Orazi, *Yona Friedman: The Dilution of Architecture*, ed. Nader Seraj (Zurich: Park Books, 2015), 563.
3. Yona Friedman, *Voyage au pays des licornes* (Paris: Semiose, 2017).
4. Yona Friedman, transcript from an interview with Philippe Chiambaretta and Gilles Coudert in Yona Friedman's studio apartment on September 21, 2017, with the assistance of the Jérôme Poggi Gallery.
5. Yona Friedman, *Vous avez un chien. C'est lui qui vous a choisi(e)* (Paris/Tel Aviv: Éditions de l'Éclat, 2004).
6. Yona Friedman, *L'ordre compliqué et autres fragments* (Paris: Éditions de l'Éclat, 2008).
7. Manuel Orazi, "Conversation with Yona Friedman," *Log*, no. 26 (Fall 2012): 61–75.
8. "7 Questions for Bernard Tschumi," in Orazi and Friedman, *Yona Friedman*, 560.

Vulture

1. See also Rudolf Wittkower, "Eagle and Serpent: A Study in the Migration of Symbols," *Journal of the Warburg Institute* 2, no. 4 (April 1939): 293–325.
2. From Pikionis's notes for his inaugural speech to the Academy of Athens, which was never completed. Published in Agni Pikionis, ed., *Dimitris Pikionis: Architectural Work*, vol. 8 (Athens: Bastas-Plessas, 1994), 15.
3. Kostas Tsiambaos, *From Doxiadis' Theory to Pikionis' Work: Reflections of Antiquity in Modern Architecture* (London: Routledge, 2018).

4. Dimitris Pikionis, “Sentimental Topography” (1935), in *D. Pikionis, Keimena*, ed. Agni Pikionis and Michalis Paroussis (Athens: MIET, 2000), 79.

Wild Boar

1. Reinhard Döhl, “Hermann Finsterlin: Eine Annäherung,” in Döhl, *Hermann Finsterlin: Eine Annäherung* (Stuttgart: Staatsgalerie Stuttgart, 1988), 24–25.
2. Hermann Finsterlin, “Biographie in grossen Zügen,” reprinted in Döhl, “Hermann Finsterlin: Eine Annäherung,” 9. Finsterlin rewrote this biography many times and altered many of the facts, so it has to be read with a skeptical eye.
3. *Hermann Finsterlin (1887–1973): Ideenarchitektur 1918–1924: Entwürfe für eine bewohnbahre Welt* (Krefeld: Kaiser Wilhelm Museum, 1976).
4. Heinrich Beck, *Das Ebersignum im Germanischen* (Amsterdam: De Gruyter, 2018), 154; Christopher R. Clason, “Animals, Birds, and Fish in the Middle Ages,” in *Handbook of Medieval Culture* (Amsterdam: De Gruyter, 2015), 32.
5. Clason, “Animals, Birds, and Fish in the Middle Ages,” 19.
6. Johannes Langner, “‘Seelengletschermühlensystem’: Hermann Finsterlin und die Tradition architektonischer Mimesis,” in Döhl, *Hermann Finsterlin*, 143.
7. Reinhard Döhl, “Auch mein Ziel und mein Stil ist das Spiel—der Gesamtkünstler Hermann Finsterlin,” in *Hermann Finsterlin: in der Hamburger Kunsthalle*, ed. Uwe Schneede (Stuttgart: Hatje, 1995), 58.
8. Döhl, “Hermann Finsterlin: Eine Annäherung,” 10; Döhl, “Auch mein Ziel und mein Stil ist das Spiel,” 51.
9. “Hybrid” was Finsterlin’s word for his compositions; Hermann Finsterlin, “Die Genesis ist der Weltarchitektur oder die Dezendenz der Dome als Stilspiel,” *Frühlicht* 3 (1922): 76.
10. Hermann Finsterlin, “Casa Nova (Zukunftsarchitektur),” *Wendingen* 3 (1924).
11. Finsterlin, “Die Genesis ist der Weltarchitektur,” 75.
12. Döhl, *Hermann Finsterlin*, 407.

X-tinct Dodo

1. *The Times* [London], July 9, 1870.
2. *The Builder*, February 5, 1876.
3. *The Cornhill Magazine* 15 (December 1890): 629–644.
4. George Edwards, *A Natural History of Uncommon Birds, and of Some Other Rare and Undescribed Animals* (London: the author, 1743–1764), vol. 6 (variously titled), plate 294.
5. Edward Ingress Bell, “The New Natural History Museum,” *Magazine of Art* 4 (1881): 358–362, 463–465.
6. *The Times*, November 16, 1886.
7. For sources, see especially Maurice B. Adams’s drawings of the terracotta ornament as installed in thirty plates for weekly issues of *The Building News* (October–December 1878); Carla Yanni, “Divine Display or Secular Science: Defining Nature at the Natural History Museum, London,” *Journal of the Society of Architectural Historians* 55, no. 3 (1996): 276–299; Colin Cunningham, *The Terracotta Designs of Alfred Waterhouse* (London: John Wiley & Sons, 2000); J. B. Bullen, “Alfred Waterhouse’s Romanesque Temple of Nature: The Natural History Museum,” *Architectural History* 49 (2006): 257–285; and Jolyon C. Parish, *The Dodo and the Solitaire: A Natural History* (Bloomington: Indiana University Press, 2013), 69–105, which gives a thorough account of the early representational history.

Yellowjacket

1. Henri Milne-Edwards, *Histoire naturelle des crustacés*, vol. 1 (Paris: Librarie enyclopédique de Roret, 1834), 5.
2. Camille Limoges, "Milne-Edwards, Darwin, Durkheim and the Division of Labour: A Case Study in Reciprocal Conceptual Exchanges between the Social and the Natural Sciences," in *Emile Durkheim: Critical Assessments of Leading Sociologists*, ed. W. F. Pickering (London: Routledge, 2001), 199–200.

Zebra

1. For a more in-depth discussion of this cover image and related topics, see Brett M. Van Hoesen, "Postcolonial Cosmopolitanism: Constructing the Weimar New Woman out of a Colonial Imaginary," in *The New Woman International: Representations in Photography and Film from the 1870s through the 1960s*, ed. Elizabeth Otto and Vanessa Rocco (Ann Arbor: University of Michigan Press, 2011), 95–114.
2. For Max Raabe's 2022 album cover with zebra, see his website, https://www.maxraabe.net/ (accessed July 17, 2023).
3. Pepper Stetler, *Stop Reading! Look! Modern Vision and the Weimar Photographic Book* (Ann Arbor: University of Michigan, 2015), 32.
4. László Moholy-Nagy, *Painting Photography Film* (Cambridge, MA: MIT Press, 1969), 12; originally *Malerei, Fotografie, Film*, volume 8 of the Bauhausbücher series, 1925.
5. Moholy-Nagy, "On the Objective and the Non-Objective," in *Painting, Photography, Film*, 13.
6. Christian Leborg, *Visual Grammar* (New York: Princeton Architectural Press, 2004), 34–35.
7. Margaret Livingstone, *Vision and Art: The Biology of Seeing* (New York: Abrams, 2002), 84–91.
8. Katherine Hessling was the wife of filmmaker Jean Renoir and starred in many of his films. This particular image of Hessling was clipped from a 1929 issue of *Münchner Illustrierte Presse*, the source for a number of Brandt's photomontages.
9. Christopher Plumb and Samuel Shaw, *Zebra* (London: Reaktion Books, 2018), 71.
10. Plumb and Shaw, *Zebra*, 58.
11. Elizabeth Otto, *Tempo, Tempo! The Bauhaus Photomontages of Marianne Brandt* (Berlin: Jovis Verlag/ Bauhaus-Archiv, 2005), 104.
12. Van Hoesen, "Postcolonial Cosmopolitanism," 104–111. See also Anne Anlin Cheng, *Second Skin: Josephine Baker and the Modern Surface* (2011; reprt., Oxford: Oxford University Press, 2023).
13. Kenhelm W. Stott Jr., *Exploring with Martin and Osa Johnson* (Chanute, KS: Martin and Osa Johnson Safari Museum Press, 1978), 69.
14. John Berger, "On Visibility," in *The Sense of Sight* (New York: Random House, 1985), 219.

Contributors

Gregorio Astengo is an architect. He holds an MSc from Turin's Polytechnic and a PhD from the Bartlett School of Architecture, UCL, and has been a postdoctoral researcher at ETH Zurich. Gregorio was Postdoc Mobility Fellow of the Swiss National Science Foundation (2023–2025) and is adjunct professor at IE University Madrid. His research, which involves early modern property development and representation, has appeared in international journals such as *RA. Revista de Arquitectura*, *gta Papers*, *Architectural Histories*, and *Oase*. He coedited the books *Amphibious Habitats* (Recolectores Urbanos, 2022) and *Architecture and Real Estate* (gta Verlag, 2026).

Vera Simone Bader is an art historian and was a research assistant at TUM and curator at the TUM Architecture Museum in the Pinakothek der Moderne from 2013 to 2023. There she curated the exhibitions *Lina Bo Bardi 100: Brazil's Alternative Path to Modernity* (2014), *World of Malls: Architectures of Consumption* (2016), *Experience in Action! DesignBuild in Architecture* (2019), and *Marina Tabassum Architects: In Bangladesh* (2023). She was awarded the Hans Janssen Prize of the Göttingen Academy of Sciences and Humanities for her dissertation in 2014. Since April 2023, she has been responsible for a DFG project at the Institute for European Art History at the University of Heidelberg on the topic of the discourse of the vernacular in modern and contemporary architecture.

Deborah Ascher Barnstone is professor and head of Architecture at the University of Sydney. Her primary research interests are in interrogating the origins of modernism and exploring the relationships between art, architecture, and culture more broadly. She has published widely in journals, edited volumes, and monographs including *The Break with the Past: German Avant-Garde Architecture, 1910–1925* (Routledge, 2018), *Beyond the Bauhaus: Cultural Modernity in Weimar Breslau, 1918–1933* (University of Michigan Press, 2016), and *The Color of Modernism: Paints, Pigments and the Transformation of Modern Architecture in 1920s Germany* (Bloomsbury Academic, 2022).

Viola Bertini is a PhD architect and a researcher in architecture and urban design at Sapienza University of Rome, Department of Architecture and Design. Her research has been published in international journals and collective volumes. Her books include *Hassan Fathy: Earth & Utopia*, with S. S. Damluji (London: Laurence King, 2018). She was a research fellow at Università Iuav di Venezia, a research consultant at the American University of Beirut, a visiting researcher for short periods at the University of Évora, and a visiting researcher and professor at the University of Sevilla. Her recent research focuses on the relationship between architecture, UNESCO sites, and heritage tourism.

M. Christine Boyer is the William R. Kenan Jr. Professor at the School of Architecture, Princeton University. She is the author of *Not Quite Architecture: Writings around Alison and Peter Smithson* (MIT Press, 2017), *Le Corbusier: homme de lettres* (Princeton Architectural Press, 2011), *CyberCities: Visual Perception in the Age of Electronic Communication* (Princeton Architectural Press, 1996), *The City of Collective Memory:*

Its Historical Imagery and Architectural Entertainments (MIT Press, 1994), *Manhattan Manners: Architecture and Style 1850–1890* (Rizzoli, 1985), and *Dreaming the Rational City: The Myth of City Planning 1890–1945* (MIT Press, 1983).

Martín Cobas is a professor of architectural history and design at FADU, Universidad de la República, Montevideo, where he serves as chair of the Department of the History of Architecture and research advisor of the Department of Architecture and Urbanism. Cobas's work primarily focuses on Brazil and examines architecture and the territory at their intersection with a variety of fields and the environmental humanities. His work articulates the creaturely modern—an architecture beyond-the-human, which he explores in his forthcoming book through Lina Bo Bardi's engagement with the zoological and botanical. His writing has appeared in specialized journals and edited volumes. As a founding principal of Fábrica de Paisaje, his work has been exhibited and awarded internationally.

Thomas Daniell is professor of architectural history, theory, and criticism at Kyoto University, Japan, and a founding board member of ADAN (Architectural Design Association of Nippon). A two-time recipient of publication grants from the Graham Foundation for Advanced Studies in the Fine Arts, his books include *FOBA: Buildings* (Princeton Architectural Press, 2005), *After the Crash: Architecture in Post-Bubble Japan* (Princeton Architectural Press, 2008), *Houses and Gardens of Kyoto* (Tuttle, 2010, 2nd ed. 2018), *Kiyoshi Sey Takeyama + Amorphe* (Equal Books, 2011), *Kansai 6* (Equal Books, 2011), and *An Anatomy of Influence* (AA Publications, 2018).

Daniela Fabricius is a historian and theorist of architecture and urbanism. She is an assistant professor in Architecture at the University of Pennsylvania. She holds a PhD in architectural history and theory from Princeton University and an MArch from Columbia University, and was a fellow in the Whitney Museum Independent Study Program. She is the author of the forthcoming book *The Ethics of Calculation: Architecture and Rationalism in Postwar Germany*, as well as an edited volume of the writings of the feminist theorist Jennifer Bloomer. Her recent research includes the history of spatial forms of social and ecological reparations, and the contested transformations of East Germany after 1989.

Françoise Fromonot is an architect and critic based in Paris, currently professor (design, history and theory) at the ENSA Paris-Belleville. In 2008 she was a founding member of criticat (www.criticat.fr), and the coeditor of a selection of articles from the first ten issues, *Yours Critically* (2016). She is also the author of numerous books and essays, including *Glenn Murcutt—Buildings and Projects* (1995 and 2003), *Jørn Utzon—The Sydney Opera House* (1999), *La Campagne des Halles* (2005), a critical account of the latest renovation of central Paris, followed in 2019 by its sequel, *La Comédie des Halles*. Her latest monograph, *Transforming Landscapes* (2020), deals with the large-scale projects of Michel Desvigne. She is currently the coeditor, with Thomas Weaver, of the book series Gumshoe (Park Books), featuring detective stories on famous modern buildings, launched in 2025 by her volume on OMA's Villa dall'Ava, *The House of Dr Koolhaas*.

Konstantina Kalfa is an architectural and urban historian, assistant professor at the Department of Art Theory and History of the Athens School of Fine Arts. Her publications on architecture's political economy and production mechanisms appear in several edited volumes as well as in the leading journals *Architectural Histories* (forthcoming), *PLATFORM*, *Journal of the Society of Architectural Historians*, *Rethinking Marxism*, and *Architecture and Culture*. In 2022, she coedited a dossier on small-scale entrepreneurship in housing for *ABE Journal* 20. She is the author of the book *Self-Sheltering Now! The Hidden Side of US Aid to Greece* [in Greek] (Futura, 2019). Her recent research titled "How the Middle Class Housed Itself in the Eastern Mediterranean" is funded by the European Research Council (ERC starting grant, 2024–2029).

Pavel Kuznetsov is a researcher of twentieth-century architecture, museologist, and curator; since 2022 he has been a lecturer on the Soviet avant-garde at the Accademia di Architettura (Mendrisio, Switzerland). He was first deputy director of Shchusev State Museum of Architecture, Moscow (2010–2022) and director of the State Museum of Konstantin and Viktor Melnikov (2014–2022). He led the preconservation survey of the Melnikov house (2017–2019) supported by the Getty Foundation and is the author of *The Melnikov House: Icon of the Avant-Garde, Family Home, Architecture Museum* (Berlin, 2017 and 2021). He curated the exhibitions *Melnikov/Le Corbusier: rencontre à la villa Savoye* (Villa Savoye, 2017), *Melnikoff* (Shchusev State Museum of Architecture, Moscow, 2022), *Melnikov: Architect of the Impossible* (2023), and *Soviet Architectural Avant-Garde: Utopias, Theories and Practice* (2024)—both in Accademia di Architettura, Mendrisio.

Gabriele Mastrigli is an architect and critic based in Rome. He has taught at the Berlage Institute Rotterdam and Cornell University Rome Program. He is now associate professor of theory and architectural design at University of Camerino (Italy). His articles and essays have appeared, among others, in *Arquitectura Viva*, *Domus*, *Log*, *Lotus International*, and *San Rocco*. He edited Rem Koolhaas's collection of essays *Junkspace* (Quodlibet, 2006, Payot, 2011, Puente Editores, 2024) and the complete archival study *Superstudio Opere 1966–1978* (Quodlibet, 2016). On the occasion of the 50th anniversary of the Florentine group's foundation, he curated the complete retrospective exhibition *Superstudio 50* which opened at MAXXI, Rome in 2016 and traveled to the Power Station of Art, Shanghai in 2017–2018.

Nicholas Olsberg, former director of the Canadian Centre for Architecture, is an archivist, curator, critic, and historian with a particular interest in architectural ideas and artifacts as an expression of the society and temper of their times. His exhibitions and published works range from the civic architecture of Enlightenment France to the recent work of Herzog & De Meuron. A major study of *William Butterfield and His Times* (Lund Humphries) appeared in 2024.

Rebecca O'Neal is professor of architecture at Auburn University. O'Neal's research focuses on architecture representation. She was awarded a Graham Foundation research grant in 2017 for a project on the paintings and drawings of the late architect Samuel Mockbee. An architecture educator for over 20 years, she teaches upper-level architecture studios, history and theory of modern architecture, and seminars on modern architecture history, theory, and representation. She served as president of the National Architectural Accrediting Board (2021–2023) and was a board director from 2019–2023. She earned her MArch at Harvard University Graduate School of Design.

Manuel Orazi is visiting professor in city and territory at the Academy of Architecture in Mendrisio of Università della Svizzera italiana. His research has been published in *Domus*, *Log*, *Volume*, and other magazines. He curated the exhibition held at the Triennale of Milan, *Carlo Aymonino: Loyalty to Betrayal* (catalogue published by Electa, 2021). He works for the Italian publishing house Quodlibet based in Macerata.

Rodrigo Pérez de Arce, PhD, is an architect and associate professor at the School of Architecture, Catholic University, Santiago. He has taught at the Architectural Association, University of Pennsylvania, Cornell, and other schools. His practice has realized a Cultural Centre, the renewal of a major public square, and a Crypt for the Metropolitan Cathedral, all in Santiago. Recent publications include *City of Play*, an architectural and urban history of recreation and leisure (Bloomsbury, 2018), *Las Vidas de San Francisco* (coauthor) (Ediciones UC, Santiago, 2023), and "Not a Playground," in *Francis Alÿs: The Nature of the Game* (Leuven University Press, 2023.) He is currently researching organic and inorganic interfaces in architecture.

Enrique Ramirez is a writer and a historian of art and architecture. His work considers histories of buildings, cities, and landscapes alongside larger cultures of textual, literary, and object production in Europe and the Americas from the Renaissance onward. He is the Frances and Gilbert P. Schafer Visiting Professor of Architecture at the University of Michigan's Taubman College of Architecture and Urban Planning.

Joseph M. Siry is professor of architectural history, and William R. Kenan Jr. Professor of the Humanities, at Wesleyan University in Connecticut. His books are *Carson Pirie Scott: Adler and Sullivan and the Chicago Department Store* (University of Chicago Press, 1988); *Unity Temple: Frank Lloyd Wright and Architecture for Liberal Religion* (Cambridge University Press, 1996); *The Chicago Auditorium Building: Adler and Sullivan's Architecture and the City* (University of Chicago Press, 2002); *Beth Sholom Synagogue: Frank Lloyd Wright and Modern Religious Architecture* (University of Chicago Press, 2012); and *Air-Conditioning in Modern American Architecture, 1890–1970* (Pennsylvania State University Press, 2021). His current research focuses on US green buildings since the 1970s.

Robin Skinner lectures in architectural history and the architecture of the Pacific at Victoria University of Wellington, New Zealand. As an architectural historian he specializes in nineteenth- and early twentieth-century architecture of New Zealand and the British world, with a special interest in issues of postcoloniality in architecture through the nineteenth and twentieth centuries.

Martin Søberg is an art historian and associate professor of architectural theory, artistic research, and poetics at the Institute of Architecture and Culture, Royal Danish Academy in Copenhagen. He is author of *Kay Fisker: Works and Ideas in Danish Modern Architecture* (Bloomsbury, 2021) and coeditor of several books including *Architectures of Dismantling and Restructuring: Spaces of Danish Welfare, 1970–Present* (Lars Müller, 2022) and *The Artful Plan: Architectural Drawing Reconfigured* (Birkhäuser, 2020). His current research focuses on housing ideals in Denmark c. 1930–1960. He is chair of do.co.mo.mo. Denmark.

Teresa Stoppani is professor of architecture and director of architecture and interior design at Norwich University of the Arts, and lectures in history and theory studies at the AA School of Architecture. She is a member of the steering group of the Architectural Humanities Research Association, and executive editor of the AHRA journal *Architecture and Culture*. Her books include *Paradigm Islands: Manhattan and Venice* (Routledge, 2010), *Unorthodox Ways to Think the City* (Routledge, 2019), and the coedited *This Thing Called Theory* (Routledge, 2016). Her current project Architecture_Dusts explores the undoing of form in architecture, studying its materiality and minor and aberrant practices (Atomised, Invisibles, Monsters).

Iwan Strauven is an engineer-architect, associate professor in history and theory of architecture at the La Cambre Horta Architecture Faculty of the Université libre de Bruxelles, and chief architecture curator at the Centre for Fine Arts, Brussels. His research focuses on twentieth-century modern and contemporary architecture and on the mediation of architecture through exhibitions. His recent publications include *Victor Horta: The Grammar of Art Nouveau* (Mercatorfonds, 2023), *Exploring NU architectuuratelier* (Walther und Franz König, 2023), and *Victor Bourgeois (1897–1962): Modernity, Tradition and Neutrality* (Nai010, 2021).

André Tavares is an architect and researcher at the Faculty of Architecture at the University of Porto, where he is the principal investigator of the project Fishing Architecture funded through an ERC consolidator grant. Since 2006 has been founding director of Dafne Editora, based in Porto. He was a research fellow at the Institute for the History and Theory of Architecture of ETH Zurich (2017–2018) and at the Observatoire de la Condition Suburbaine, Université Paris-Est (2021–2023). His book *The Anatomy of the Architectural Book* (Lars Müller/Canadian Centre for Architecture, 2016) addresses the crossovers between book culture and building culture. He is also the author of *Raw Material: A View of Álvaro Siza's Archive* (Serralves, 2017), *Vitruvius without Text* (gta Verlag, 2022), and *Architecture Follows Fish* (MIT Press, 2024).

Kostas Tsiambaos is an architect and associate professor in history and theory of architecture at the School of Architecture of the National Technical University in Athens. He is chair of do.co.mo.mo. Greece. He studied in Athens (NTUA) and New York (Columbia GSAPP). His research has been published in international journals and collective volumes; his books include *From Doxiadis' Theory to Pikionis' Work: Reflections of Antiquity in Modern Architecture* (Routledge, 2018 and 2020). In the fall semester of the academic year 2019–2020, he was a Stanley J. Seeger Visiting Research Fellow at Princeton University. His recent research focuses on animals in the architecture of the twentieth century.

Brett M. Van Hoesen is associate professor and area head of Art History at the University of Nevada, Reno. She holds a PhD from the University of Iowa and an MA from the University of Massachusetts, Amherst. Her recent publications include a chapter on Max Ernst's collages and colonial botany in the volume *Compressed Utterances: Collage in a Germanic Context after 1912*, edited by Cole Collins (Peter Lang Press), and a chapter on the contemporary artist Mwangi Hutter's postcolonialism(s) in the volume *German Colonialism in Africa and Its Legacies*, edited by Itohan Osayimwese (Bloomsbury Press).

Aron Vinegar is a theorist and historian working at the intersection of visual studies, art history, architecture, aesthetics, and philosophy. His writing, research, and teaching are concerned with the relationships between habit, repetition, and representation; the concept of indifference; and critical perspectives in preservation. His publications include *Subject Matter: The Anaesthetics of Habit and the Logic of Breakdown* (MIT Press, 2023); *Grey on Grey: At the Threshold of Philosophy of Art* (coedited, Edinburgh University Press, 2023); *Heidegger and the Work of Art History* (coedited, Ashgate, 2014); *I Am a Monument: On Learning from Las Vegas* (MIT Press, 2008); and *Relearning from Las Vegas* (coedited, University of Minnesota Press, 2009). Current projects are *What Wings Raise to the Second Power*, a book about birds, experience, and meaning, and *Apokatastasis: Angles of Vision, Citing the Past and the Drive to Totality.* He has been Professor of Art History and Visual Studies in the Department of Philosophy, Classics, History of Art and Ideas, University of Oslo; Director of Art History and Visual Culture at the University of Exeter; and Associate Professor of Art History at Ohio State University.

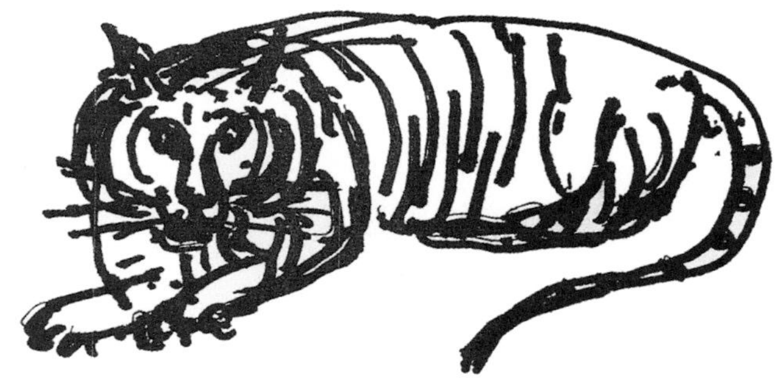

Figure 27.1